saur

Thomas P. Slavens

A Great Library through Gifts

K·G·Saur
New York·Munich·London·Paris 1986

To Cora

CIP-Kurztitelaufnahme der Deutschen Bibliothek

Slavens, Thomas P. :
A great library through gifts / Thomas P.
Slavens. – New York ; Munich ; London ;
Paris : Saur , 1986.
  ISBN 3-598-10621-1

© 1986 by K.G.Saur Verlag, München
Printed and bound in the Federal Republic of Germany
by WS-Druckerei Werner Schaubruch, Mainz
and Verlagsbuchbinderei Kränkl, Heppenheim

ISBN 3-598-10621-1

Contents

Chapter   Page

List of Illustrations

Preface

It has been the purpose of this book to investigate the scattered materials concerning the development of the Library of the Union Theological Seminary in the City of New York, the greatest collection of religious materials in the western hemisphere, with a view to determining the means by which this collection was developed through gifts and to demonstrate how other libraries may profit from Union's experience.

The Library has comprised for many years one of the finest and most widely-used collections of theological literature in the world. Because the development of the collection is an integral part of the Seminary itself, it has been necessary to relate the development of the Library to the educational objectives, faculty, curriculum, physical facilities, and financial program of the school.

This study has been made in the belief that its results may provide guidelines for the development of other libraries. The book has relevance for administrators, faculty members, benefactors, librarians, and the general public interested in the improvement of libraries.

Thanks are due to these publishers for permission to use
materials listed below by Thomas P. Slavens: School of Library
and Information Studies, Florida State University, for material
on the Van Ess Collection as well as Henry Preserved Smith in
Library History Seminars held in 1968 and 1969, the University of Texas Press for material on William Walker Rockwell,
as well as Charles Ripley Gillett in The Journal of Library
History in 1976, and Union Seminary Quarterly Review for
material on Charles Briggs published in 1969, and the
Library History Review for material on Henry B. Smith as well
as other data about the development of the Library at Union
Seminary. Appreciation also is expressed to Shirley A.
Culliton and Donna J. Perry of the School of Library Science
at The University of Michigan for their work on the
manuscript.

Introduction

Historical Studies of Union Theological
Seminary and Its Library

Much has been written about the history of Union
Theological Seminary in the City of New York, but only a
résumé of the studies which deal with the history of the
Library will be given here. This will be followed by a list
of the primary sources of the data investigated.

One of the earliest sketches of the history of the
Seminary is found in <u>Extracts from a Speech Delivered by</u>
<u>Dr. McAuley at the Dedication of the Edifice Belonging to</u>
<u>the New-York Theological Seminary, 12th Dec. 1838</u>. The
address was important for this study because of its description of the means by which the library of Professor Leander
van Ess of Marburg and Alzey was acquired. The recorded
speech is so brief, however, that it is hardly possible to
call it a history of the Seminary.

The first history of the school, then, is a twenty-
seven-page document, <u>The Early Annals of Union Theological</u>
<u>Seminary in the City of New York</u>, written in 1876 by Edwin
F. Hatfield, a fund-raiser for the school. This brief study
also has a good treatment of the acquisition of the Van Ess
materials, which included approximately 14,000 volumes, containing about 37 manuscripts and 430 incunabula, in addition
to a rich collection of materials on the Reformation in

1

original editions, Biblical literature, church history, and
theology. Hatfield's history is, however, incomplete in its
presentation of other aspects of the early development of
the Union Library.

When George Lewis Prentiss, a professor in the Seminary, wrote the next major histories of the institution,
The Union Theological Seminary in the City of New York: Historical and Biographical Sketches of Its First Fifty Years in
1889 and The Union Theological Seminary in the City of New
York: Its Design and Another Decade of Its History, with a
Sketch of the Life and Public Services of Charles Butler, LL.D.
in 1899, he gathered information concerning the history of
the Seminary, which has been valuable for understanding the
institution in which the Library was developed; but the materials about the collection itself were sketchily presented.

Brief accounts of the development of special collections within the Library were given also from time to time in
newspaper and magazine articles. A description of the acquisition and contents of the Van Ess Library was, for example,
written by T. F. Crane in The Evening Post: New York on May 8,
1888 and by William Walker Rockwell in The Columbia University
Quarterly in 1911. A short history of the development of the
McAlpin Collection of British History and Theology was published in the Union Theological Seminary Bulletin for January
1924; and when the first volume of the Catalogue of that
Collection was published in 1927, a copy of this history appeared in that work.

Nine years after the publication of the McAlpin
Catalogue, a booklet was prepared for the celebration of the
centennial of the Seminary entitled Union Theological Seminary
in the City of New York, One Hundredth Anniversary; and the
speeches of Henry Sloane Coffin and William Adams Brown which
are recorded there are pertinent for the material they include
on the history of the Library. Yet they, like the other literature mentioned, were not intended to be thorough studies
of the history of the collection.

A brief chronological account of some of the major
events in the history of the Library is included in an unpublished manuscript entitled "Detailed History of the Union
Theological Seminary in the City of New York" prepared during
this period by Charles Ripley Gillett. One of the major
values of this study is that the "Archives," which are cited
as one source of the author's data, are now missing.[1] The
only form in which some of these records endure is as quoted
by Gillett and in the notes he used in the preparation of his
study.

The section devoted to the Library in this work includes almost no interpretation nor evaluation. Neither are
conclusions drawn about the importance of the collection for
other institutions; nor is correlation shown between the
growth of the Library and that of the educational objectives,
Faculty, curriculum, physical facilities, or finances of the
school.

Much information pertinent to an understanding of the
evolution of the Library is omitted also in Gillett's account.

The description and evaluation of his own long and important
tenure as Librarian is, for example, especially brief and
inadequately treated. The fact that the work has neither
footnotes nor bibliography has limited its usefulness for
this study.

Two surveys of the Library have been presented to the
School of Library Service at Columbia University as masters'
projects; but they have been of no value to this study because
they were written with only incidental interest in historical
aspects. "A Survey of the Library of the Union Theological
Seminary in New York City" by Donn Michael Farris contains
only a few pages on the Library's history, and the "Report
of a Study Made of the Library of Union Theological Seminary
in The City of New York" has only two pages on that subject.

When Ellouise W. Skinner wrote Sacred Music at Union
Theological Seminary, 1836-1953; An Informal History a few
years later, she included a few pages on the development of
the Sacred Music Library. Soon after the publication of this
work, Henry Sloane Coffin's A Half Century of Union Theological Seminary, 1896-1945, An Informal History was published
by Scribner's. This study has not only a limited amount of
information about the growth of the Library from 1896 to 1954
but also some data about the earlier period of its history.
The development of the collection, nevertheless, is only a
minor theme in this work.

Primary Sources for Investigating
the History of the Library

Some of the primary sources for the study have been
minutes of the Board of Directors, the Faculty, the Alumni
Association, the Building Committee, 1881-84, the Committee
on Site and Buildings, 1905-11, the Executive Committee, and
the Finance Committee. The reports of the Treasurer were
also useful for financial information. The most important
primary material was, however, the reports of the Librarian
to the Directors, which were available for most of the years
since 1884.

Related to these sources is a scrapbook of newspaper
articles and other materials in a volume entitled "Registrar's
Archives." Other archival materials include promotional
pamphlets in which needs and endowments of the Library are
sketched and a manuscript catalogue in the handwriting of
Leander van Ess of the collection which bears his name.

"An Act to incorporate the Union Theological Seminary,
in the city of New-York" was valuable also for an understanding
of the early organization of the school, as were the various
editions of the Constitutions and By-Laws. The Catalogues,
too, provide information. Similar data were gathered from other
publications of the school, such as the Alumni Bulletin,
The Union Seminary Tower, and the Missionary Research Library's
Occasional Bulletin.

Information on Union's classification scheme is,
further, available in Classification of the Library published
in 1939, the Cumulated Supplement which came out in 1957, and

in the <u>List of Theological Subject Headings and Corporate
Church Names Based upon the Headings in the Catalogue of the
Library of Union Theological Seminary</u> published by the American
Library Association in 1947. Critiques of the system were
found in library journals, such as <u>Library Trends</u>, <u>The Library
Quarterly</u>, <u>Catholic Library World</u>, and <u>Library Journal</u>, as
well as in Maurice F. Tauber's <u>Technical Services in Libraries</u>.

Several letters by one of the librarians also proved
to be interesting in the study as did some of the booklets
published in connection with special events in the development
of the institution. Aside from these materials, a biography
of Henry Boynton Smith, one of the librarians, was used; and
articles about the Library were located in such media as the
<u>New York Observer</u>, the <u>New York Evangelist</u>, <u>Harper's Weekly</u>,
the <u>New York Times</u>, and <u>Time</u>.

Descriptions of the collection were also found in
such reference works as Lane and Bolton's <u>Notes on Special
Collections in American Libraries</u>, <u>The New Schaff-Herzog
Encyclopedia of Religious Knowledge</u>, Dawson and Mudge's
<u>Special Collections in Libraries in the United States</u>, Downs's
<u>Resources of New York City Libraries</u>, and De Ricci and Wilson's
<u>Census of Medieval and Renaissance Manuscripts in the United
States and Canada</u>.

Many of the standard biographical works were consulted
for information on librarians, directors, Faculty members,
and benefactors. These tools included <u>Who's Who in America</u>,
<u>Who's Who in New York</u>, <u>Who's Who in the Protestant Clergy</u>,

<u>Religious Leaders of America</u>, <u>Who's Who in Library Service</u>,
<u>Who's Who in Music</u>, <u>Leaders in Education</u>, <u>Who Was Who in
America</u>, <u>The National Cyclopaedia of American Biography</u>, and
<u>Dictionary of American Biography</u>.

FOOTNOTES

[1]Charles Ripley Gillett, "Detailed History of the Union Theological Seminary in the City of New York." [New York, 1937]. (Typewritten.), p. iv. Note by C.C.R. [Cyril C. Richardson].

Chapter I

THE FOUNDING OF THE SEMINARY
AND ITS LIBRARY, 1835-40

The Era of the Founders, 1835-36

Union Theological Seminary was founded in New York
in 1836 during a period of intense controversy in American
Presbyterianism. A division between conservatives and liberals in the denomination began at Yale University where its
first Professor of Theology, Nathaniel William Taylor, taught
a liberalized brand of Calvinism which was unsatisfactory to
a strong segment that came to be known as the "Old School"
Presbyterians, in contrast to the "New School" Presbyterians
who found their theological position in the teachings of
Taylor. The "Old School" leaders objected especially to his
ideas that man's freedom is not an illusion but a reality and
to his contention that man is not born totally depraved.[1]
The "New School" men also wanted to continue Presbyterian
support of undenominational missionary and educational organizations, while the "Old School" leaders advocated the dis-
continuance of such support and the establishment or strengthening of Presbyterian groups to accomplish their purposes.[2]

The Early Meetings of the Founders

As the controversy developed, Princeton Seminary increasingly became identified with the "Old School," while the

9

"New School" leaders began planning for the formation of a seminary in New York.[3] The first meeting of the latter for this purpose was held on October 10, 1835 at the house of Knowles Taylor at 8 Bond Street in New York.[4] Taylor was one of the leading merchants of New York and a ruling elder in the Bleecker Street Presbyterian Church. He had given generously to several religious institutions, including the Union Theological Seminary in Virginia. He presided over the first meeting, attended by four clergymen and five laymen, to establish a "New School" seminary in New York.[5] A committee of Ways and Means was appointed at this meeting and was given the power to call another session as soon as it would be able to report.[6]

The next meeting was held on October 19 and was attended by five more men in addition to those who were at the first meeting. Two committees were appointed at this meeting, one for setting forth the goals of the proposed seminary and an outline of a curriculum for it and another to prepare recommendations for the best means of organizing a Board of Directors for the institution.[7]

The Founders' Plans for the Directorate

The planning group had grown by November 9 to twenty-seven members. At the meeting on that date the committee on the organization of the proposed seminary recommended that the government of the school be vested in a Board of Directors of twenty-eight members from New York and Brooklyn, one-half of whom should be clergymen, with the further provision that

all members of the Board should be members of the Presbyterian
Church.[8]

The Founders' Subscriptions

The Committee on Ways and Means reported in another
resolution that $65,000, or $13,000 per year for five years,
would be required to establish the institution which was to
be called the "New-York Theological Seminary." They planned
that this amount would not only provide for the current expenses but also would leave a building and a Library debt-free.
A subscription paper was thereupon presented in the meeting
and $31,000 toward the $65,000 was pledged.[9] This Committee
reported at the next meeting that additional subscriptions of
$4,500 had been obtained; and $5,500 was raised at this meeting, making a total of $41,000.[10] An announcement was made
at a meeting two months later that, despite a fire in New York
which had destroyed 500 buildings and $17,000,000 worth of
property on December 16, 1835,[11] the subscriptions to the
Seminary stood at $61,000.[12]

The Founders' Constitution

A draft of a constitution for the Seminary was accepted,
amended, adopted, and recommitted to a committee for alterations with plans for resubmission to the Directors at this
meeting. A resolution, too, that the Directors be authorized
to apply to the New York Legislature for an act of incorporation was also adopted at this meeting.[13]

The Aims of the Founders

The goals of the founders in the establishment of the Seminary were stated in a suggested preamble to this constitution:

> That the design of the founders of this Institution may be fully known to all whom it may concern, and be sacredly regarded by the Directors, Professors, and Students, it is judged proper to make the following preliminary statements.
>
> 1. A number of christians, Clergymen and Laymen in the cities of New York and Brooklyn, deeply impressed with the claims of the world upon the church of Christ to furnish a competent supply of well educated and pious ministers of correct principles to preach the gospel to every creature; impressed also with the inadequacy of all existing means for this purpose, and believing that large cities furnish many peculiar facilities, and advantages for conducting Theological education, after several meetings for consultation and prayer. Resolved unanimously, in humble dependence on the grace of God to attempt the establishment of a Theological Seminary in the city of New York.
>
> 2. This institution (while it will receive others to the advantages it may furnish) is principally designed for such young men in the cities of New York, and Brooklyn, as are or may be, desirous of pursuing a course of Theological study and whose circumstances render it inconvenient for them to go from home for this purpose.
>
> 3. It is the design of the Founders to furnish the means of a full and thorough education in all the subjects taught in the best theological Seminaries in the United States, and also to embrace therewith a thorough knowledge of the standards of the Faith and Discipline of the Presbyterian Church.
>
> 4. Being fully persuaded, that vital godliness well proved, a thorough education, and a wholesome practical training in works of benevolence and pastoral labours are all essentially necessary to meet the wants, and promote the best interests of the Kingdom of Christ, the Founders of this Seminary design, that its students living and acting under pastoral influence and performing the important duties of church members, in the several churches to which they belong, or with which they worship, in prayer meetings, the instruction of Sabbath schools, and Bible classes, and being conversant with all the social benevolent efforts, in this important location shall have the opportunity of adding to solid learning and true piety, enlightened experience.
>
> 5. By the foregoing advantages, the Founders hope and expect, with the blessing of God, to call forth from

the two flourishing cities, and to enlist in the
service of Christ and in the work of the ministry,
genius, talent, enlightened piety, and missionary
zeal, and to qualify many for the labours, and management of the various religious Institutions, Seminaries of learning, and enterprises of benevolence,
which characterize the present times.
6.   Finally. It is the design of the Founders to
provide a Theological Seminary in the midst of the
greatest, and most growing community in America, around
which all men, of moderate views and feelings, who desire to live free from party strife, and to stand
aloof from all the extremes of doctrinal speculation,
practical radicalism, and ecclesiastical domination,
may cordially and affectionally rally.[14]

Although the principal concern of the founders, ac-

cording to this preamble, was to provide an institution for

the education of ministers, they felt that their venture had

some unusual advantages for the accomplishment of this purpose.

First, the school, unlike the other seminaries of that era,

was to be located in a large city. They thought that this

would provide not only unusual opportunities for self-support

for the students but also experiences which would help them

to understand urban problems as they worked under the tutelage

of local pastors. They hoped also to recruit young men from

Brooklyn and New York for the ministry.

Second, they hoped that the atmosphere of moderation

which they envisaged for the Seminary would be a corrective

to the extremism which they thought existed in other schools.

As they solicited the support of men of "moderate views and

feelings," they specifically appealed to those who would

"stand aloof from all the extremes of doctrinal speculation,"

in which were included, in their opinion, not only the Uni-

tarians of Harvard and many of the New York Congregationalists

but also the "Old School" supporters of Princeton. That the
founders were moderate in their toleration of the "Old School,"
however, was demonstrated in the fact that one of them, Henry
White, the first Professor of Theology at Union, remained in
the "Old School."[15] The reference to "practical radicalism"
in the preamble probably referred to the anti-slavery movement,
for though these men desired emancipation, they thought that
it could be accomplished through legal and peaceful means.[16]
The "extremes of . . . ecclesiastical domination" in the document referred to the fact that the government of the Seminary
was under a Board of Directors which was not responsible to
any ecclesiastical organization.

The Founders' Plan for Ecclesiastical Relations

Despite this freedom from ecclesiastical control, however, each director, according to the Constitution, was to
promise to sustain "the Confession of Faith and Form of Government of the Presbyterian Church."[17] Each professor, moreover,
was to be required to make the following declaration:

> I believe the Scriptures of the Old and New Testaments
> to be the word of God, the only infallible rule of Faith
> and practice, and I do now in the presence of God, and
> the Directors of this Seminary, solemnly and sincerely
> receive and adopt the Confession of Faith of the
> Presbyterian Church . . . and I do also in like manner
> approve of the form of government and discipline of said
> church, and I do solemnly promise that I will not teach,
> nor inculcate any thing which shall appear to me, to be
> subversive of the said system of doctrine, or of the
> principles of said government, so long as I shall con-
> tinue to be a Professor in this seminary.[18]

Thus, although the Seminary was not responsible to
the General Assembly of the Presbyterian Church, it was considered by its founders to be a Presbyterian institution. Yet

they insisted that the institution be "equally open to every denomination of evangelical Christians." Unlike the Directors and the members of the Faculty, the students were not required to swear allegiance to the Presbyterian Church but were rather expected to promise to obey the Faculty and the Board of Directors.[19]

The Founders' Plans for the Library

One of the articles of this constitution specifically directed that the Board of Directors should form a set of rules for the protection, use, and management of the Library and should appoint and prescribe the duties of a Librarian.[20]

The Early Directorate

The First Board of Directors

The first meeting of the Directors was announced for January 18, 1836 with the provision that the Board would meet "afterward on their own adjournment," thus creating the independent existence of the Directorate.[21] The first meeting of these Directors was held at the American Tract Society's House on the designated date. Committees appointed that night included those on Faculty, Finance and Building, By-laws, Incorporation, and Library.[22]

The First Faculty

Thomas McAuley was elected by these Directors on September 30, 1836 as President and Professor of Pastoral Theology and Government.[23] He was born in 1777 and graduated from Union College in 1804. He was appointed Professor of

Mathematics and Natural Philosophy at this school in 1814.
Eight years later he became Pastor of the Rutgers Street
Presbyterian Church in the city of New York. He remained
with this congregation for six years, after which he became
the Pastor of Tenth Presbyterian Church in Philadelphia. He
returned to New York in 1833 as Pastor of the Murray Street
Presbyterian Church, in which capacity he was serving when
he was chosen to be the President of the new school.[24] He
was instrumental in securing both retrospective and current
materials for the Library. His appreciation of scholarship
was indicated by his support of the appropriation of funds
for the collection.

The other full-time member of the Faculty was Henry
White, Professor of Theology.[25] He, like McAuley, was a
graduate of Union College, having received a degree with honor
in 1824. His education at this school was financed by a
Ladies' Education Society in the Presbyterian Church at
Catskill, because he came from a poor family. He studied
theology at Princeton and in 1828 was installed as Pastor of
the Allen Street Presbyterian Church in New York. He was a
man of medium height and of "rather spare form." He also was
said to have a "keen eye, a lofty, expansive forehead, . . .
and premature and unusual whiteness" of hair. One friend
said of him, "You knew not only where to find him, but where
he would remain." His teaching was thoroughly Calvinistic
and rigidly orthodox.[26] His recommendations for current materials probably reflected his conservative theological

position, and he was responsible for the inclusion of books
by members of the "Old School."

Part-time members of the Faculty were Thomas H. Skinner,
Professor of Sacred Rhetoric; Ichabod S. Spencer, Professor
of Biblical History; and Erskine Mason, Professor of Ecclesiastical History.[27] Skinner was educated at the College of
New Jersey and Princeton. After several pastorates he became
Professor of Sacred Rhetoric in the Theological Seminary at
Andover. A year before classes began at the New York Seminary
he became the Pastor of the Mercer Street Presbyterian Church
in that city. He was especially effective in this post in
securing funds for the new school. He was said to be highly
diligent in the preparation of his sermons and lectures. As
a member of the "New School," he was committed to the theology
of the Reformed Churches but tolerant in his approach to minor
differences in doctrine.[28] He attempted to read all of the
new books in the fields of Church Government, Sacred Rhetoric,
and the Pastoral Office and, undoubtedly, recommended many of
them for purchase for the Library.

Ichabod S. Spencer was also a graduate of Union College.
Following a three-year term as Principal of the Grammar School
in Schenectady, he was appointed to a similar post at the
Academy in Canandaigua, New York. He was called to the Congregational Church in Northampton, Massachusetts in 1826; and in
1832 he became the Pastor of the Second Presbyterian Church
in Brooklyn, where he stayed until his death. His best known
work was <u>A Pastor's Sketches, or Conversations with Anxious</u>

Inquirers respecting the Way of Salvation.[29] His recommendations for library acquisitions probably reflected his interest
in evangelism as well as his teaching field.

Another part-time teacher was Erskine Mason, Professor
of Ecclesiastical History.[30] He graduated from Dickinson
College, where his father was President, in 1823 and from
Princeton Seminary in 1825. Following a pastorate in Schenectady,
he became Pastor of the Bleecker Street Presbyterian Church
in New York. A volume of his sermons was published under the
title, A Pastor's Legacy.[31] Any works which he recommended
in his teaching field for the Library probably reflected his
scholarly yet pragmatic approach to the ministry.

The Faculty having been chosen, the Recorder was instructed to announce that the Seminary would begin giving instruction on December 5, 1836. Application for admission was
to be made to President Thomas McAuley, 112 Leonard Street.[32]

The First Students

Thirteen young men appeared at the house of the President on the designated day for enrollment in the new Seminary,[33]
and ten additional students enrolled during the first academic
year.[34] Because the school had no buildings, these students
lived at home and reported to the apartments of the professors
for instruction.[35]

The First Curriculum

The Directors planned the following curriculum for
these students:

1. . . . First or Junior year . . .

The Hebrew language with such exegetical exercises on
   the Greek and Hebrew Scriptures as the professor may
   direct
Biblical Archaeology
Natural Theology
Evidences of the Christian religion
Elements of the philosophy of rhetoric
The Sacred Canon . . .
Sacred Chronology
Mental and Moral Science
Ancient Mythology . . .

2. . . . Second or Middle year . . .

Theology
Biblical History . . .
Exegetical study of the Hebrew and Greek scriptures
Pastoral Theology
Sacred Rhetoric
Ecclesiastical History
History of Biblical criticism . . .

3. . . . Third or Senior year

Ecclesiastical History
Pastoral Theology
Church Government
Exegetical study of the Greek and Hebrew scriptures
Theology
Sacred Rhetoric
Biblical History . . .[36]

The First Building Plans

The beginning of plans for a building for the developing institution was made at the February 10, 1836 meeting of
the Directors when the Committee on Finance and Building suggested that eight city lots be purchased under a lease from
the Sailors' Snug Harbor for $8,000 and provisions for an
annual ground rent of $700. Four of these fronted one hundred
feet on University Place between Seventh and Eighth Streets;
and four, attached to the rear, were on Greene Street. The
depth of the plot was 175 feet.[37]

This location was at that time on the outskirts of the city, for between Tenth Street and the village of Harlem lay open country. The only ecclesiastical institutions north of Tenth Street and south of Harlem were General Theological Seminary of the Protestant Episcopal Church, which had been erected outside the city near another Episcopal institution, St. Peter's Chapel on Twentieth Street, and several mission stations in the country. The building for the University of the City of New-York was under construction one block from the site, which was chosen for its proximity to the business section of the city but with sufficient remoteness to provide a quiet retreat.[38]

Construction on the building for the Seminary on these lots was begun in March of 1837 without adequate financial support. The first installment of the subscriptions, payable June 1, 1836, had produced approximately $10,000; but nearly all of this had been used for the purchase of the lease on the lots on University Place, the ground rent and assessments.[39]

For two reasons this was a poor time to begin construction on Presbyterian seminary buildings. First, the nation was shaken by the panic of 1837, in which many banks defaulted and which began an era of hard times in America.[40] Second, the Presbyterian Church was divided in that year into two groups; and the New York Seminary had support on both sides.[41] Because of these conditions, the second installment of the subscription amounted to only $8,000. The Directors, therefore, approved a recommendation of the Finance Committee to discontinue

the construction on the buildings until more adequate financial
means could be secured.[42]

The First Library

Long before the building was begun, however, plans
were made for a Library for the Seminary. The first Library
Committee had been appointed by the Directors on January 18,
1836 and was composed of the Rev. Thomas McAuley, D.D.; the
Rev. Thomas H. Skinner, D.D.; the Rev. Absalom Peters, D.D.;
the Rev. William Patton; and the Rev. Ichabod S. Spencer.[43]
The Committee included no laymen perhaps because it was thought
that clergymen were better qualified to make decisions about
the Library; on the other hand, it may have been deemed wise
to appoint the laymen to other committees which were considered
to have been more important. The Library Committee, at any
rate, was charged with the responsibility of appropriating
the funds placed at its disposal to buy works "appropriate
for a theological library and to seek gifts of books for the
collection."[44]

The first allocation for the Committee was made nearly
eleven months later when $1,000 were allocated for the purchase
of books, and Professor Henry White was appointed one week
later to be in charge of the Library.[45] The first gift made
to the collection was by Messrs. Gould and Newman of New York,
who presented thirty-one volumes.[46] Other gifts presented to
the school during this period included a set of Jonathan
Edwards' works in ten volumes given by Micah Baldwin, a set
of the Missionary Herald by the American Board of Commissioners

for Foreign Missions, a set of reports by the American Education Society, and a copy of the <u>Reiver Bible</u> in five volumes
from Col. William Edwards of Green County, New York.[47]

Still other gifts included:

Donor	Author	Title
William Patton	Grotius, Hugo	De Veritate Religionis Christianae
	Flavel, John	Pneumatologia
Thomas McAuley		The Christian Observer, 13 volumes
		Religious Intelligencer, 7 volumes
		The Christian's Magazine, 3 volumes
	Montaigne, Michel Eyquem de	Works
Latimer R. Shaw	Henry, Matthew	An Exposition of the Old and New Testament
	Heber, Reginald	The Life of Reginald Heber
	Ainsworth, Robert	Ainsworth's Latin Dictionary
	Owen, John	An Exposition of the Epistle to the Hebrews[48]

A document important in the development of the Library,
<u>The Plan of the New-York Theological Seminary</u>, was published
on May 5, and its provisions were basic for later constitutions
and by-laws. It provided that the Librarian was to be appointed by the Directors for a term of three years, subject
to dismissal at any time by them. The Library was, according
to the document, to be for the "exclusive use" of the Faculty,
Directorate, and students; but provisions were made for loan-
ing books to others who had permission in writing from a member of the Faculty. Provisions were made also for an annual
inspection of the library by the Faculty, with a subsequent
report to the Directors. The Librarian was also assigned the
task of keeping an alphabetical catalog of the collection

"in which the title, size, place and number of copies and volumes of every author" was to be recorded.[49]

The Acquisition of the Van Ess Library

The Purchase of the Library

An important development in the history of the Library occurred when the Directors received a letter of acceptance for the position of Professor of Biblical Literature from Edward Robinson, whom they had elected at their meeting on December 20, 1836[50] on the condition that he be granted a leave of absence for the academic year 1837-38, during which he planned to visit Europe. The primary purpose of his trip was to visit his family there; but while he was there, he wrote that he hoped to purchase materials for the Seminary Library and also to establish connections in Europe which would be of benefit to the institution in the future in the procurement of books. The Directors promptly accepted this condition.[51] His appreciation of scholarship was indicated in a paragraph in his letter of acceptance.

> On the general subject of a Library, it is here only proper to remark that a full apparatus of books in every department of Theology is, of course, indispensable to the prosperity of the Institution. In particular, the Library should also contain a complete series of the works of the Fathers so called, in the best editions, and with proper apparatus, and likewise the best edition of every Greek and Roman writer, with the necessary aids for their elucidation. There is not a page of any Greek writer which does not in the same way yield illustration to the sacred text, and the same is true also in a modified sense of all the Roman writers.[52]

While it is questionable that it would be necessary to have the complete writings of the Greeks and the Romans in

a theological library and while it is, further, doubtful that
all of these would be useful in Biblical interpretation, the
liberal view of that science expressed in this letter was
commendable. The classical tradition in which he had been
educated was to have many consequences for the development of
the Library.

Harriet Beecher Stowe's husband, Professor Calvin E.
Stowe, who had recently returned from Europe, wrote to
Robinson from Lane Seminary on April 3, 1837 that an unusual
collection of books was for sale on that continent.[53] Stowe
had been in Europe buying books for Lane Seminary, where he
was a professor, and already having purchased a large collection, he was offered the Library of Leander Van Ess of Marburg
on moderate terms. The president of the New-York Theological
Seminary said later that Stowe had not needed this addition
to "the extensive collection he had already purchased" and,
thus, transferred the offer to the New York school.[54] Stowe's
problem was probably related more to finances than to an over-
abundance of materials, but his hesitancy proved to be the
New York Seminary's opportunity, although subsequent action
on the acquisition of the collection was deferred until July.
The Library Committee recommended then that on his trip to
Europe Robinson be requested to examine the Library which had
been recommended for the New-York Seminary by Stowe and be
asked also to report to the Directors on the condition of the
collection, its value to the institution, its price, and the
terms of payment. That he "secure the refusal of it, until

he can receive the answer of the Board" was, moreover, recommended.[55]

He wrote, upon his arrival in Europe, an encouraging letter about the value of the Library, and the Finance Committee was authorized by the Directors to raise the money to purchase it.[56] After an examination of the materials by Wolff of the University of Erlingen, a brother of Mrs. Gordon Philip Buck of New York,[57] they were purchased by the Directors in April, 1838 for 10,000 florins, although they had cost Van Ess 50,000 florins.[58] Wolff spent fourteen weeks examining and packing the Library without charge. It was shipped from Alzey in Germany[59] and arrived in New York in October, 1838, at a total cost to the Seminary of $5,070.08.[60] The firm of Caspar Meier Co. attended to its importation without expense to the school.[61]

This collection was characterized in Special Collections in Libraries in the United States by W. Dawson Johnston and Isadore G. Mudge as "for many years . . . the most important . . . in the United States"[62] and in The Evening Post: New York for May 8, 1888, by Professor T. F. Crane of Cornell University, as the most valuable library which had been brought into the United States.[63] Further testimony as to the importance of the collection was given by Justin Winsor in an address at the public exercises on the completion of the Library of the University of Michigan in 1883:

> In the fifty or sixty years which followed the first work of the press, and within the fifteenth century, it is usually reckoned that there were at least 16,000

volumes printed at all of the presses of the forty-
two cities which are known to have had printing
offices. It is not an unfair estimate to place the
average edition of those days at 500 copies, and
this would give a round eight million of incunabula--
cradle books--of which the number which have come
down to us is comparatively small. Of this 8,000,000
I doubt if there are more than a very few thousand
on this continent. I do not regard the possible
excess in some of the libraries of Spanish America,
when I say that the largest number which I know in
this part of the world is the four or five hundred
which belong to the Union Theological Seminary, of
New York.[64]

The History of the Library

This Library was begun as a collection of Reformation

literature[65] in the Benedictine Monastery of Marienmünster,

near Marburg,[66] in the Diocese of Paderborn in Westphalia,

during the time of the Reformation. Approximately 600 volumes

by the Reformers and their critics[67] were collected in the

monastery at that time and kept in a room, the door of which

was inscribed, "Libri Prohibiti."[68]

The key to this door was kept in the latter part of

the eighteenth century by a monk whose secular name was Johann

Heinrich Van Ess but who was known in the monastery as Brother

Leander. He had been born in Marburg on February 25, 1770

and had been educated in the Dominican Gymnasium there. He

entered Marienmünster as a novice in 1790 and was ordained

in 1796. He was appointed in 1799 to supervise the parish

of Schwalenburg, in the principality of Lippe; but his super-

vision was to take place from the abbey.[69]

Events were occurring, in the meantime, which were

to change radically his future. The success of the French

Republic in battle had resulted in the treaties of Campo
Formio in 1797 and Lunéville in 1800, through which France
was given Belgium and the left bank of the Rhine. The Germans
who surrendered their states by these treaties were recom-
pensed by lands within the empire, and to accomplish this the
ecclesiastical territories were secularized and divided among
them. Paderborn was given to Prussia and became a hereditary
principality in 1803, although Prussia had taken possession
on August 3, 1802.[70]

The monks at Marienmünster anticipated the sequestra-
tion of the monastic property and attempted to save as much
of the Library as they could by dividing it among themselves
and moving the parts to places of safety.[71]

Van Ess took as his share the "Libri Prohibiti," which
contained among other things at least 500 works which bore
the name of Luther. He moved to Schwalenburg, where he administered his parish, and remained in that place until 1812,
when, through the influence of the Superintendent of Instruction of Westphalia, he was called on July 30 to the positions
of Extraordinary Professor of Catholic Theology in the
University of Marburg and Curate of the town, which included
the directorship of a seminary for teachers.[72]

The kingdom of Westphalia was abolished in 1813 and
its parts were returned to their former governments. Marburg
reverted to the Electorate of Hesse, and in 1814 Van Ess was
appointed by that government as an Extraordinary Professor
and teacher of canon law. During this period he made a

translation into German of the New Testament and in the
process brought together a Library of

> Bibles, polyglots, lexicons, concordances, commen-
> taries, the Latin and Greek Fathers, the decrees of
> councils and popes, church histories, and other
> similar literary treasures, including a large col-
> lection of Incunabula . . . in all, with what he
> had saved from the wreck at Paderborn (more than
> 13,000 volumes), about 6000 separate works.[73]

His New Testament in German was published in 1810; and with
the coöperation of the British and Foreign Bible Society, he
circulated several thousand copies of this work.[74] He also
prepared editions of the Septuagint in 1824, the Vulgate in
1822-24 and the Greek New Testament with the Vulgate in 1827.[75]

Grown old and with financial problems, he retired to
Alzey, in Hesse-Darmstadt, and in 1837[76] offered his Library,
which had required forty years and approximately $25,000 for
him to acquire,[77] for sale for 11,000 florins.[78] Calvin
Stowe heard of the sale and wrote to Robinson about it, whereupon it was purchased for the New York Seminary.

The Contents of the Library

The collection contained approximately 14,000 volumes,
representing 6,000 works.[79] The manuscripts in the collection
are listed in a catalog in the handwriting of Van Ess, which
may be found in the Union Theological Seminary Library,[80] and
also in Ricci and Wilson's Census of Medieval and Renaissance
Manuscripts.[81] The authors and dates in the descriptions by
W. W. Rockwell in this work are given below:

Author	Date
1. Biblia	XVIIIth c.
3. Missale	(XVth c.)
4. Origenes	(XIVth c.)
5. S. Thomas de Aquino	XVth c.
6. Smaragdus	XIVth c.
7. Chronicon	Early XIXth c.
8. Johannes Andreae	(24 Nov. 1483)
9. Isidorus Hispalensis	1472
10. Biblia	XVth c.
11. Liber miraculorum	(XIIth, XVIth c.)
12. Hildebertus Lavardinensis	(1473-1476)
13. Johannes Gerson	(XVth c.)
14. Albertus Magnus	(1463)
15. Graduale	(XVIth c.)
19. Collectarius	(XVth c.)
20. Aldenberg	(XVIIth c.)
21. Summa	(XVth c.)
24. Vocabularius	(1463)
29. Expositiones Evangeliorum	(XIIIth c.)
30. Preces variae	XIXth c.
31. Commonplace book	(XVIIth c.)
37. [Early Deeds and documents]	(XIIIth to XVIIIth c.)[82]

The collection also included 430 incunabula[83] and
1,246 works of Reformation literature[84] in original impressions,
dealing principally with the earlier period of the Lutheran
reformation.[85] It also included approximately 200 editions
of the Vulgate and German Bibles from 1478,[86] 2,000 volumes
of patristic literature, and 1,000 volumes from the sixteenth
and seventeenth centuries.[87] Its subjects included

> . . . the works of the Fathers; an extensive collec-
> tion of works on Church History; on Ecclesiastical
> Law; on the acts of the councils of all ages of the
> Church; and on Didactic and Polemic Theology. . . .
> It also . . . [contained] an extensive collection of
> . . . Commentaries, of Concordances, of Lexicons, of
> Polyglotts, of Harmonies, and of other works needed
> by the student of scripture.[88]

It included, too, works on

> . . . Roman Catholic theology, liturgies, Canon law,
> and Casuistry . . . collections of councils and of
> lives of saints, such as the Acta Sanctorum . . .
> and German theological periodicals.[89]

Although a catalog of the Van Ess collection was not made nor, except for the manuscripts and the incunabula, was it kept separate from the rest of the acquistions of that period, most of the following works probably came from that Library:

Author   Title

General Works

Despont, ed.	Bibliotheca maxima veterum patrum
Gallandius	Bibliotheca graeco-latina veterum patrum
Martène and Durand	Veterum scriptorum amplissima collectio
Martène and Durand	Thesaurus anecdotorum novus
D'Archery	Spicilegium

Sermons

Johannes von Paltz	Celifodina
Gritsch	Quadragesimale
Herolt Haselbach	Sermones discipuli super epistolas dominicales
Lochmair	Sermones
Meffreth	Hortulus reginae
Michaelo Carchano	Quadragesimale
George Morgenstern	Sermones Disertissimi
Paulus Florentinus	Quadragesimale
Robert Caraczoli	Sermones Dormi Secure
Nyder	Preceptorium
Peraldus	Summa virtutum et vitiorum
Petrus de Natalibus	Catalogus Sanctorum

Miscellaneous

St. Bridget	Revelationes
Boethius	De consolatione philosophiae
Abbott Joachim	Vaticinia
Petrarch	De Vita Solitaria
Vincent of Beauvais	Speculum Doctrinale

Classics

Catullus	Carme[n] hexametrum nuptiale edylion
Seneca	Epistolae etc.
Cato	Moralia instituta
Josephus	De antiquitatibus ac de bello Judaico
Perotti	Grammatica

Author	Title
	Oriental History
M. Crusius	Turcograeciae libri octo
Haythorn	Liber historiarum partium
	Orientis
Laonicus Chalcocdndylas [sic]	De Origine et rebus gestis
	Turcorum libri decem[90]

An Era of Growth with Problems, 1838-40

The Growth of the Institution

The bill for this collection was paid through a loan
of $5,000 from the President of the institution, Thomas
McAuley; and it was mortgaged as security. It arrived in
New York as the new building for the Seminary was being completed and was housed in a room provided for it there.[91]
This building was financed through loans from two friends of
the Seminary in the amount of $27,000 secured by mortgage on
the land and the building itself,[92] which included, in addition to the Library, a chapel,[93] three lecture rooms, a
reading room, and a few dormitory rooms.[94]

Despite heavy indebtedness, the school was moving
forward rapidly. It had, within a period of two years, secured an enrollment of ninety-two students,[95] constructed a
new building, acquired a Faculty of ten,[96] and purchased an
unusual Library. Although the remark of the President that
its curriculum was "not, in its extent, its variety, and its
excellence of arrangement, inferior to that of any other seminary in our country"[97] was probably not justified, the New
York Seminary offered courses in Arabic and Syriac in addition
to the courses taught in other similar institutions.[98]

Because of this growth the school appeared to be assured of continuity; thus, an act of incorporation was secured for the Seminary from the Legislature of the State of New York on March 27, 1839 under the name, "The Union Theological Seminary in the city of New-York;" and it provided "equal privileges of admission and instruction" for "students of every denomination of christians."[99] The name, "Union," was probably chosen to differentiate the school from the General Theological Seminary, which was also a "New-York Theological Seminary," and also because of the friendship of some of the founders for Union Theological Seminary in Virginia; yet it was a prophetic name for the unitive role which the Seminary was to hold.

While other phases of the institution were developing, its Library was growing too. Yet President McAuley estimated that approximately 5,000 or 6,000 more volumes, chiefly in the English language, would be minimal to fulfill the purposes of the institution.[100] This was probably one of the few occasions when an American theological library was disproportionately strong in materials in languages other than English. He, therefore, promised, to help correct this deficiency, by promising that

> when any individual or individuals, society, church, or other association, shall contribute in books or money any sum not less than $250, the name of the donor or donors shall be engraven on a suitable plate, and firmly and permanently fixed on an appropriate alcove in the Library.[101]

The institution had a new collection, a new building, and a new plan for gifts; it was next to secure a new Librarian.

Robinson, who was to fill this position when he returned from Europe, had been granted another year's leave of absence for his stay there; thus, plans were laid for employing two instructors to replace him, one of whom would give exegetical instruction and serve as Librarian. R. B. Patton was appointed to this position,[102] and five members of the Faculty were assigned to direct and superintend him in the preparation of an alphabetical catalog.[103] Another of his duties was to open the Library for public inspection of the Van Ess Collection for three days during February, 1839.[104]

The Directors had been working for months on the Constitution and By-Laws of the Seminary, and at about this time the document was referred to the Faculty for publication.[105] In the appendix to this document the Library was said to have 15,000 volumes; and because the Van Ess Collection included approximately 14,000 volumes, the remainder of the collection must have included only about 1,000 volumes. Since much of it would have been unusable because of its antiquity and foreign languages, the 1,000 volumes, which were presumably chiefly in English, constituted an impoverished collection for a professional school with nearly 100 students.

The librarianship of Patton, under whose administration these provisions were published, was short-lived, for he died on May 6, 1839[106] and was replaced by Herman Bokum, who was appointed as Assistant Librarian to work under the supervision of Professor White. One of his principal duties was to be the completion of the catalog of the Library.[107] A student

in the Seminary, he was born in Königsberg, Prussia on
January 2, 1807 and taught German at Harvard before coming
to New York.[108] His facility with German would have been
helpful to him in cataloging the Van Ess Collection.

Problems with Finances

Although the school's enrollment, curriculum, and
Library were growing, the institution in 1839 was in serious
financial difficulty. Only $50,000 of the original subscrip-
tion had, for instance, been paid, while more than this had
been spent.[109] The Treasurer, further, reported $16,287.04
in bills for which he had no money, plus these current expenses:

Annual interest on loans	$3,080
Annual ground rent	800
Taxes	160
Insurance premium	92
	4,132
Needed for payment of professors' salaries, etc.	5,500
	$9,632 110

The professors' salaries had mostly been unpaid for
two years.[111] Henry White, for example, had been forced to
borrow a year's salary, to operate a boarding house in his
home, to do supply preaching, and to solicit in person funds
for his own salary.[112]

The school received another blow that winter when
President McAuley resigned and presented a bill for funds
owed to him by the Seminary. The Directors decided at the
meeting at which the resignation was offered that one of the
chief duties of the new President would be to raise funds
for the institution.[113]

Agents were sent, in view of these circumstances, throughout the country to solicit funds for the desperate institution,[114] and enough money was raised in pledges "to justify the Board in continuing the Seminary in operation for the ensuing year."[115]

FOOTNOTES

[1] Kenneth Scott Latourette, *The Nineteenth Century outside Europe* ("Christianity in a Revolutionary Age," Vol. III; New York: Harper & Brothers, Publishers, 1961), p. 160.

[2] Robert Ellis Thompson, *A History of the Presbyterian Churches in the United States* ("The American Church History Series," edited by Philip Schaff et. al., Vol. VI; New York: The Christian Literature Co., 1894), pp. 105-08.

[3] *Ibid.*, p. 114 and *New York Evangelist*, April 16, 1836.

[4] Minutes of the Board of Directors of Union Theological Seminary in the City of New York, October 10, 1835.

[5] George Lewis Prentiss, *The Union Theological Seminary in the City of New York: Historical and Biographical Sketches of Its First Fifty Years* (New York: Anson D. F. Randolph and Co., 1889), pp. 134-36.

[6] Directors, *op. cit.*, October 10, 1835.

[7] *Ibid.*, October 19, 1835.

[8] *Ibid.*, November 9, 1835.

[9] *Ibid.*, November 9, 1835.

[10] *Ibid.*, November 16, 1835.

[11] Edwin F. Hatfield, *The Early Annals of Union Theological Seminary in the City of New York* (New York: No. 30 Clinton Place, 1876), p. 9.

[12] Directors, *op. cit.*, January 11, 1836.

[13] *Ibid.*

[14] *Ibid.*

[15] Union Theological Seminary in the City of New York, *One Hundredth Anniversary, 1836-1936* (New York: Union Theological Seminary, 1936), p. 19.

[16] *Ibid.*

[17]Directors, op. cit., January 11, 1835.

[18]Ibid.

[19]Ibid.

[20]Ibid.

[21]Ibid.

[22]Ibid., January 18, 1836.

[23]Ibid., September 30, 1836.

[24]Prentiss, op. cit., pp. 149-50.

[25]Minutes of the Faculty of Union Theological Seminary in the City of New York, p. 1; and Hatfield, op. cit., pp. 11-12.

[26]Prentiss, op. cit., pp. 251-54.

[27]Faculty, op. cit., p. 1.

[28]Ibid., pp. 254-57.

[29]Ibid., p. 152.

[30]Faculty, op. cit., p. 1.

[31]Prentiss, op. cit., pp. 130-34.

[32]Directors, op. cit., November 24, 1836.

[33]Hatfield, op. cit., p. 12.

[34]Prentiss, op. cit., p. 25.

[35]Faculty, op. cit., p. 1.

[36]Directors, op. cit., December 12, 1836.

[37]Ibid., February 10, 1836; and Union Theological Seminary, Services in Adams Chapel at the Dedication of the New Buildings of the Union Theological Seminary, 1200 Park Avenue, New York City, December 9, 1884 (New York: Printing House of William C. Martin, 111 John Street, 1885), p. 3.

[38]Hatfield, op. cit., p. 11.

[39]Ibid., p. 13.

[40]Samuel Eliot Morison and Henry Steele Commager, The Growth of the American Republic, Vol. I (New York: Oxford University Press, 1956), p. 562.

[41]Hatfield, _op. cit._, p. 14.

[42]Directors, _op. cit._, April 26, 1837.

[43]_Ibid._, January 18, 1836.

[44]_Ibid._

[45]_Ibid._, December 12, 1836.

[46]_Ibid._, January 8, 1837.

[47]_Ibid._, January 6, 1837.

[48]_Ibid._, April 18, 1838.

[49]New-York Theological Seminary, _The Plan of the New York Theological Seminary_ ([New York: New-York Theological Seminary] 1837). This document has been lost but these provisions are cited in Charles Ripley Gillett, "Detailed History of the Union Theological Seminary in the City of New York" [New York, 1937.] (Typewritten.), p. 1089 and Charles Ripley Gillett, "Extracts from Source Materials Used in Preparing a History of Union Theological Seminary" [New York, 1937.] (Typewritten.), p. 1A.

[50]Directors, _op. cit._, December 20, 1836.

[51]_Ibid._, January 20, 1837.

[52]_Ibid._

[53]Hatfield, _op. cit._, p. 2.

[54]Thomas McAuley, _Extracts from a Speech Delivered by Dr. McAuley at the Dedication of the Edifice Belonging to the New-York Theological Seminary, 12th Dec. 1838_ [New York, 1839?], p. 2.

[55]Directors, _op. cit._, July 5, 1837.

[56]_Ibid._, December 22, 1837.

[57]McAuley, _op. cit._, p. 2.

[58]Hatfield, _op. cit._, p. 15.

[59]McAuley, _op. cit._, p. 2.

[60]Hatfield, _op. cit._, p. 15.

[61]Directors, _op. cit._, November 20, 1838.

[62]W. Dawson Johnston and Isadore G. Mudge, Special Collections in Libraries in the United States, U. S. Bureau of Education Bulletin, 1912, No. 23 (Washington: U. S. Government Printing Office, 1912), p. 10.

[63]The Evening Post: New York, May 8, 1888.

[64]Justin Winsor, "Address," Public Exercises on the Completion of the Library Building of the University of Michigan, December 12, 1883 (Ann Arbor: University of Michigan, 1884), p. 33.

[65]McAuley, op. cit., p. 3.

[66]The Evening Post: New York, May 8, 1888.

[67]Hatfield, op. cit., p. 14.

[68]McAuley, op. cit., p. 3.

[69]The Evening Post: New York, May 8, 1888.

[70]Ibid.

[71]McAuley, op. cit., p. 3.

[72]The Evening Post: New York, May 8, 1888.

[73]Hatfield, op. cit., p. 14.

[74]Ibid., pp. 14-15.

[75]The Evening Post: New York, May 8, 1888.

[76]Ibid.

[77]McAuley, op. cit., p. 3.

[78]Hatfield, op. cit., p. 15.

[79]McAuley, op. cit., pp. 3-4.

[80]Union Theological Seminary, Library, Catalogue of the Van Ess Collection [n.p., 18-?].

[81]Seymour De Ricci and W. J. Wilson, Census of Medieval and Renaissance Manuscripts in the United States and Canada, Vol. II (New York: Kraus Reprint Corporation, 1961), pp. 1637-44, 2322.

[82]Ibid.

[83]Johnston and Mudge, op. cit., p. 10 and Union Theological Seminary, Catalogue of the Officers and Students of the Union Theological Seminary in the City of New York, 1877-78 (New York: Wm. C. Martin, 111 John Street, 1877), p. 5.

[84]Ibid. and Johnston and Mudge, op. cit., p. 17.

[85]Ibid.

[86]Union Theological Seminary, Catalogue . . . 1877-78, p. 5.

[87]William Coolidge Lane and Charles Knowles Bolton, Notes on Special Collections in American Libraries ("Library of Harvard University, Bibliographical Contributions," edited by Justin Winsor, No. 45; Cambridge, Mass.: Issued by the Library of Harvard University, 1892), p. 49.

[88]McAuley, op. cit., p. 4.

[89]Prentiss, The Union Theological Seminary in the City of New York: Its Design . . . , p. 352.

[90]The Evening Post: New York, May 8, 1888.

[91]Hatfield, op. cit., p. 15.

[92]Ibid., p. 13.

[93]McAuley, op. cit., p. 2.

[94]Union Theological Seminary, Services in Adams Chapel . . . , p. 3.

[95]Hatfield, op. cit., p. 15.

[96]McAuley, op. cit., p. 2.

[97]Ibid.

[98]Ibid.

[99]New York (State) Laws, Statutes, etc., Laws of the State of New-York Passed at the Sixty-Second Session of the Legislature Begun and Held at the City of Albany, the First Day of January, 1839 (Albany: Printed for W. & A. Gould & Co. [etc.], 1839), pp. 83-84.

[100]McAuley, op. cit., p. 4.

[101]Ibid.

[102]Directors, op. cit., December 26, 1838.

[103] *Ibid*., January 9, 1839.

[104] Faculty, op. cit., February 8, 1839.

[105] Directors, op. cit., February 1, 1839.

[106] Gillett, Detailed History, p. 1104.

[107] Directors, op. cit., June 21, 1839.

[108] Union Theological Seminary, General Catalogue of Union Theological Seminary In the City of New-York, 1836-1876 (New York: S. W. Green, Printer, 16 and 18 Jacob Street, 1876), p. 21.

[109] Prentiss, The Union Theological Seminary in the City of New York: Historical . . . , p. 27.

[110] Minutes of the Finance Committee of Union Theological Seminary in the City of New York, February 5, 1840.

[111] Prentiss, The Union Theological Seminary in the City of New York: Historical . . . , p. 27.

[112] Hatfield, op. cit., p. 17.

[113] Directors, op. cit., February 12, 1840.

[114] Hatfield, op. cit., p. 17.

[115] Directors, op. cit., May 6, 1840.

Chapter II

THE LIBRARIANSHIP OF EDWARD ROBINSON, 1840-51

The Pre-Union Background of Robinson

Edward Robinson, who took charge of the Library of New-York Theological Seminary in 1840, had a good background for his position. He was born on April 10, 1794 in Southington, Connecticut, where his father was Pastor of the Congregational Church, a farmer, and owner of a grist-mill and saw-mill, in which roles he was the wealthiest man in Southington. Young Robinson in 1812 entered Hamilton College, where he was academically at the head of his class and where, upon graduation, he accepted a tutorship in mathematics and Greek. He was married in 1818 to Eliza Kirkland, sister of John Thornton Kirkland, president of Harvard. After her death within a year following their marriage, he received possession from her estate of a valuable farm where he lived until 1821, when he moved to Andover, Massachusetts. He published there an edition of eleven books of the Iliad. He was appointed, in the fall of 1823, Instructor in Hebrew in the Theological Seminary at Andover.[1]

He resigned this position in 1826 and went abroad for four years for study with such theological and philosophical scholars as Tholuck and Gesenius at Halle and Neander and Ritter at Berlin. He was married in 1828 to Therese Albertine

Louise, a daughter of Staatsrath von Jacob, a professor at
Halle; and he brought her to the United States in 1830 when
he became Professor Extraordinary of Sacred Literature and
Librarian in the Theological Seminary at Andover. Here he
remained for three years, during which he founded and wrote
nearly one-half of the articles for The Biblical Repository.
Because of poor health, he resigned and moved to Boston, where
in 1836 he published his Greek and English Lexicon of the
New Testament and his translation of Gesenius' Hebrew Lexicon.
Almost simultaneously with their publication, he was appointed
at the New-York Theological Seminary, but he was on leave of
absence for the first four years of his appointment while
doing research in Europe and Palestine and preparing his
Biblical Researches for publication.[2] The Directors, thus,
had secured for their Professor of Biblical Literature and
Librarian a mature scholar.

The Financial Limitations
during His Librarianship

The Seminary's General Financial Condition

His ten years during the 1840's, while profitable to
the institution for his teaching, scholarship, and publication,
were not distinguished ones in the development of the Library.
This was true largely because of the serious financial condition
in which the school was involved throughout the decade. He,
in fact, apparently had little, if any, budgeted funds with
which to buy books during the entire decade. His most important
contribution to the development of the collection, therefore,

was probably in connection with his responsibility in the
acquisition of the Van Ess Library before he began his duties
at the Seminary. When he returned from Europe and began his
work there on December 1, 1840,[3] only about $50,000 on the
initial $65,000 subscription had been paid. Mortgages had,
therefore, been acquired against the building and the Van Ess
Library to secure funds for the operation of the school.[4]

The institution received a new President, Joel Parker,
at this time. He had studied at Hamilton College as well as
at Auburn Seminary and had served as Pastor of churches in
Rochester, New York, New Orleans, and New York City.[5] He was
unable to raise enough money to pay the Professors' salaries
and the other accounts due the Seminary,[6] however, and two
years later left the school to become Pastor of the Clinton
Street Presbyterian Church in Philadelphia.[7] Because of the
dire straits of his administration, his contributions to the
development of the collection were few. Any recommendations
he may have made for contemporary materials probably reflected
his intense interest in evangelism.

In view of these circumstances, three years after he
had been appointed, Robinson, along with the only other full-
time Professor, Henry White, proposed to the Directors that
their salaries be reduced from $2,500 per year to $2,000 per
year with the understanding that they would be paid promptly
in quarterly installments. They indicated that unless they
were paid more regularly, they would be forced to seek other
employment. Although the Directors agreed to pay them more

promptly on these reduced terms,[8] they were unable to do so;
therefore, on June 27, 1843, they received from the two
teachers another communication in which it was stated that
only one-half of the first quarter's salary had been paid to
one of them and a little more than one-fourth to the other.
They, furthermore, gave notice that unless the arrearages for
1843 were paid along with provision for their future support,
they would resign on the first day of October.[9]

Professor White notified the Board on September 19
that he had received an appointment in Auburn Theological Seminary which he would accept if he were not assured of permanent
support at Union.[10] Although he refused the appointment at
Auburn, he demanded that his salary from May 1, 1843 be paid
and that $25,000 be subscribed by November 1 if he were to
stay at the New-York Seminary.[11] Robinson joined him that
week with another letter threatening to resign by October 1
unless "proper provisions were made."[12]

A meeting of friends of the Seminary was called in
response to these demands, and $26,000 were pledged for an
endowment for the Professorship of Theology and another $2,000
per year for five years for current expenses. Robinson was
promised his salary by the Directors from any collections from
churches or from any other funds made available to the school.[13]
These plans were accepted by both men.[14]

The desperate circumstances of the institution during
this period were revealed in this financial statement:

The expected receipts to be used for instruction were

From endowment of chair of systematic theology	$1.786.75
" Young men's professorship	750.00
" Philadelphia professorship	850.00
" Five-year subscriptions	1.795.00
" Investment for professorship of Biblical literature	439.00

. . .

Debts and assets:
        To ensure the subscriptions of $25.525 and the sum of $6.283.57 it was necessary to pay off the floating debt, estimated on November 1, 1844

To W. M. Halsted	$ 8.325.37	
G. O. Halsted	1.100.00	
R. T. Haines	300.00	
E. Robinson	3.370.00	
Henry White	1.709.33	
Thomas McAuley	2.204.21	
Isaac Nordheimer	500.00	
Absalom Peters	487.87	
Miscellaneous bills	1.400.00	
	$19.396.78	$19.396.78
To meet the above, subscriptions payable and good		4.450.00

. . .

Pledges received toward payment of floating debt	12.737.87
Other items, and students' dues, would bring to	14.000.00
Amount received in cash by Treasurer on account	1.192.00

Expenses for the year

Salary Dr. Robinson	$2.000	
" Dr. White	2.000	
" Mr. Turner	500	
" Librarian	100	
Janitors (2)	125	
Fuel: coal and wood	100	
Light, cleaning	37	
Rent: students' housing	550	
	5.412	
Add to this instruction in music	500	$5.912
Expense on land etc.		
Interest on mortgage on Seminary buildings	1.050	
Interest on mortgage on library ($5.000)	350	
Interest on buildings etc.	36	
Ground rent on Seminary lots	300	
	1.736	
	7.148	
To meet endowments etc.	5.621.35	
To meet interest etc. charges	759.35	15

The Demand for Payment of the
McAuley Mortgage

About this time former President McAuley requested that the mortgage of $5,000 on the Van Ess Library for funds he had advanced for its purchase, which was due September 1, 1843, be paid in full.[16] The Alumni were notified that unless the mortgage were paid, the Library would be sold;[17] but the money was not forthcoming from them nor the Van Ess books sold. McAuley wrote again on January 2, 1844 and demanded that at least the interest on his claims be paid by March 1, 1844 or that he would be forced to take "the necessary measures."[18]

Although the means whereby the money was secured is unknown, $1,000 on the principal and the interest were paid on November 1, 1845 and a bond and mortgage in the amount of $4,000 were executed to McAuley.[19] Despite this attempt to pacify him, the Directors received on December 21, 1846 a letter from him, through his attorney, demanding that the Van Ess Library, on which he held a mortgage of $4,000, be delivered to him,[20] whereupon $2,000 more were paid on the principal.[21] Another $1,000 were paid on the mortgage on February 2, 1847,[22] and the last payment on the mortgage was made on August 2, 1847.[23]

A Legacy from James Roosevelt

A ray of light into this financially gloomy situation was cast by the announcement at the March 1, 1847 meeting of the Directors of a legacy from James Roosevelt, a Director of the Seminary.[24] His grandson had been educated for and

ordained to the priesthood of the Protestant Episcopal Church
but left that church and was ordained in 1842 to the Roman
Catholic priesthood. His grandfather, because of this, devised
to Union Seminary the inheritance valued at $30,000, which was
originally designed for the grandson. The will was contested
successfully at first, but the provisions were finally sustained by the New York Court of Appeals;[25] yet none of these
funds became available during Robinson's tenure as Librarian.

Library Development without Budget

Because of these dire financial conditions, the Library
had for nearly a decade no budget for the purchase of books
and periodicals; yet some progress was made in the development
of the collection on the basis of gifts. A gift of 700 books
was, for example, received on June 20, 1842 from the Society
of Inquiry, a student organization. Because the group, to
which nearly everyone in the Seminary belonged, had as one of
its principal purposes the cultivation of interest in the world
mission of the church,[26] the books were probably largely on
that subject.

Another means which was utilized to increase the collection was through the sale of duplicate copies by using the
proceeds thus acquired for the purchase of books in English.[27]
The need for books in English was obvious, yet some valuable
duplicate copies from the Van Ess Library were probably sold
for this purpose.

One of the Directors purchased 300 books at this time
from the Library of the Rev. Matthias Bruen, Pastor of the

Bleecker Street Presbyterian Church, who had died on December 6, 1829.[28] These books were given to the Seminary in 1847. This gift was followed on January 3, 1848 by a gift of 270 volumes from the same collection from Caleb O. Halsted.[29] He had come early in life to New York and had become a dry goods merchant in William Street. He later became President of the Manhattan Company. He was a member of the University Place Church and a generous contributor to the Seminary.[30] This gift, however, was made to the Halsted Literary Society for the use of the Seminary, which was to have charge of them, arrange them, and keep them in its stacks.[31] Eight members of the Mercer Street Presbyterian Church in New York also contributed $430 for the purchase of books.[32]

Thus, the 2,000 which were added to the collection during Robinson's librarianship[33] were probably acquired in the form of gifts and funds rather than through regular budgeted accounts.

New Faculty Appointments

Even though the collection was not growing rapidly, it was strengthened indirectly during the latter part of this administration through two appointments to the faculty. The first of these was Thomas H. Skinner, who was appointed as Professor of Sacred Rhetoric and Pastoral Theology in February, 1848, with assurances of his salary having been underwritten by members of the Mercer Street Presbyterian Church, of which he had been Pastor.[34]

Next, the Financial Agent reported on June 19, 1850
that five-year subscriptions of $2,000 had been secured for
a Chair of Ecclesiastical History,[35] and soon afterward
Henry B. Smith of Amherst was elected to this position.[36]
While the Seminary had gained these two new Professors, it
lost one through the death of Henry White on August 28, 1850.[37]

Smith began his responsibilities in December, 1850,[38]
whereupon Robinson, while retaining his appointment as Pro-
fessor of Biblical Literature, resigned as Librarian on
January 7, 1841 and was replaced on the same date by the new
Professor of Ecclesiastical History,[39] who, in a letter to
George Lewis Prentiss on September 17, 1850, had written,

> I go to New York in full view of all the uncertain-
> ties and difficulties of this position. The literary
> character of the Seminary is slight, its zeal in
> theological science is little, the need of a compre-
> hensive range of theological studies and books has
> got to be created.[40]

He had a high opinion of his predecessor in the Library,
however; and this appreciation was reflected in his bribute
following his death,

> A "large roundabout common sense" characterized all
> he did and said; an inflexible honesty presided over
> his investigations. . . . he stood aloof from doctrinal
> controversy, and ever showed a truly catholic and mag-
> nanimous spirit.[41]

Yet this admiration for Robinson did not deflect Smith
from attempting to improve on the older professor's librarianship. The development which was to be attempted was implied
by the appointment of a committee to act with the new Librarian
in determining changes which could be made to increase the
usefulness of the Library.[42]

FOOTNOTES

[1] George Lewis Prentiss, _The Union Theological Seminary in the City of New York: Historical and Biographical Sketches of Its First Fifty Years_ (New York: Anson D. F. Randolph and Co., 1889), pp. 243-44.

[2] Ibid., pp. 244-49.

[3] Minutes of the Faculty of Union Theological Seminary in the City of New York, p. 27.

[4] _New York Evangelist_, February 13, 1841.

[5] Prentiss, _op. cit._, 1889, pp. 211-12.

[6] Minutes of the Board of Directors of Union Theological Seminary in the City of New York, June 29, 1841.

[7] Prentiss, _op. cit._, 1889, p. 212.

[8] Directors, _op. cit._, May 31, 1843.

[9] Ibid., June 27, 1843.

[10] Ibid., September 19, 1843.

[11] Letter from Henry White, September 28, 1843, cited in Charles Ripley Gillett, "Archives," "Extracts from Source Materials Used in Preparing a History of Union Theological Seminary" [New York, 1937] (Typewritten), p. 7.

[12] Letter from Edward Robinson, September 30, 1843, cited in ibid., p. 8.

[13] Directors, _op. cit._, October 4, 1843.

[14] Ibid., October 11, 1843 and October 16, 1843.

[15] Charles Ripley Gillett, "Detailed History of the Union Theological Seminary in the City of New York" [New York, 1937] (Typewritten), pp. 231-32.

[16] Directors, _op. cit._, May 31, 1843.

[17] Letter to the Alumni, cited in Gillett, "Detailed History," pp. 1098-99 and "Archives," "Extracts," p. 7.

[18]Letter from Dr. McAuley, cited in Gillett, "Detailed History," p. 1099 and "Archives," "Extracts," p. 11.

[19]Directors, op. cit., November 4, 1845.

[20]Ibid., December 21, 1846.

[21]Bond and Mortgage in Favor of Dr. Th. McAuley, cited in Gillett, "Detailed History," p. 1101 and "Archives," "Extracts," p. 17.

[22]Ibid.

[23]Directors, op. cit., August 2, 1847.

[24]Ibid., March 1, 1847.

[25]Ibid., May 10, 1847 ff. and Edwin F. Hatfield, The Early Annals of Union Theological Seminary in the City of New York (New York: No. 30 Clinton Place, 1876), pp. 18-19.

[26]Directors, op. cit., June 20, 1842.

[27]Ibid., January 5, 1847.

[28]Prentiss, op. cit., 1889, p. 132.

[29]Directors, op. cit., June 29, 1847.

[30]Prentiss, op. cit., 1889, pp. 153-54.

[31]Directors, op. cit., January 4, 1848.

[32]Ibid., June 19, 1850.

[33]Union Theological Seminary, Catalogue of the Officers and Students of the New-York Theological Seminary, January, 1841 (New York: Printed by William Osborn, 1841) and ibid., January, 1851 (New York: J. F. Trow, Printer, 49 & 51 Ann Street, 1851).

[34]Directors, op. cit., February 7, 1848.

[35]Ibid., July 8, 1850.

[36]Ibid.

[37]Ibid., August 28, 1850.

[38]Faculty, op. cit., December, 1850.

[39]Directors, op. cit., January 7, 1851.

[40]Prentiss, _op. cit._, pp. 65-66.

[41]_Ibid._, p. 250.

[42]Directors, _op. cit._, January 7, 1851.

Chapter III

THE LIBRARIANSHIP OF HENRY B. SMITH, 1851-77

The Pre-Union Background of Smith

Henry B. Smith was well-equipped for his role as
Professor of Ecclesiastical History and successor to Edward
Robinson as Librarian of Union Theological Seminary. Smith
was born on November 21, 1815 at Portland, Maine and graduated
from Bowdoin College in 1834. His theological education was
received at Bangor, Andover, Halle and Berlin. He became
acquainted in the German institutions with Tholuck, Ulrici,
Neander, Kahnis, and Godet. Returning to the United States,
he became a teacher in Bowdoin College for one year, following
which he was appointed Pastor of the Congregational Church in
West Amesbury, Massachusetts. He then served for three years
as Professor of Mental and Moral Philosophy in Amherst College.
He became a member of the Presbyterian Church upon his appointment at Union and was attacked, therefore, by clergymen in
New England for being unfaithful to the theological position
advocated at Yale[1] and by "Old School" Presbyterians, who said
that he was too closely attached to German theology. The
latter charge was provoked in part by a eulogy of Schleiermacher
which Smith had made in an address at Andover on the "Relations
of Faith and Philosophy" in 1849.[2] One of the critics was

Henry White, Professor of Theology at Union, a conversation
with whom was described in this way by Smith:

> Last evening I spent wholly till eleven o'clock and
> after with Dr. White talking over the whole Seminary
> and matters thereto belonging. He was rather curious
> about some of my theological opinions, and we got
> into a discussion of two hours on the person of
> Christ, in which he claimed that I advocated something
> inconsistent with the Catechism, and I claimed that
> he taught what was against the Catechism, which was
> rather a hard saying against an old-established pro-
> fessor of theology. However, it was all very well
> and kind on both sides, and did not prevent his urging
> my coming here.[3]

Despite such accusations, Smith began his duties as Professor
of Ecclesiastical History in December, 1850[4] and as Librarian
on January 7, 1851.[5]

Setting the Sights

He immediately took a greater interest in the development of the Library than had Robinson. Soon after he began
his duties, the Seminary bought eighteen volumes of The Biblical
Repository and a full set of The National Preacher from Walter H.
Bidwell.[6] Smith was also asked to report to the Directors on
the state and needs of the Library.[7] He asked for four major
items in his report of June 18, 1851 on these needs. First,
he asked for $250 for the preparation of a catalog because of
the "sad condition" of the Van Ess records. He offered his
services for this purpose without compensation and asked that
the list be printed with "names and subjects." Second, he
said that, although the students were subscribing for reprints
of four English quarterlies, the Library did not subscribe to
any reviews and asked for $100 for periodicals for the next

year. Third, he asked for $75 for binding. Finally, he asked
for $250 for current theological books. The total budget re-
quested was $750, but he asked that the finances of the Library
be raised in the future to equal that of a professorship, which
at that time was about $2,000.[8] He reported, further, that
he had given a course of fifteen lectures on theological bibliography during the year. He also said that he had spent
$200 on English historical books and that he thought that a
similar amount should be spent for German books on history.[9]

The Directors approved the first of these recommendations on July 22, when they allocated $250 for the preparation
of a catalog of the Library.[10] Robinson had recommended in
1847 that the manuscript catalog, which was in a "worn, imperfect and exposed state," be completed according to the scheme
devised by Professor Patton in 1839. This catalog had been
made by Herman Bokum, whom Robinson considered to be incompe-
tent; and it had remained in the imperfect condition in which
he had left it. Although Robinson recommended that a committee
be appointed to supervise the making of a new catalog, nothing
seems to have been done about this suggestion.[11] Work was
done on the project during the summer of 1851, however; and
in the fall $100 were paid to students who had assisted Smith
in making the catalog.[12]

The committee, to whom the report on the needs of the
Library had been referred, recommended to the Directors on
October 7, 1851 that the budget for the year be:

For periodicals	$100
For current theol. works	200
For desk, blank books etc.	25
For binding books	75
For German works in Ch. Hist.	150
	$550 [13]

The request for the catalog was, thus, approved; and the requests for periodicals and binding were sustained by the committee. The amounts suggested for theological works and for German books in church history, however, were cut fifty dollars each by the committee. The Directors, moreover, accepted the report and laid it on the table because of lack of funds.[14]

Despite the lack of proper authority, Smith purchased $250 worth of books at an auction during that month; and that amount was allocated for their payment at the meeting of the Directors on January 6, 1852, when they further authorized the expenditure of $100 for periodicals.[15]

An Era of Financial Stabilization

The 1852 Endowment Campaign and Subsequent Growth

The annual expenses of the school during this period were approximately $12,000. The yearly income, including that from the Roosevelt legacy, was about $5,000; approximately $7,000, therefore, had to be secured through contributions.[16] A meeting was called for the evening of February 9, 1852 to cope with this situation; at this session it was decided to attempt to secure additional endowment.[17] The Directors authorized a campaign to raise $100,000 for this purpose and appointed a committee to consider the matter and to prepare

a paper for publication in regard to it.[18] Plans were worked
out to raise this money, and an agent was appointed to do the
solicitation.[19] Subscriptions in the amount of $42,367 were
recorded at the March 26 meeting of the Directors.[20] Joseph S.
Gallagher of Bloomfield, New Jersey was employed as a Financial
Agent for the campaign;[21] and within a year $100,000 had been
raised. He raised a similar amount in the next few years.[22]

These funds were raised in part through the publication
of a tract entitled <u>Appeal to the Friends of the Institution
and Others</u>, in which it was stated that the Seminary was
Presbyterian but "liberal" and appealed to non-Presbyterians
for financial support. One of the principal purposes of the
proposed endowment was said in this tract to be for materials
in the field of "English and modern German literature."[23]

The resulting stabilization of the finances of the
school was immediately obvious in the development of the Library.
The budget for 1852-53 was, for example:

German works	$100
Periodicals	100
Binding	125
Current theological works	125 [24]

Although this was less than the budget for the previous
year, it was roughly equivalent to what had been spent during
that year. Smith had succeeded in 1851 in getting a budget
approved and laid on the table. He had then spent $350 for
books and periodicals and had sought authorization for payment
later. The 1852-53 school year, therefore, was the first in
which a budget for the Library was prepared and approved before
the academic year began.

The increasing strength of the financial program was, further, reflected in a plan which was approved to add another story and an attic to the building. This was to be constructed through a mortgage, which was not to exceed $10,000, on the existing property. The original building had three stories with classrooms in the front on the lower two and with a chapel in the rear on the first and the Library in the rear on the second. The third floor contained rooms for thirty students,[25] and the additional space provided room for forty-eight more.[26] When the addition was constructed, gas was introduced for heating; and on June 24, 1853 the Directors ordered that arrangements be made for gas lights for the Library.[27]

Further encouragement was given through a gift of $20,000 by James Boorman. He was a partner in the firm of Boorman and Johnston, which for many years enjoyed a monopoly of the Dundee trade. The firm was also for a long time at the head of the iron trade of New York. It also had a good tobacco business. Boorman had founded the Bank of Commerce in 1839 and was instrumental in the establishment of the Hudson River Railroad Company.[28]

The gift of $20,000 was designated, with $5,000 previously given by him, to endow the Davenport Professorship of Sacred Rhetoric and Pastoral Theology[29] in memory of the Rev. John Davenport, the first minister of New Haven and an ancestor of Mrs. Boorman.[30] The Finance Committee passed a resolution shortly thereafter that

THE OLD SEMINARY BUILDING,

UNIVERSITY PLACE, NEW YORK.

Figure 1[31]

> the subscriptions for the endowment of the Seminary
> be set apart and appropriated for the endowment of
> the professorships in the Seminary and for no other
> purpose[32]

despite the fact that publicity for raising the endowment had
stated that it would be used also for the improvement of the
Library.[33]

The Directors were informed by Dr. Robinson on the
following January 3, that he had given 900 volumes, many of
which were rare and valuable, to the Library.[34] Smith was
transferred that year from the Chair of Ecclesiastical History
to that of Systematic Theology;[35] but he retained his office
as Librarian at the salary of $250 per year,[36] which seems to
have been the standard for most of his appointment.

The man chosen to replace him in church history was
Roswell Dwight Hitchcock, who was appointed to fill the newly-
created Washburn Professorship of Ecclesiastical History,[37]
which had been endowed by Harriett W. Bell in memory of her
brother, the Reverend Samuel Washburn, former Pastor of the
Fifth Presbyterian Church in Baltimore. Hitchcock had studied
at Amherst College and Andover Theological Seminary as well
as at Halle and Berlin. He had been a Pastor in Exeter, New
Hampshire until 1852, when he was appointed Professor of
Natural and Revealed Religion in Bowdoin College, from where
he was called to Union.[38]

He was strongly influenced by Transcendentalism during
his years at Amherst, Andover, and Exeter; but his thinking
began to move in a more conservative direction following a
trip to Europe in 1847 and 1848. Although his publications

were few, his influence as a scholar was strong. He was said
to be able to condense masses of thought into single sentences
which were noteworthy for their originality and force.[39] He
was largely responsible for the selection of church history
materials for the collection during the thirty-three years
with which he was associated with the school. The strength
of the Library in this field is in part attributed to this
outstanding nineteenth-century historian.

The school had many assets by this time. Progress
had been made in the permanent endowment of the professorships;
the Seminary had an outstanding Faculty composed of Robinson,
Skinner, Smith, and Hitchcock.[40] The Library included the
Van Ess Collection of 14,000 volumes plus another 9,000.[41]
Whereas the first decade of the school's existence ended with
questions as to its continuance, it had within the second
decade become permanently established as one of the leading
seminaries of the nation.

The 1856 Endowment Campaign
and Subsequent Growth

Yet the school was unwilling to rest on its achievements. In fact, a meeting of "some of the most prominent
citizens" of New York was held in December, 1856; and it was
announced then that, although the endowment had reached
$140,000, it was desirable to raise $60,000 to make $200,000,
the interest from which would pay for the current expenses of
the school.[42] The Vice-President of the Board indicated that
the needs of the institution included additional dormitory

space, scholarships, and books and a fire-proof building for
the Library. As part of the appeal it was noted that 450
ministers, approximately one-tenth of whom were missionaries,
had been educated at Union.[43] The subscription, plus an
additional $6,000 to cover a floating loan which had been
incurred, was raised within the next few years.[44]

The Librarian reported in 1857 that the Library had
received the publications of the London Tract Society as a
donation from that organization.[45] He also reported that the
manuscript catalog had been completed in four volumes, excluding 2,000 pamphlets, and that the list consisted chiefly
of the material from the Van Ess Collection. The Recorder of
the Board was directed to discover the cost of printing 500
copies of this catalog,[46] but this project did not take place.
The manuscript catalog has, in fact, disappeared, although it
was still in existence in 1899 when Prentiss's second history
was written.[47]

The possibility of better accommodations for the
Library was suggested at this time in a paper by one of the
Directors about the selection of a "proper site." The recom-
mendation was referred to the Finance Committee.[48]

The quarrels between the "Old School" and the "New
School" were by now not as bitter as they had been in 1837.
The Faculty, therefore, in 1858 was "authorized to make an
annual statement to the General Assembly [of the Presbyterian
Church] of the condition of Seminary."[49]

Smith, in addition to his Library duties, was teaching all the courses in theology. He also founded in 1859

The American Theological Review and in the same year published
A History of the Church of Christ in Chronological Tables and
edited a revised translation of Gieseler's Church History in
four volumes. Shortly thereafter, he published a translation
of Hagenbach's History of Christian Doctrine.[50] He was also
a frequent contributor to periodicals such as Bibliotheca Sacra,
Norton's Literary Gazette, the London Evangelical Christendom,
the Presbyterian, the New Brunswick, the Methodist, the
Baptist, the Southern Quarterly Review, and the New York
Evangelist. He also contributed articles for Appleton's and
McClintock's Cyclopaedias.[51]

The amount requested for the Library budget was reduced for 1863 to $300,[52] perhaps because of the lack of space,
for he claimed that "Room for the new volumes can only be
found by hiding the old."[53] The reduction may have been related, however, to the fact that the nation was engaged in the
Civil War with an accompanying tightening of funds available
for the purchase of books. The effects of the war were also
felt in the enrollment with a drop from 133 in 1861-62 to
eighty-six in 1862-63.[54] The recommendation of advanced senior
students for ordination to enable them to become Chaplains
seems to have been practiced commonly in an attempt to aid the
war effort.[55] Other students were excused to work for the
Christian Commission,[56] while still others were graduated
while serving as Chaplains.[57] Another loss to the institution
through the war was the death of Henry Hamilton Hadley, who
had been an Instructor in Sacred Literature from 1858-64.[58]

He was killed while serving with the Christian Commission with the Army of the Potomac in Virginia.[59]

Another matter presented by the Librarian in the fall of 1864 concerned some books which were coming from Germany for Edward Robinson,[60] who had died on January 27, 1863.[61] The subject had been raised by Mrs. Robinson and was referred by the Directors to a "special committee on the interests of the Library."[62] Robinson's books, according to Gillett, later came into the possession of the institution.[63]

Robinson was replaced as Professor of Biblical Literature by William Greenough Thayer Shedd. The new Professor had been educated at the University of Vermont and Andover Theological Seminary. In 1845 he had become Professor of English Literature at Vermont, and in 1853 Professor of Ecclesiastical History at Andover. He remained in the chair of Biblical Literature until 1874, when he was transferred to that of Systematic Theology. He was said by Prentiss to have had more knowledge of Coleridge's ideas than any American theologian of his day. One of his best known works was, in fact, his edition of Coleridge's prose writings.[64]

An influential scholar, his orthodoxy was of the Calvinistic type. He wrote and spoke vigorously, for example, against higher criticism of the Scriptures. His writings included History of Christian Doctrine, Homiletics and Pastoral Theology, Sermons to the Natural Man, Theological Essays, Literary Essays, Commentary on Romans, Sermons to the Spiritual Man, The Doctrine of Endless Punishment, and Dogmatic Theology.

His interest in Coleridge probably affected the development
of the collection with respect to works about him, but his
most important contributions to the growth of the Library
must have been his recommendations for contemporary materials
dealing with Biblical studies and theology.[65]

The 1864 Endowment Campaign
and Subsequent Growth

The annual expenses of the school were running at
approximately $2,000 a year beyond its income during this
period. The Finance Committee was asked, therefore, to report
"as to the propriety of obtaining an enlarged endowment for
the institution."[66] It reported on January 27 that the sum
of $50,000 could be secured;[67] and on February 10 a campaign
for the enlargement of the endowment was approved by the
Board.[68]

A conference of the Faculty with a committee of the
Board was held later in the year, at which time the professors
suggested that $4,000 was needed for textbooks and that the
Library should be strengthened to make it a theological center
for the ministers of the city. They also wished to expand the
curriculum to include courses in introduction to the Old and
New Testaments, symbolism, relation of the Bible to modern
science, various phases of "infidelity," Christian ethics,
and philosophy. They also asked the Board to consider changing
the location of the school. They, in this connection, called
the Seminary building the "worst contrived in the city" and
the Library facilities the "worst" which could be "contrived."

The most important recommendation made was that permanent income for the support of the Library be secured.[69]

Although the confrontation was marked by exaggerated
claims on the part of the Faculty, it began to produce results.
The Directors at their next meeting referred the suggestions
concerning the physical facilities, as well as the budget and
the permanent income of the Library, to the Finance Committee,[70]
which, characteristically, raised the insurance on the Library
to $15,000. The Treasurer was directed to ask for subscriptions
in the amount of $1,000 for the textbooks or to take the
amount from available funds. The members of the Board were,
further, asked to raise at least $10,000 for the Library En-
dowment Fund; but the Committee did not consider this the
opportune time for changing the location of the school. The
other recommendation on acquiring added facilities for students
and "perhaps for the Library, in the vicinity" was left open.[71]

Although the Library budget was not increased for
1864-65, two additional funds were approved for that year
which were of benefit to the collection. The first was the
appropriation of $100 for the purchase of a portion of the
Library of the late Recorder, James W. McLane, who had graduated from Yale and Andover and had been a Pastor of two large
Presbyterian Churches.[72] The second was the appropriation of
$1,000 for the purchase of textbooks, with the provision that
they be bought under the direction of the Faculty and the
Treasurer.[73] Some of these probably became assimilated into
the collection. The Finance Committee's suggestion that

$150,000 be raised for the endowment fund was approved with the authorization of another campaign.[74]

This Committee designated the uses for which the additional endowment was to be used: $90,000 for professorial salaries, $50,000 for scholarships, and $10,000 for the Library.[75] Although permanent financing for the Library had been promised in the campaign of 1852,[76] the collection had been deprived of receiving any of the proceeds from that effort through the recommendation by the Finance Committee that the entire endowment be designated for professorships. It seemed more likely, however, that the Library would receive greater benefits from the campaign launched in 1865, as the publicity material carried a statement that $10,000 of the funds raised would be designated for that purpose. The paragraph appeared, in this connection, in the quarto pamphlet prepared for the campaign:

> The Library of the Seminary has no endowment. There ought to be in New-York one sample theological library, fully supplied with periodicals, and books both new and old, for the use of our Pastors, as well as of the Professors and Students. A fund of $10,000 would be but a beginning of what is needed for this object.[77]

The Finance Committee was asked, in connection with this campaign, to secure a change in the charter empowering the school to have an added amount of personal estate and income. The application was, therefore, for authority to hold $100,000 in addition to the endowment for professorships and the Library's value.[78] This permission was secured on May 1, 1865.[79]

Edwin F. Hatfield, who for thirty-seven years was a member of the Board of Directors and the Stated Clerk of the

General Assembly of the Presbyterian Church, was asked to
direct the campaign. He had been educated at Middlebury
College in Vermont and Andover Theological Seminary. He had
been Pastor of the Seventh Presbyterian Church in New York
from 1835 until 1856, during which time he received over 2,000
members into the congregation. He had become Pastor of North
Presbyterian Church in 1856 but had been forced to resign in
1863 because of poor health. His books included Memoir of
Elihu W. Baldwin, D.D.; The History of Elizabeth, N. J.; The
Church Hymn-Book with Tunes, and The Poets of the Church, a
Series of Biographical Sketches of Hymn Writers.[80] The institution was fortunate to secure the services of this capable
man as its Financial Agent.

The school received, in addition to its regular income
for expenses and endowment, $20,000 in 1865 for lectureships.
The first was established as the "Elias P. Ely Lectures on
the Evidences of Christianity," and the second was financed
by Samuel Morse for a series on "The Relation of the Bible to
the Sciences."[81] The latter was, however, in a sense, a loss
to the Library, for Morse had intended originally to give
$5,000 to it; whereas, this amount was diverted into the
Lectureship Fund, as was revealed in this letter:

New York. May 20th 1865.

Gentlemen.

. . . I have made up my mind that the general plan,
which at my request you submitted _____ is a
judicious one, and I have come to the conclusion to
adopt it as the Foundation of a Lectureship which
I will endow in the Seminary, and I therefore en-
close a certificate of stock in the Western Union

Telegraph Company for Fifty Shares Additional, to
be added to my previous donation of Fifty Shares
of the same stock of one hundred dollars, par value,
each, making in all One Hundred Shares, or Ten
Thousand Dollars, par value, for the purpose of
enclosing [i.e., endowing] the proposed Lectureship,
desiring by this act to change my purpose expressed
in the previous donation of Fifty Shares, my interest
then being to have it devoted to the Library. . . .[82]

The proposal was promptly accepted by the Board, and the
Morse Lectureship was thereby established.[83]

Despite this loss to the Library, Dr. Hitchcock expressed his appreciation at the May 8, 1865 meeting of the
Directors for the books supplied by it for collateral reading.
The Librarian reported also at that time on the books purchased
from the $1,000 for textbooks. He reiterated his position
that a good library budget should be equal to a professorship,
that the Library was in danger of fire, and that the physical
facilities were "the most convenient . . . ever planned."
Nothing was done about any of these problems; he was, in fact,
handed another, when the portrait of his predecessor, Edward
Robinson, was put into his care.[84] His budget was, however,
increased to $700.[85]

This increase was made possible by improved financial
circumstances at the school. Hatfield reported, for example,
on March 30, 1865, that $125,000 of the subscription had been
raised and that prospects were good for securing the additional
$25,000.[86] He succeeded in the summer in raising another
$5,000.[87] Yet, as part of the original subscription had been
designated for specific causes by the donors, it was decided
that an additional $50,000 should be solicited, $10,000 of

which was to be for the Library.[88] He asserted that $150,000
was secured in 1865.[89] The institution did not find it easy
to locate designated funds for the Library during this period
in comparison with the ease with which the professorships,
such as the new Brown Professorship of Hebrew and the Cognate
Languages, and lectureships were endowed. Permanent funds
for the Library seem, in fact, to have been among the most
difficult causes for which to raise money.

This was a period of inflation; and, in order to help
meet it, the professors' salaries were raised $500 to $3,500.
Henry Smith's salary for serving as Librarian was also increased from $250 to $400 per year.[90] The budget was not
covered, however, by receipts, for the financial report for
that year showed a large excess of expenditures above the
income.[91] The school was plagued also by a serious decline
in enrollment, especially from the western states, because of
the War; and the physical facilities were becoming increasingly
inadequate. The need for housing for Faculty members and
students was especially acute.[92]

The 1866 Endowment Campaign
and Subsequent Growth

The Librarian visited Europe in 1866 and purchased
materials for the collection. He made a report of these
acquisitions to the Board in the fall of 1866, and an increased appropriation of $600 was made to cover their cost.[93]
Other financial appropriations made that fall included an
increase of $1,000 for each professorial salary and $250 for
a course in theological bibliography to be taught by Philip

Schaff.[94] A campaign was also approved to raise $100,000 for the permanent funds.[95] The endowment required for the naming of a section in the Library was soon after raised from $200 to $500.[96] The effort for increased endowment was partially successful; and the balance sheet on April 30 showed endowment in the amount of $311,285 and permanent scholarships in the amount of $43,000.[97]

A suggestion, which was to have long-term effects in the development of the institution, was made at the beginning of the next year by Daniel Willis James.[98] The proposal was significant, in part, because it was made by one of the leading American philanthropists of the latter part of the nineteenth century. James had been born in Liverpool, England, where his father was a partner in the American firm, Phelps, Dodge & Company, which dealt in metals. His mother was the daughter of the head of the firm. Young James came to New York at the age of seventeen; and within five years he had become a junior partner in the Company, which owned copper mines in Arizona and which built branch railroads in the South-west and in Mexico. Other institutions, in addition to Union, in which he was interested included the Children's Aid Society of New York, Amherst College, and the American Museum of Natural History.[99]

Noting the inadequacy of the location of the school and that it would be too expensive to acquire more land in the neighborhood, he recommended moving to an area north of Central Park. He was asked by the Finance Committee to pursue the

matter further and to report to them again.[100] He later presented an expanded recommendation to the Directors and proposed
that enough land be purchased to provide residences for the
Faculty "as well as other buildings useful for the Library,
Chapel etc."[101]

Several gifts were recorded at the fall meeting of
the Directors that year. Dudley, Stephen J., Cyrus, and Henry M.
Field, for example, gave 400 volumes, many of them said to be
rare, and 2,500 pamphlets from the Library of David Dudley
Field of Stockbridge, Massachusetts. These were to be assigned
to a special case or alcove and designated as the Field Library.
A second gift reported on this date was the donation by Sarah
Cummings of Portland, Maine, of part of the Library of her
father, Asa Cummings,[102] "one of the most influential religious
editors of New England."[103] A third gift was presented by a
Mr. Wigram and consisted of thirty volumes of the works of
Darby and other Plymouth Brethren.[104]

The Directors voted at this meeting, because of the
growth of the city and the related high cost of lots, that a
committee be appointed with powers to select and purchase
suitable lots after seeking the approval of the Finance and
Executive Committees.[105] The committee was asked to consider
especially the high ground south of 125th Street or a section
on the east side below 90th Street.[106]

The health of the Librarian broke during the midst of
this, and he was forced to abandon his work. He left in early
1869 for a year and a half in Germany, Italy, and Palestine.[107]

Henry Zwingli McAlin was appointed as the student assistant in the Library for the next academic year.[108] While Smith was abroad, his classes were taught by Professor Shedd.[109]

Soon after his departure, the Seminary was asked to introduce into its constitution the principle of "synodical or assembly supervision," for which it was promised "official recognition and approbation" by the General Assembly of the Presbyterian Church.[110] The willingness of the Directors to consider such a step may have been related to the growing need for better physical facilities for the school. They were in the midst of purchasing lots for a new location and probably were glad to have the endorsement of the national organization of the church for this venture.

The Committee on the Site had been appointed on November 11, 1868; and on December 3, the Finance Committee approved its recommendation that eight-five lots on St. Nicholas Avenue be purchased.[111] A contract for sixty of these, with an option for twenty-five more, was signed on December 13. These lots between 130th and 134th Streets were reported to be for sale for $250,000 less $20,000 which represented a donation of Miss Susan A. King, a part-owner. She, further, promised to take twenty-five lots at $4,000 each, leaving eight to the school, and, thereby, reducing the cost to $130,000. Five were to be sold to friends of the institution, thus cutting the cost of the remaining fifty-five lots to $110,000. The Board approved this plan and appointed a committee to raise the funds for the purchase of the lots and the preparation of plans for the new buildings.[112]

The 1869 Endowment Campaign
with Subsequent Growth

This committee reported on December 29 that $500,000
would be needed for the proposed project: $110,000 for the
property; $250,000 for a fire-proof Library, chapel, lecture
rooms, dormitories and professors' houses; and $140,000 for
endowment. The sale of the old buildings was to provide the
funds to purchase the additional twenty-five lots or additions
to the endowment, and an appeal was to be made throughout the
united Presbyterian Church for funds.[113] The Faculty recommended that the new buildings include four lecture rooms,
facilities for 100,000 volumes, a chapel to seat 500, a parlor,
a dormitory for 300 students, professors' houses, a dining
hall, and other rooms.[114]

A campaign was launched to raise the proposed $500,000,
and a good beginning was made in raising it through the gift
of property worth $60,000 from the estate of John C. Baldwin.[115]
He was a merchant in Baltimore and New York, who gave away
over $1,000,000 to such institutions as Wabash, Hamilton,
Middlebury, and Williams Colleges.[116] Shortly before this
gift was announced, an anonymous donor in New York proposed
to contribute $15,000 to found a Lectureship and Library on
social, commercial, and political ethics at Union;[117] but the
money for this project was never received.

A series of important gifts to the collection was
made, however, that spring. Charles Gillett claimed to have
seen a report made by the Assistant Librarian, in the absence
of Smith, in which mention was made of the gift of approximately

400 volumes by David H. McAlpin.[118] The donor, a long-time
Director of the Seminary, made a fortune in the tobacco business,
employing at this time approximately 250 men in his plant where
"Virgin Leaf" and "Navy" tobaccos were manufactured. He also
was involved in the real estate business, owning, for example,
the land on which the Alpine Building and the McAlpin Hotel
stood, as well as having interests in insurance and banking.
He contributed to the Metropolitan Museum of Art, the American
Museum of Natural History, and the American Geographical Society,
as well as to the Library of Union Seminary.[119]

It was implied, according to Gillett, that his gifts
to the Library had been begun in 1868-69. It was, further,
reported that because of lack of shelf-room, many of the books
had remained unpacked.[120] This early donation in a long series
of gifts was acknowledged at the May 8, 1871 meeting of the
Directors; and it was ordered that an alcove in the new
building be named for McAlpin.[121]

The idea for this collection, which was to become the
famous McAlpin Library of British History and Theology, originated in the mind of Ezra Hall Gillett, who was, at the time,
Pastor of the Harlem Presbyterian Church in New York. He was
interested in the Deistic movement in England and especially
in the literature which had motivated the writing of Bishop
Butler's _Analogy_. He purchased as many of these materials as
his meager salary would permit and was, afterward, assisted
by generous parishioners. The collection, through the aid of
these interested persons, chief among whom was McAlpin, came

to include nearly all of the literature of this controversy. His purchases were selected in these early years by Gillett with the stipulation that they should find their permanent location in the Union Library.[122]

Another important event that spring was associated with the appointment of Philip Schaff as Professor of Theological Encyclopedia [Bibliography] and Christian Symbolism.[123] He had studied at Coire, Stuttgart, Tübingen, Halle, and Berlin and lectured at the latter school as privat-docent on Exegesis and Church History. He had been called in 1844 to a chair in the Theological Seminary of the German Reformed Church at Mercersburg, Pennsylvania. He had been in charge of preparing a hymnal and a new liturgy which were widely used in the denomination represented by that school. He later was transferred to the Hebrew chair, that of Sacred Literature, and finally to the post of Professor of Church History. Later he was to serve as President of the American Bible Revision Committee.[124]

He translated several theological works from German into English and was the author of many books, some of the more important of which were History of the Apostolic Church, History of the Christian Church, and The Creeds of Christendom.[125] Two of his most important undertakings were the editing of an English translation of a Nicene and Post-Nicene Library of the Fathers and the New Schaff-Herzog Encyclopedia of Religious Knowledge. He must have recommended many titles for purchase for the Library in the fields of theological

bibliography, symbolism, Biblical studies, and church history
during his years at Union. With his tremendous scholarly background, it is almost certain that these included the most
recent and learned tomes available on those subjects.

He was not only to introduce succeeding generations
of students to the contents of the Library but was also to
write the volume which was the standard textbook for courses
in theological bibliography in other seminaries for many years.
Many of his other books, moreover, have found permanent importance in theological collections around the world.

The most far-reaching decision of the Directors that
spring was the one included in an overture to the General
Assembly. A uniform system of ecclesiastical supervision
over the seminaries of the Presbyterian Church had been suggested in connection with negotiations for reuniting the "Old
School" and the "New School" branches of the denomination.
The Directors agreed in 1870 to submit their suggestions for
appointment of Professors to the Assembly for approval.[126]

This plan was approved by the Assembly on June 1,
1870; and thus, Union, for the first time established an
official relationship with an ecclesiastical organization,
although the Directors had been required to advocate the
Presbyterian form of church government and every Faculty member had been required to announce his approval of that form
of polity and to promise not to teach anything contrary to
the Westminster Confession. The constitution, further, had

prohibited any amendments "inconsistent with the doctrinal basis contained in" these declarations.[127]

Union entered this relationship in part in the interest of reunion and to assist other Presbyterian seminaries in rectifying a system of professorial appointment which had become intolerable. The members of the various faculties were at that time selected by the General Assembly, which was too large a body to determine the qualifications of the candidates. Thus, it was proposed by the Directors at Union that in the united church each Presbyterian seminary be permitted to appoint its own professors, who would, thereupon, be approved by the Assembly.[128] Coffin said that the resolution was prepared by William Adams, the Chairman of the Board of Union, in response to an appeal by the authorities of Princeton to obtain relief from the impossible system of academic appointment which had been established by the Assembly.[129]

This decision to surrender some of their freedom to the ecclesiastical body was one of the most serious errors made in the history of the Seminary, as was demonstrated in the rancor connected with the heresy trial of Charles Augustus Briggs in the last decade of the nineteenth century. The agreement of 1870 was, following that, repealed; but it was, as D. Willis James of Union's Board said in opposing it at the time of its passage, "A very serious mistake, and calcu-lated to produce great and unfortunate mischief."[130]

The school came to the end of the calendar year, therefore, with plans for relocating and for entering a new

relationship with the Presbyterian Church. The most important
events in the Library during this year were the acquisition
of the first of a long series of gifts from David H. McAlpin,
and the return of the Librarian from Europe in an improved
condition.[131]

The new building program had received $300,000 in
pledges by this time, but by the spring of the next year only
$58,081.65 had been paid. The Directors decided, therefore,
that construction on the Library, the chapel, and the professors' houses would be deferred and that only the central
building would be built, with R. M. Hunt as the architect.[132]

The Treasurer's report that fall showed on November 22,
1871 that subscriptions to the new building and the endowment
funds amounted to $334,299.52, which included pledges due in
1872 and 1873. The estimated value of the old building was
$50,000; Clinton Place at $16,500; and Greene Street House at
$12,500 for a total of $79,000, which was about equal to the
mortgage on the new property in the amount of $70,000. Because
it was estimated that the new buildings would cost $318,000,
it was claimed that $166,000 more was needed.[133] Concern was
also expressed about the institution's inability to meet its
current expenses. Additional endowment of $100,000 to meet
costs on the existing basis was, therefore, said to be required.
The Directors, nevertheless, "substantially adopted" Hunt's
plans and approved a resolution that the Committee on Plans
become the Building Committee.[134] The proposed building was
to have four stories and was to include the temporary Library,
classrooms, refectory, dormitory, and other rooms.[135]

The collection received some generous gifts during this period.[136] During the period 1868-71, for example, 2,010 gift volumes were received, 1,050 of which had been given by D. H. McAlpin. Other notable gifts were the Sprague Collection of 2,000 pamphlets bound in ninety-eight volumes and seventy-six books from the Misses Marsh of Brooklyn.[137]

E. H. Gillett during this period secured and bound the Sprague and Marsh tracts in manila paper covers and was paid fifty dollars by the Board for this service.[138] Another gift from Hanson K. Corning, a wealthy merchant in the Brazilian trade,[139] must have been fairly substantial, for an alcove was named for him; its worth, therefore, must have exceeded $500.[140]

The Librarian, the Recorder, and the Treasurer were appointed as a committee to inquire about another gift, the library of the late Rev. James Mathews, which had been willed to Union;[141] but no indication was found that this gift was received. Another "gift" to the Library, an "indenture" dated March 18, 1872 by which the Willard Parker Lectureship was founded, provided that unused income from the endowment could be used for Library books, preferably in the natural sciences,[142] probably resulted in nothing for the collection.

Another attempt to improve the Library was made by the Alumni, thirty-three of whom met at the home of the Librarian on May 8, 1872. They passed four resolutions at this meeting. The first endorsed the plans for the new buildings. The second authorized the appointment of a committee

of one from each class to raise an endowment fund of $50,000
for the Library to be called the "Alumni Library Fund." The
third approved the appointment of a committee to designate
this committee and to supervise the execution of the proposed
plan. The last suggested to the Directors that an alcove in
the Library be designated as "The Alumni Alcove." The committee of three in the third resolution was composed of Ezra H.
Gillett, Gardiner Spring Plumley, and Charles H. Payson.[143]

An appeal was sent subsequently to the Alumni. The
committee claimed in this letter that the Library of the
Seminary was unrivaled in the United States in works of the
church fathers and in mediaeval and reformation works but that
it was deficient in philology, archaeology, philosophy, and
"older English theology." The proposal, therefore, was made
to divide the $50,000 into 1,000 shares of $50 each and to
solicit subscriptions from each Alumnus and clergyman in
New York and the vicinity in an attempt to help to remedy the
situation. Friends of the school were also invited to send
materials for "The Alumni Alcove." A form was enclosed for
making subscriptions.[144]

A new chair, The Skinner and McAlpin Professorship
of Pastoral Theology, Church Polity and Mission Work, was
proposed in the meantime.[145] George Lewis Prentiss was appointed to fill this vacancy. He had studied at Bowdoin, and
Halle and had been the Pastor of the South Trinitarian Church
in New Bedford, Massachusetts as well as the Mercer Street
Presbyterian Church and the Church of the Covenant in New York.

His books included, in addition to his histories of Union,
a work entitled Our National Bane: or, the Dryrot in American
Politics. A frail man, who rarely enjoyed robust health, he
was said by William Walker Rockwell not to have excited much
enthusiasm in his preaching or lecturing.[146] He probably
recommended many current titles in the field of Practical
Theology for inclusion in the Union Library.

In the discussion of the recommendation to create
this chair, a Treasurer's report was prepared which showed
the financial circumstances of the school and of which the
following is a condensation:

Treasurer's Report

Property and indebtedness of permanent funds		$686.674
Estimated value of Seminary bldg. 9 University Place		50.000
		736.674
From this must be deducted [Scholarships, lectureship, building and endowment funds]		232.803
		503.671
Of this is unproductive		295.265
		208.605
Estimated income from above	$14.802	
Student fees etc.	1.600	
Probable donations	300	16.502
Expenditures for the last year to Oct. 31		
Salaries, professors and instructors	22.850	
Teacher of elocution	500	
Paid Trow (for printing)	2.000	
Library and librarian	500	
Monitors	105	
Janitors and laundress	1.116	
		27.071
Incidentals		8.144
Income as above		35.215
Overdrawn		16.502 [147]

The current expenses were during this period paid
almost entirely from the interest on the permanent funds.
The Library received less than two per cent of the total expenses; and this meager financial support was responsible for
the fact that the collection grew by only 4,000 volumes between
1868 and 1872,[148] over half of which growth was accounted for
by gifts.

The Special Committee and the Building Committee
visited the proposed location on St. Nicholas Avenue during
this period; and, upon the recommendation of the Executive
and Finance committees and the Faculty, they were advised to
recommend to the Directors that work on the site be postponed
for six months. They were, further, advised to reconsider
the plans of the architect.[149] The Directors, on the recommendation of the Finance Committee, voted at their meeting
two days later that

> as Isaac T. Smith [attorney for St. Nicholas property
> owners] has applied for the cancellation of certain
> agreements in relation to the St. Nicholas Avenue lots,
> on entering upon new agreements, the Finance Committee
> be authorized to grant the application, subject to
> the approval of the President and counsel of the board.[150]

Other important business affecting the Library at this
meeting included the acknowledgement of a letter from David
McAlpin for a gift of $25,000 toward the endowment of the
Skinner and McAlpin Professorship, the acceptance of a letter
from George Prentiss agreeing to fill this position, and the
election of Philip Schaff as Professor of Hebrew.[151]

An Era with an Incapacitated Librarian

A vote of thanks was also extended at this meeting to McAlpin for a gift of 183 books, which, according to the Librarian, constituted a "valuable addition." The materials were selected principally, as usual, by E. H. Gillett. The announcement was also made at this meeting that Smith had been prevented from working full-time during the latter part of the year because of poor health.[152]

The Alumni Association received a report two days later that, as a result of its campaign, subscriptions in the amount of $2,200, $2,000 of which had been pledged by Professors and members of the campaign committee, had been received. The Association was told at this meeting by the President of the Directors that the plans for the new building on St. Nicholas Avenue had been suspended and that plans were being made to recondition some of the quarters at 9 University Place.[153]

The Directors that fall appointed the Rev. William Adams as President and Professor of Sacred Rhetoric.[154] He had graduated from Phillips Academy, Yale College, and Andover Theological Seminary and had been a Pastor of the Congregational Society in Brighton, Massachusetts, as well as Central and Madison Square Presbyterian Church in New York. He had been Moderator of the New School General Assembly in 1852. His books included The Three Gardens, Eden, Gethsemane and Paradise, Redemption, Restoration, Thanksgiving, Memories of the Day and Helps to the Habit, In the World and not of the

World, and <u>Conversations of Jesus Christ with Representative Men</u>. Some of his friends were Samuel Morse, Daniel Webster, and General George B. McClellan, who was a parishioner.[155] His chair was financed by a gift of $40,000 from James Brown, "a merchant whose name was known and highly esteemed throughout the commercial world,"[156] and promises of three men to contribute $1,700 each year during Adams' lifetime.[157] As President, he helped to raise thousands of dollars for the support of the Library; and as Professor of Sacred Rhetoric he recommended many titles for purchase in his area of responsibility.

Several important decisions were made at this time by the Directors, such as the one to include only the President on the Board, excluding the other Professors, and the setting of four instead of two meetings of the Board each year. The Librarian was also asked to thank Walter H. Bidwell, the Editor of the <u>American Theological Review</u>, for a gift of a copy of the <u>Codex Vaticanus</u>.[158]

The Board received an exciting letter three weeks later from James Brown, who wrote:

> . . . Having in my note of September 24th, signified my purpose to give $40,000 to the endowment of the chair of Sacred Rhetoric in the Seminary under your care, I hereby inform you of my purpose to add to that sum, sufficient to make the total amount $300,000.

> . . . It is my wish that no part of this sum be expended in the erection of buildings, but that it be so treated as a part of your present general endowment fund, that its annual income shall go to what in your judgment [shall be] a wise provision for a full teaching faculty, and for their adequate support.[159]

The decision was reached at the same time to discontinue plans for building on the St. Nicholas property; and a committee was appointed to select a suitable site elsewhere.[160]

The Executive Committee received a letter from the Librarian on December 15 that year, in which he explained that he had been forced to go away "for a season, with but faint prospect of speedily resuming his place."[161] The Directors received a letter from him on January 14, 1874, in which he resigned his professorship because of his health. Although his doctors had told him that he might be able to resume some of his duties after a long period of rest and recuperation, he was, at the time the letter was written totally disabled. The esteem in which he was held by the Board is reflected in the action of its members on his resignation:

> Whereas the Board has heard with profound grief of the serious illness of Prof. Henry B. Smith, D.D., disabling him entirely, at present, from performing the duties of that chair which he has so long graced and honored; and

> Whereas this illness, protracted already through such a length of time, makes his return to the full activities of his professorship so uncertain that he has felt constrained to tender the resignation of his office;

> Therefore, be it Resolved, That with the tenderest sympathy for Professor Smith in view of the necessity which has arisen in his case for absolute exemption from official service, and out of regard to the public trusts which they are charged to administer, this Board, though with utmost reluctance, hereby accept his resignation.

> Whereas the Board cherish the highest and most grateful sense of their obligation to Professor Smith for his past services, his indefatigable exertions in behalf of the Seminary for so many years, his preeminent ability as a theological teacher,

and his well-earned renown as a Christian scholar,
and indulging the hope, that, by the season of
entire repose which medical authority has pre-
scribed, he may yet be enabled to resume his usual
intellectual pursuits and this Seminary again enjoy
the benefit of his invaluable services;

Therefore be it, Resolved, First that the salary
of Prof. Smith be continued to the end of this
academic year, and

Second, that it be referred to a committee . .
to consider and report what arrangements should be
made whereby Dr. Henry B. Smith may be retained in
connection with the Union Theological Seminary as
Professor emeritus. . . .162

Professor Shedd was elected to teach his classes, and

Professor E. H. Gillett of New York University was asked to

be in charge of the Library until Smith was able to return or

until other arrangements could be made.163   Charles Augustus

Briggs, who was to become the Librarian in 1877, was appointed

at this meeting as Provisional Professor of Hebrew and Cognate

Languages at the salary of $2,500.164 The salaries of the

Professors had been, by this time, raised to $5,000 per annum.165

A report of the Committee on the Site was received at

this time. The members suggested that because the plans for

the construction of dormitories for the students had been

abandoned that a fire-proof library "lighted from the roof,"

a chapel, and a classroom building be built. They, further,

suggested that a corner lot 150 feet square be purchased for

these buildings. This, they said, would be ample space for

a library fifty by eighty feet, a classroom building fifty by

eighty feet, and a chapel fifty by seventy feet. They called

attention to a plot at Lexington Avenue and 37th Street and

to twelve lots at Lexington Avenue and 75th Street which were for sale at $120,000.[166]

The Finance Committee reported two months later that a document had been received from James Brown constituting the transfer of an "indenture of mortgage" dated January 1, 1874 "to secure payment of the sum of $300,000" maturing January 1, 1879. The bulk of the proceeds of the mortgage was designated for the endowment of existing professorships, but $28,000 was pocketed for the "General Endowment."[167]

Smith's report as Librarian was presented to the final meeting of the Board that year, at which time the Directors decided to commit the selection of books for the Library to the Faculty. Improvement in his health was noted, and he was appointed as Professor Emeritus. He was relieved of administrative and instructional duties for the ensuing academic year and yet, insofar as his health would permit, was requested to prepare his lectures in theology for publication. He was, further, asked to lecture occasionally on this subject, and his salary was fixed for the following year at $3,500.[168]

The Alumni Association heard at their meeting two days later that only $3,200 had been pledged to their campaign for the Library.[169] Still, evidence that things were going well with the school was to be seen in an act of the New York Legislature on May 11, when the amount of personal estate for the Seminary was raised from a ceiling of $50,000 to $500,000

. . . exclusive of the Library, and of such Professorships, Scholarships, and Lectureships, or other offices connected with the Educational Department of the Seminary as are now or may hereafter be, from time to time, endowed.[170]

The institution became increasingly concerned with
the quality of its work during this period; the accompanying
self-examination was reflected in at least two records which
were made at this time. The first was a suggestion from the
Committee on Examinations that higher requirements be made for
graduation.[171] The second was a Faculty minute that allowed
a Greek student to proceed with his class with the provision
that because of his lack of Hebrew, he would receive a certificate instead of a diploma at commencement.[172] This emphasis
on Hebrew was reflected in the Library appropriation this
year for $1,000 plus the price of the _Talmud_,[173] which was
subsequently given to the school after having been purchased
by a donor for $200.[174]

The new constitution went to press at the beginning
of the new year; and in it the provision that the Library was
to be restricted to ministers, theological students and other
persons of professional or literary standing who had been
introduced by a Director or Faculty member[175] was abolished.
The rules for the use of the Library, according to the new
by-laws, were to be made by the Faculty according to the needs
of the institution.[176]

The school still was financially unable to change its
location; but an extensive remodeling and expansion program
of the existing quarters, including those of the Library, was
suggested.[177] An additional property at 259 Greene Street
was also purchased for $14,000. Suggestions for steam heat,
Croton water, bathrooms and closets on each floor, and

remodeling of this property, in addition to an extension at the rear of 30 Clinton Place, were also made at this time.[178]

The ailing Librarian was advised during this period to give up his responsibilities in the Library and to give himself entirely to preparing his lectures for the press. He wrote, however, in a letter to George Prentiss:

> I intend, of course, to begin this work on my lectures as soon as I can; but in doing it, I must be where I can have access to the library, etc. It will be my hardest work. My lectures at the Seminary on Apologetics and Natural Theology, etc., could all be worked in and made a part of it. And I and all other men need to be where there is something definite to do every day. The library is a kind of recreation to me, and a change of work.[179]

He wrote, in another letter to Prentiss from Clifton Springs, on February 25, 1875:

> . . . As to the library, I should say that fully two-thirds of it could not be replaced excepting at great additional (to what it cost) expense. One-third of the two-thirds could not be replaced at all. This is true of a large part of the Van Ess collection, which numbered about seventeen thousand titles. The Incunabula (earliest printed editions between 1487 and 1510), one hundred and fifty in number, are, as a whole, invaluable; and so is the Reformation literature, about two thousand original editions. If there is any plan about a fire-proof building, I should like to see it, for it is quite imperative that the alcoves and shelves should be so arranged that we be not obliged to rearrange and renumber all the books and the whole catalogue.[180]

The suggestion about the rearrangement of the Library was followed by a plan for the accomplishment of this goal, which was brought before the Faculty on April 17 by Smith.[181] Although nothing seems to have been done about the plan at this meeting, his salary as Professor Emeritus was fixed for the following year at $2,000.[182]

The occasion for the rearrangement, the construction
of the new Library building, was considered again on May 3
by the Finance Committee at the same time that suggestions
for improving the dormitory were made.[183] Two days later a
recommendation was made to the Board that the Library building
be constructed outside the existing walls of 9 University
Place.[184] One week later the proposed enlargement of the
Library and chapel was estimated at $5,000, the addition of
steam heat at $6,800, the improvement of the dormitories at
$2,900 and the construction of bathrooms at $4,500.[185] These
plans were carried out as a result of gifts from Frederick
Marquand in the amount of $45,000.[186]

That summer a new building was constructed, joining
259 Greene Street with 30 Clinton Place; an addition was made
to the north side of the central building, in part to house
the growing library; and the main building was remodeled. The
total cost amounted to $46,362.[187]

Another important event in the history of the Library
that year was the death of E. H. Gillett. His contributions
included the selection of approximately 1,200 volumes of
Deistic, Dissenting, Unitarian and Universalist works which
were controversial in England and in America.[188] He also
played an important role in the development of the Alumni
Library Committee and replaced Smith as Librarian during the
latter's illness.

The Librarian suggested at this time that the Library
be rearranged by subjects during the summer vacation. He also

announced that Mrs. E. H. Gillett wanted the Seminary to have
the books from her husband's Library which would be useful
and needed.[189] These gifts, which eventually came to Union,
included a strong collection of materials on American theology
and history.[190]

The enthusiasm with which the academic year ended was
reflected in the commencement address by E. H. Hatfield, in
which he said:

> . . . In this respect [enrollment] Union Seminary
> now ranks every other in the land. By the grace
> of God, it has, through much and severe tribulation,
> attained to a position of influence excelled by
> none other. During the forty years of its opera-
> tions, it has sent forth 1778 students, of whom
> 1070 have graduated here. . . . They are found in
> every section, in nearly State, of the Union. . . .
> They are found in our academies, colleges, and
> seminaries. . . . On every continent and ocean
> group of islands they are toiling. . . . Union
> Seminary is a mighty power in the world.[191]

The Directors ordered that this address be printed;
and it became, thereby, the first published history of the
school. They decided at the same meeting that the Library
should be "rearranged and put in complete order." They, therefore, appointed Directors Brown, McAlpin, and Kingsley to
assure that this was done.[192] The report was given at the
September meeting of the Board that the collection had been
rearranged "substantially as directed" under the supervision
of Professor Briggs at a cost of approximately $1,000.[193]
The Directors further expressed their appreciation to Briggs
for his time and work

> during the heat of the last summer, in superintending
> and inspection and dusting of the whole Library; and

in arranging and cataloguing a large part of it, after a new method, thus making it more convenient and available for all who are entitled to its use.[194]

The rearrangement must have been modest to have been accomplished at this cost and in the period of three months. The inadequacy of the work was, in fact, later acknowledged by Briggs.

The annual catalog issued for that fall had two relevant paragraphs about the Library:

The Board of Directors have granted the alumni a room for the executive committee where it is proposed to gather a library of all the publications of the alumni, whether books or pamphlets.

. . . The leading Theological and Literary Reviews of England, Germany, France, and the United States are taken.[195]

The Death of and Tributes to the Librarian

Smith's health had improved to the point that he was invited that fall to deliver the Ely Lectures in the spring of 1877.[196] He was involved in preparing for a course on evolution[197] when he died at five o'clock in the morning on February 7, 1877.[198] The funeral was held in the Church of the Covenant on the afternoon of February 9.[199]

Many tributes were made to him. Dr. Hitchcock spoke for his colleagues on the Faculty, for example, in a minute recorded in their proceedings. In recognizing Smith's twenty-seven years of service to the institution, the President spoke of his "genial temper, his profound, exact, and various learning, his rare skill . . . as a teacher, and his unflagging zeal.[200]

Dr. Dorner of Berlin wrote to Professor Briggs in referring to Dr. Smith:

> Sehr schmertzlich hat mich der Tod von Henry B.
> Smith berührt. Ich habe ihn als einen der ersten,
> wenn nicht als ersten Amerikanischen Theologen der
> Gegenwart angesehen; festgegrundet in christlichen
> Glauben, frei und weitzen Herzens und Blickes,
> philosophischen Geistes und für systematische
> Theologie ungewöhnlich begabt.[201]

Professor Goden of Neuchatel wrote, in a similar vein, to Mrs. Smith:

> La première fois que nous nous sommes recontrés,
> c'était à Berlin, chez notre père spirituel,
> l'excellent Neander. J'ai appris alors à connaître
> en lui l'un des jeunes chrétiens les plus aimables,
> l'un des gentlemen les plus chrétiens que j'ai
> jamais recontrés. Plus tard j'ai eu la joie de
> revoir M. Smith en Suisse. Devenus professeurs
> l'un et l'autre, nous causâmes naturellement de
> theólogie, et j'appris alors à connaître l'un des
> espirits les plus profonds, les plus judicieux et
> les plus perspicieux [i.e., perspicaces] que j'ai
> jamais recontrés. Il dominait chaque sujet et me
> dominait en en parlant. En apprenant la mort de
> cet homme éminent, j'ai eu le sentiment bien
> profond: Voilà un citoyen rentré dans sa patrie![202]

Another friend's vivid recollection of the man as Librarian is recalled in Prentiss's history:

> . . . Who can forget that room [the library], walled
> and double-walled with books, the baize-covered desk
> in the corner by the window, loaded with the fresh
> philosophical and theological treasures of the
> European press, and the little figure in the long
> gray wrapper seated there,--the figure so frail and
> slight--the beautifully moulded brow, crowned with
> its thick, wavy, sharply parted, iron-gray hair, the
> strong aquiline profile, the restless shifting in
> his chair, the nervous pulling of the hand at the
> moustache, as the stream of talk widened and deepened,
> the occasional start from his seat to pull down a
> book or to search for a pamphlet--how inseparably these
> memories twine themselves with those of high debate,
> and golden speech, and converse.[203]

Henry Sloane Coffin credited him with the introduction of the historical method into the teaching of theology;[204]

and while this may be exaggerated, Charles R. Gillett's statement that

> The whole [systematic theology] collection shows
> evidences of the formative hand of that master
> of theological science, Dr. Henry B. Smith[205]

was unquestionably justified.

FOOTNOTES

[1]George Lewis Prentiss, The Union Theological Seminary in the City of New York: Historical and Biographical Sketches of Its First Fifty Years (New York: Anson D. F. Randolph and Co., 1889), pp. 260-61.

[2]George Lewis Prentiss, The Union Theological Seminary in the City of New York: Its Design and Another Decade of Its History, with a Sketch of the Life and Public Services of Charles Butler, LL.D. (Asbury Park, N. J.: M., W., & C. Pennypacker, 1899), p. 242.

[3]Union Theological Seminary, One Hundredth Anniversary, 1836-1936 (New York: Union Theological Seminary, 1936), p. 27.

[4]Minutes of the Faculty of Union Theological Seminary in the City of New York, December, 1850.

[5]Minutes of the Board of Directors of Union Theological Seminary in the City of New York, January 7, 1851.

[6]Ibid., February 12, 1851.

[7]Ibid., March 31, 1851.

[8]"Report of Librarian, Needs of the Library, 1851-60," "Extracts from Source Materials Used in Preparing a History of Union Theological Seminary," ed. by Charles Ripley Gillett [New York, 1937] (Typewritten), p. 29-A.

[9]"Report of Dr. H. B. Smith: Church History, June 18, 1851," ibid., p. 30.

[10]Directors, op. cit., July 22, 1851.

[11]Ibid., June 29, 1847.

[12]Ibid., October 7, 1851.

[13]Ibid.

[14]Ibid.

[15]Ibid., January 6, 1852.

[16]Edwin F. Hatfield, _The Early Annals of Union Theological Seminary in the City of New York_ (New York: No. 30 Clinton Place, 1876), p. 19.

[17]Prentiss, _The Union Theological Seminary in the City of New York: Historical_ [etc.], p. 53.

[18]Directors, _op. cit._, February 13, 1852.

[19]_Ibid._, February 23, 1852.

[20]_Ibid._, March 25, 1852.

[21]Hatfield, _op. cit._, p. 19.

[22]Prentiss, _The Union Theological Seminary in the City of New York: Historical_ [etc.], p. 55.

[23]_Appeal to the Friends of the Institution and Others, April 30, 1852_, "Extracts," ed. by Gillett, p. 31-A.

[24]Directors, _op. cit._, June 16 and 25, 1852.

[25]Gillett, _op. cit._, p. 32.

[26]Hatfield, _op. cit._, p. 20.

[27]Directors, _op. cit._, January 24, 1853.

[28]Prentiss, _op. cit._, 1889, pp. 195-96.

[29]Directors, _op. cit._, May 6, 1853.

[30]Prentiss, _op. cit._, 1889, p. 197.

[31]Union Theological Seminary, _Services in Adams Chapel at the Dedication of the New Buildings of the Union Theological Seminary, 1200 Park Avenue, New York City, December 9, 1884_ (New York: Printing House of William C. Martin, 111 John Street, 1885), p. 11.

[32]Minutes of the Finance Committee of Union Theological Seminary in the City of New York, May 16, 1853.

[33]_Appeal to the Friends of the Institution and Others, April 30, 1852_, "Extracts," ed. by Gillett, p. 31-A.

[34]Directors, _op. cit._, January 3, 1854.

[35]Directors, _op. cit._, March 3, 1854.

[36]_Ibid._, May 8, 1854.

[37]Prentiss, _op. cit._, 1889, p. 279.

99

[38] Ibid., p. 274.

[39] Ibid., pp. 275-80.

[40] Directors, op. cit., June 20, 1855.

[41] Union Theological Seminary, Catalgue of the Officers and Students of the Union Theological Seminary in the City of New York: January, 1857 (New York: John F. Trow, Printer, 1857).

[42] New York Evangelist, December 18, 1856.

[43] New York Observer, December 18, 1856.

[44] Charles Ripley Gillett, "Detailed History of the Union Theological Seminary in the City of New York" [New York, 1937] (Typewritten), p. 265.

[45] Directors, op. cit., January 6, 1857.

[46] Ibid., May 11, 1857.

[47] Prentiss, The Union Theological Seminary in the City of New York: Historical [etc.], p. 353.

[48] Ibid.

[49] Ibid., May 10, 1858.

[50] Prentiss, The Union Theological Seminary in the City of New York: Historical [etc.], pp. 264-65.

[51] [Elizabeth L. Smith], Henry Boynton Smith, His Life and Work (New York: A. C. Armstrong & Son, 714 Broadway, 1881), p. 175.

[52] Directors, op. cit., May 7, 1862.

[53] "Reports of Librarian," "Extracts," ed. by Gillett, p. 2-A.

[54] Prentiss, The Union Theological Seminary in the City of New York: Its Design [etc.], p. 79.

[55] Faculty, op. cit., March 13, 1863.

[56] Ibid., April 29, May 6, 1884.

[57] Ibid., June 7, 1864.

[58] Prentiss, op. cit., 1889, p. 48.

[59] Faculty, op. cit., September 14, 1864.

[60] Ibid.

[61] Prentiss, The Union Theological Seminary in the City of New York: Historical [etc.], p. 250.

[62] Directors, op. cit., May 11, 1863.

[63] Ibid., p. 48.

[64] Prentiss, op. cit., 1899, pp. 418-19.

[65] Ibid., pp. 419-20.

[66] Directors, op. cit., January 11, 1864.

[67] Ibid., January 27, 1864.

[68] Ibid., February 10, 1864.

[69] "Conference of Faculty with Committee of Board," "Extracts," ed. by Gillett, p. 45-B.

[70] Directors, op. cit., April 18, 1864.

[71] Finance Committee, op. cit., May 16, 1864.

[72] Prentiss, op. cit., 1889, p. 178.

[73] Directors, op. cit., June 8, 1864.

[74] Ibid.

[75] Finance Committee, op. cit., September 30, 1864.

[76] Appeal to the Friends of the Institution and Others, April 30, 1852, "Extracts," ed. by Gillett, p. 31-A.

[77] Appeal in Behalf of The Union Theological Seminary in the City of New York, December 7, 1864, in Union Theological Seminary, Registrar, "Registrar's Archives, 1864.

[78] Finance Committee, op. cit., January 17, 1865.

[79] Directors, op. cit., November 8, 1865.

[80] Prentiss, op. cit., 1889, pp. 182-84.

[81] Directors, op. cit., May 8, 1865 and Finance Committee, op. cit., May 29, 1865.

[82] Directors, op. cit., November 8, 1865.

[83] Ibid.

[84] Ibid., May 8, 1865.

[85] Ibid., November 8, 1865.

[86] Finance Committee, op. cit., March 30, 1865.

[87] Ibid., October 2, 1865.

[88] Directors, op. cit., November 8, 1865.

[89] Hatfield, op. cit., p. 21.

[90] Directors, op. cit., November 15, 1865.

[91] Finance Committee, op. cit., May 7, 1866.

[92] "Faculty Report," "Archives," "Extracts," ed. by Gillett, p. 49.

[93] Ibid., December 5, 1866.

[94] Finance Committee, op. cit., November 23, 1866.

[95] Directors, op. cit., December 5, 1866.

[96] Directors, op. cit., March 11, 1867.

[97] "Balance Sheet, April 30, 1867," "Archives," "Extracts," ed. by Gillett, p. 50.

[98] Finance Committee, op. cit., January 22, 1868.

[99] William Bristol Shaw, "James, Daniel Willis," in Dictionary of American Biography, ed. by Allen Johnson & Dumas Malone, IX (New York: Charles Scribner's Sons, 1937), pp. 573-74.

[100] Finance Committee, op. cit., January 22, 1868.

[101] Directors, op. cit., May 11, 1868.

[102] Directors, op. cit., November 11, 1868.

[103] Prentiss, op. cit., 1889, p. 276.

[104] Directors, op. cit., November 11, 1868.

[105] Ibid.

[106] "Report of Committee on New Site," "Archives," "Extracts," ed. by Gillett, p. 52.

[107] Prentiss, The Union Theological Seminary in the City of New York: Historical [etc.], p. 261.

[108]Faculty, op. cit., May 8, 1869.

[109]"Report of Faculty, May 9, 1870," "Archives," "Extracts," ed. by Gillett, p. 55.

[110]"Concurrent Declaration of the General Assemblies of 1869, May 27, 1869," Ibid., p. 53-A.

[111]Finance Committee, op. cit., December 3, 1869.

[112]Directors, op. cit., December 15, 1869.

[113]Ibid., December 29, 1869.

[114]Ibid.

[115]Ibid., May 9, 1870.

[116]Prentiss, op. cit., 1889, pp. 184-86.

[117]Directors, op. cit., March 23, 1870.

[118]Gillett, "Detailed History," p. 1121.

[119]"McAlpin, David Hunter," The National Cyclopaedia of American Biography, XXXIII (New York: James T. White Company, 1947), pp. 304-05.

[120]Gillett, "Detailed History," p. 1121.

[121]Directors, op. cit., May 8, 1871.

[122]Charles R. Gillett, "The McAlpin Collection of British History and Theology, Union Theological Seminary Bulletin, VII, No. 2 (January, 1924), p. 3.

[123]Directors, op. cit., May 16, 1870.

[124]Prentiss, op. cit., 1899, pp. 420-22.

[125]Ibid., p. 423.

[126]Ibid., May 16, 1870.

[127]Hatfield, op. cit., p. 27.

[128]Directors, op. cit., May 16, 1870.

[129]Henry Sloane Coffin, A Half Century of Union Theological Seminary, 1896-1945, An Informal History (New York: Charles Scribner's Sons, 1954), p. 17.

[130]Ibid.

[131]Prentiss, The Union Theological Seminary in the City of New York: Historical [etc.], p. 261.

[132]Directors, op. cit., February 20, 1872.

[133]Ibid.

[134]Ibid.

[135]"Circular," "Archives," "Extracts," ed. by Gillett, p. 58.

[136]Directors, op. cit., May 8, 1871.

[137]"Librarian's Report, May 8, 1871," "Archives," "Extracts," ed. by Gillett, p. 56.

[138]Directors, op. cit., May 8, 1871.

[139]Prentiss, op. cit., 1889, p. 218.

[140]Directors, op. cit., May 8, 1871.

[141]Ibid.

[142]Gillett, "Detailed History," p. 1129.

[143]Minutes of the Alumni Association of Union Theological Seminary in the City of New York, May 8, 1872.

[144]Ibid., May 7, 1873.

[145]Directors, op. cit., November 13, 1872 and December 23, 1872.

[146]William Walker Rockwell, "Prentiss, George Lewis," Dictionary of American Biography, ed. Allen Johnson and Dumas Malone, XV (New York: Charles Scribner's Sons, 1937), 189-90.

[147]Finance Committee, op. cit., October 31, 1872.

[148]Union Theological Seminary, Catalogue of the Officers and Students of the Union Theological Seminary in the City of New York, 1867-68 (New York: W. C. Rogers & Co., 1868) and ibid., 1871-72 (1871).

[149]Directors, op. cit., May 5, 1873.

[150]Ibid.

[151]Ibid.

[152]Ibid.

104

[153] Alumni, op. cit., May 7, 1873.

[154] Directors, op. cit., September 24, 1873.

[155] Prentiss, op. cit., 1889, pp. 266-67, 273-74.

[156] Ibid., p. 239.

[157] Directors, op. cit., September 24, 1873.

[158] Directors, op. cit., October 20, 1873.

[159] Ibid., November 12, 1873.

[160] Ibid.

[161] Minutes of the Executive Committee of Union Theological Seminary in the City of New York, December 15, 1873.

[162] Directors, op. cit., January 14, 1874.

[163] Ibid.

[164] Ibid., April 11, 1873.

[165] Ibid., January 14, 1874.

[166] "Archives," "Extracts," ed. by Gillett, p. 62.

[167] Directors, op. cit., March 11, 1874.

[168] Ibid., May 11, 1874.

[169] Alumni, op. cit., May 13, 1874.

[170] Hatfield, op. cit., p. 25.

[171] "Report of Committee on Examinations," "Archives," "Extracts," ed. by Gillett, p. 52.

[172] Faculty, op. cit., September 29, 1874.

[173] Finance Committee, op. cit., October 5, 1874.

[174] Ibid., December 7, 1874.

[175] Union Theological Seminary, Constitution and Laws of The Union Theological Seminary in the City of New York, Founded on the 18th of January, A. D. 1836, As Revised and Amended A. D. 1867 (New York: W. C. Rogers & Co., 1867) General Laws: Chap. VII, Sec. 6.

[176] Ibid., 1876 (New York: John F. Trow & Son, 1875).

[177]Directors, op. cit., January 29, 1875.

[178]Ibid., March 10, 1875.

[179][Elizabeth L. Smith], Henry Boynton Smith, His Life and Work (New York: A. C. Armstrong & Son, 714 Broadway, 1881), p. 387.

[180]Ibid.

[181]Faculty, op. cit., April 17, 1875.

[182]Directors, op. cit., May 10, 1875.

[183]Finance Committee, op. cit., May 3, 1875.

[184]Ibid., May 5, 1875.

[185]Ibid., May 12, 1875.

[186]Directors, op. cit., May 8, 1876.

[187]Union Theological Seminary, Services in Adams Chapel at the Dedication of the New Buildings of the Union Theological Seminary, 1200 Park Avenue, New York City, December 9, 1884 (New York: Printing House of William C. Martin, 1885), p. 4.

[188]William Coolidge Lane and Charles Knowles Bolton, Notes on Special Collections in American Libraries ("Library of Harvard University, Bibliographical Contributions," edited by Justin Winsor, No. 45, Cambridge, Mass.: Issued by the Library of Harvard University, 1892), pp. 48-49.

[189]"Archives," "Extracts," ed. by Gillett, p. 63-A.

[190]Lane, op. cit., pp. 48-49.

[191]Hatfield, op. cit., pp. 22-23.

[192]Directors, op. cit., June 5, 1876.

[193]Ibid., September 4, 1876.

[194]Ibid., May 13, 1877.

[195]Union Theological Seminary, Catalogue of the Officers and Students of the Union Theological Seminary in the City of New York, 1876-77 (New York: Wm. C. Martin, 1876), p. 23.

[196]Faculty, op. cit., October 25, 1876.

[197]Prentiss, The Union Theological Seminary in the City of New York: Historical [etc.], p. 261.

[198]Faculty, op. cit., February 8, 1877.

[199]Prentiss, The Union Theological Seminary in the City of New York: Historical [etc.], p. 262.

[200]Faculty, op. cit., February 14, 1877.

[201]Prentiss, The Union Theological Seminary in the City of New York: Historical [etc.], p. 263.

[202]Ibid.

[203]Ibid. pp. 265-66.

[204]Henry Sloan Coffin, "The Centennial Sermon," in Union Theological Seminary, One Hundredth Anniversary, 1836-1936, p. 23.

[205]Charles R. Gillett, "The Library, General Catalogue and the Alumni" in Prentiss, The Union Theological Seminary in the City of New York: Its Design [etc.], p. 359.

Chapter IV

THE LIBRARIANSHIP OF CHARLES
AUGUSTUS BRIGGS, 1877-83

Charles Augustus Briggs, Professor of Hebrew and
Cognate Languages of Union Theological Seminary was appointed
by the Faculty as Librarian Pro Tem one week following the
death of Henry B. Smith.[1] One month later the Directors
elected him as Librarian for two years with the date of appointment set at May 1, 1877. E. F. Hatfield, M. R. Vincent, and
D. H. McAlpin were asked to act with him as a Standing Committee on the Library.[2] Although his salary for his services
there probably did not begin until May 1, he had been by this
time in charge of the Library for nearly a year.

The Pre-Union Background of Briggs

He, like his predecessors, was a good choice to fill
this office. He was born in the city of New York on January 14,
1841. His father's ancestors were English, and his mother's
family were partly Huguenot and partly German Reformed and
Scottish Presbyterian. Both families had been early settlers
in New York and the New England colonies.[3]

A letter, written by him as a youth to an uncle, re-
veals his tenaciousness:

I am going back to school to prepare for college.
I intend to finish Caesar and Virgil, and get along
considerable in Greek. . . . I intend to go right
at it, when I get back to school. I am going in
strong. When I start once, I am going to finish.
My mind is made up.[4]

He entered the University of Virginia at the age of
sixteen and studied there for three years. He united with
the Presbyterian Church in Charlottesville during his second
year and decided to become a minister. His studies were
interrupted by the war, in which he served with the seventh
regiment of the New York State Volunteers for a brief time
before leaving the service to enter Union Seminary in 1861.[5]
He left school in 1863[6] and went to work for his father as a
merchant. He went abroad in 1866, accompanied by his wife,
and spent three years in Germany,[7] studying at the University
of Berlin[8] with Dorner and making vacation trips during this
period to Italy, France, Russia, Egypt, and Palestine.[9]

He was ordained, shortly after returning to the United
States, in the Presbyterian Church in Elizabeth, New Jersey
and was Pastor of the First Presbyterian Church of Roselle,
in that state from 1870-74.[10]

The First Two-Year Appointment as Librarian

Following his appointment as Librarian Pro Tem, the
Library received some income from the Prize Fellowship Endowment,[11] which had been established the previous year through
a gift of $10,000[12] from Francis Peoples Schoals, a member of
the Spring Street Church.[13] The income had been designated
as a gift to the student who

> shall have made in the judgment of the faculty, the
> greatest proficiency in his studies, particularly
> in the original languages of the Bible.[14]

Yet a provision had been made that if it were not expedient
to continue the awards, the income could be appropriated to
the Library;[15] and the first year's income was used in this
way. Another gift was received at this time from Mrs. R. M.
Galloway of New York through the presentation of 538 volumes
from the Library of her brother, the Rev. F. W. Williams of
the class of 1852.[16]

Gillett reported on a study presented by Briggs in
the spring, which was still in the archives in 1937 but which
has subsequently been lost. Briggs had been asked by the
Board to report on the condition of the Library and reported
that it had been "neglected from the beginning." He said
that he was impressed by the collection, the extent of which
was unknown to anyone. He insisted that it was in a chaotic
condition, with many volumes lost by misplacement.[17]

The newer books, Briggs said, had been moved during
the previous summer to the new long room adjoining the old
Library. He claimed that many faults in the collection had
been discovered at the time of moving. He thought, for
example, that the collection was suited more for scholarly
research than for the needs of the students, faculty, and
ministers who were using it most.[18]

He attacked, further, the administration of the Library,
claiming that it had been open only two hours a day under the
direction of an inexperienced student. He also said that the

34,000 volumes reported in the 1876-77 catalog were not all
in the Library, as an actual count had revealed only 26,997.[19]
Many of the recent acquisitions, such as the Marsh, Cox, and
Gillett gifts, had not been cataloged. The four-volume manuscript catalog, he said, was interlined and interleaved; a new
catalog on the card system was, therefore, necessary.[20]

His report praised Dr. and Mrs. E. H. Gillett as the
"leading benefactors" of the Library and proposed to begin
the Gillett Collection for many of the materials from his
library. He also recommended that the collection of Henry B.
Smith be purchased at the cost of $3,000 to fill some of the
gaps in Union's holdings.[21] He concluded that the principal
needs of the Library were for an endowment of $50,000 and a
full-time librarian.[22]

The financing required for accomplishing some of these
goals was outlined in this report to the Finance Committee:

Rearrangement and re-cataloguing	$ 500
Forming a reference library	1,000
Bindings and repairs	2,000
Reviews and deficiencies of last year	700
Purchase of books	600
Purchase of H. B. Smith's library	3,000
	7,800

The following amounts were appropriated following a
discussion of these requests:

To meet the deficiency of last year	$ 431
For reviews, etc.	269
For the purchase of books	100
For re-cataloguing and rearranging	500
For repairs	100
	1,400 [23]

They, further, voted that $1,000 from the Ely Lecture-
ship Fund be set aside for the Library, with the consent of

the founder,[24] which was given on September 3.[25] A campaign by the Library Committee to raise $5,000 for the purchase of Smith's library was also approved.[26]

The Alumni Association met at this time and resolved to raise $10,000 to endow the Henry Smith Memorial Reference Library. This amount was to be divided into 2,000 shares of $5.00 each with the date for the completion of the campaign set for one year later.[27]

The reclassification of the Library with the construction of a card catalogue began the following summer under the direction of Briggs,[28] with Charles R. Gillett assisting.[29] The scheme for the cataloging of the materials was that of the Astor Library,[30] with cards of the same shape and size as those used in that library.[31] The adaptation of this scheme by Briggs, the details of which have been lost, was said by his successor to have been

> . . . a very large task, embodying an application of the current principles of Theological Encyclopedia, and representing an advance upon any scheme that had been employed previously in any theological library.[32]

The Finance Committee authorized at this time the purchase of H. B. Smith's Library for $2,500, $1,400 of which had been raised by subscription and $1,000 of which had come from the interest on the Ely Lectureship Fund.[33] The Directors approved this expenditure the following week.[34]

The Alumni Association heard a report the following day that $1,790 had been contributed to the Smith Memorial Fund, which was being held open for future gifts. Z. S. Ely,

H. K. Corning, D. H. McAlpin, M. O. Roberts, I. N. Phelps,
A. Van Rensselaer, and H. G. DeForest were said to have contributed the funds for the purchase of the Smith Library.[35]

The Second Two-Year Appointment

Briggs's two-year appointment expired at this time,
and he was re-appointed for two more at the spring meeting of
the Directors. He mentioned at this session the desirability
of securing the works of the Westminster divines.[36] Evidence
that McAlpin money was used for this purpose was to be found
in the fact that the catalog for that year showed that its
scope had been expanded to include Westminster materials as
well as the Deistic and Trinitarian controversies of the
eighteenth century.[37]

A development began at this time which was to have
long-range effects upon the growth of the Library. Two seniors
of the class of 1879 asked to remain for a year of graduate
study, and they were given permission to do this with rooms
provided free of charge.[38] The fall term began, however, with
seven post-graduate students enrolled; Hitchcock and Briggs
were appointed, therefore, to bring a report to the Faculty
about a course for these students.[39]

Francis Brown, who, along with Professor S. R. Driver
and Professor Briggs edited the Hebrew dictionary which is
still considered standard, began teaching at Union at this
time.[40] Two Assistants in the Library, one of whom was Charles
R. Gillett of the class of 1880, were also appointed.[41]

Gillett was later made Fellow of his class,

> to remain one year in the Seminary as assistant
> librarian, and then to study one year abroad under
> the direction of the faculty.[42]

The Morgan Gift

All events in the Seminary in this academic year became secondary, however, to those caused by a letter from Edwin Denison Morgan. He had established himself in New York the same year that Union was opened; and in a few years he had become one of the leading businessmen of the city. He was elected Governor of New York in 1859. He is said to have "raised, equipped, and sent" 220,000 men into the field during the Civil War. He represented New York in the Senate of the United States from 1863 to 1869; and he was offered the Secretaryship of the Treasury by Presidents Lincoln and Arthur. On March 29, 1880 he sent the following letter to the Directors of Union:

> I desire to show my appreciation of the useful-
> ness of the Union Theological Seminary, and to aid
> it in the great work that it is now doing for the
> country.
>
> I therefore forward herewith, One Hundred Thou-
> sand (100.000) Dollars of Seven per cent (7 %)
> Rail Road Bonds. . . .
>
> I desire this fund to be held upon the following
> Trusts for the following purposes.
>
> First.   The principal shall be held perpetually as
> from all other funds of the Seminary.
>
> Second. The income of this fund shall be applied
> to the improvement, increase, and support
> of the Library of the Union Theological
> Seminary.

Third. When the Seminary shall be <u>permanently located</u>
so much of this fund as may be necessary shall
be expended in the erection of a new Library
Building.

It is my earnest desire that there should be no
unnecessary delay in beginning this new building, and
I trust that <u>in no case</u> this delay may Exceed the limit
of three years; meantime during this interval of three
years the Directors of the Seminary, after using so
much of the annual income of this fund, as may be necessary for the support and enlargement of the Library,
are permitted to use the remainder of said income in
such manner as in their judgements shall best subserve
the general purposes of the Seminary. . . .

(signed) E. D. Morgan

. . . Resolved . . . that the amount thus received be
retained distinct from all other funds, and that it
shall always be known and designated as the Edwin D.
Morgan Library Fund, and secondly, that whenever a
permanent location shall be chosen, the building to be
erected in accordance with the terms of the gift shall
be designated as the Morgan Library.[43]

The enthusiasm with which the gift was received was

recalled by Gillett:

. . . During the winter of 1879, Dr. Richard S. Storrs
delivered the Ely Lectures . . . in the hall of the
Young Men's Christian Association at 23d St. and 4th
Avenue. At the close of the courses, speeches were
made thanking all concerned, and particularly the
speaker. It had recently become known that Governor
Morgan had made a large donation to the funds of the
Seminary--making removal to a new site possible at
an early date. It was known to a number that Governor
Morgan was present at the meeting mentioned above, and
at the first opportunity there came calls for "Governor
Morgan!.speech.! I happened to sit directly behind
the Governor, and saw how disagreeable the situation
was becoming to him. Dr. Adams was presiding, and he
was also quite conscious of the growing tension. In
the course of a few moments the calls for the governor
came from all parts of the house. They ceased as Dr.
Adams rose to his full height, and slowly advanced to
the edge of the platform. . . . With a gesture which
was almost a benediction, he said: "Ladies and
gentlemen; Governor Morgan is a man whose modesty is
only exceeded by his generosity," and then proceeded
to dismiss the gathering.[44]

The income from the endowment was used immediately to pay the expenses of the Library,[45] which were increased to $3,500; and the insurance on the collection was raised to $5,000.[46] The Librarian's report at the meeting of the Board in May stated that the following gifts had been received during the academic year, in addition to the budget and the Morgan money: D. H. McAlpin, whose collection was increased by 350 volumes and 790 tracts, $500; Marshall O. Roberts, $500; George W. Childs of Philadelphia, $500; and J. R. Skidmore, $100. Despite these gifts, he claimed that $3,000 worth of books, a list of which was presented, and $2,000 worth of binding, were needed before the move to the new location.[47] A committee was appointed on this date to recommend "the best available site."[48] The Alumni Association met the following day and heard a report that $1,845 had been received for the Smith Memorial Library Fund.[49] Apparently the fund was not increased substantially beyond that amount, in part because of Morgan's provision for the Library.

The President of the school died in the summer,[50] and Professor Hitchcock was appointed to fill that office.[51] Thomas Hastings was elected to the Chair of Sacred Rhetoric.[52] He was the son of Thomas Hastings, a distinguished author of hymns. The son graduated from Hamilton College in 1840 and from Union Seminary in 1851. Following his ordination in 1852, he became Pastor of the Presbyterian Church in Mendham, New Jersey for four years. He was then called to become Pastor of the West Presbyterian Church in New York, where he remained from 1856 to 1881. He was granted an honorary doctorate by the University of New York in 1865. He had been a Director of the Seminary since 1864. Although he was known more for his scholarly preaching and his administrative ability than for his writing, he had assisted his father in the preparation of Church Melodies in 1857 and was the author of many published essays and addresses. He stood firmly for freedom of inquiry in theological education and helped to shape Union's tradition in this area.[53] He helped build the Seminary's collection of works on homiletics and sermon materials by preachers of that era. His devotion to intellectual freedom in the preparation of ministers helped the Library to become less parochial.

Late in the winter the Directors decided that the new site for the Seminary should be as near as possible to the Lenox Library; and a committee was appointed to raise $150,000 to purchase such a site.[54] Again, E. D. Morgan came to the aid of the school with a letter:

> Understanding that you desire to purchase a portion of the block of land on Lenox Hill bounded by Madison & Park Avenues, 69th and 70th Streets as a site for the Chapel, Library, and other buildings of the Seminary, I hereby make to the Board of Trustees of the Seminary the following proposition.
>
> I will sell them ten lots of land comprising the easterly end of said block, and extending in depth from Park avenue One hundred and twenty feet, for $275,000. In case they purchase the property I will donate towards the purchase money, the sum of $100,000.
>
> The above offer is made on the condition that the buildings of the Seminary are to be erected on the lands so sold and that the erection of the same shall be commenced on or before the first day of April next. . . .[55]

The Board accepted these terms, and President Hitchcock
announced that subscriptions amounting to $50,000 for the new
site had been raised.[56] The Finance Committee instructed the
Treasurer ten days later to execute the contract, giving Morgan
$50,000 in cash and a mortgage for $125,000.[57]

The Building Program

Plans for the new building were, in the meantime, proceeding. The Committee on Plans suggested that the Library
be a separate and fire-proof building, that the chapel and
lecture rooms be a second structure, and that the dormitory
buildings occupy the remaining area.[58] The Building Committee
appointed on May 26 selected William A. Potter and James Brown
Lord as the architects for the new facilities and specified
that the Library and reading room, and perhaps a Librarian's
office, should cover about sixty by seventy feet.[59] The cost
of the building was limited to $200,000 at this time.[60] The
plans of the architects were accepted with minor changes, such
as the addition of a turret at the southwest corner of the
Library, the raising of the ceilings on the first floor to
sixteen feet from fourteen feet, the enlargement of the ground
area of the Library, and the inclusion of the museum in the
area assigned to the collection.[61] The cost of the buildings
was estimated a few months later to be:

Land, 10 lots	$275.000
Excavation	12.500
Foundation and basement walls	41.500
Heating and plumbing	20.000
Interest on bond and mortgage	15.000
Superstructure	289.000

Furniture	10.000
Architects' fees	17.500
Miscellaneous	4.500
Total	685.000 [62]

The school at this time had $515,000 for the building program, including $75,000 anticipated from the sale of the St. Nicholas Avenue lots.[63] The bid for the superstructure was, therefore, let to the Norcross Brothers,[64] who began the construction immediately.[65]

The McAlpin Collection

At the same time that a new Library building was being planned and built, a strong collection of materials on British history and theology was being gathered by Briggs and being paid for by McAlpin. Although the McAlpin Collection was begun by E. H. Gillett, its scope was changed upon his death. In contrast to the elder Gillett's interest in ecclesiastical disputes, especially those concerning the Deistic controversies of the late seventeenth and early eighteenth centuries, Briggs was more interested in literature by the Westminster and Puritan divines and materials written during the period of the Civil War and the Commonwealth.[66]

The collection also came to include materials by members of such sects as the Baptists, Brownists, Independents, Family of Love, and Muggletonians, as well as the Roman Catholic disputes of the sixteenth and seventeenth centuries. It also included general and local histories of Great Britain, church histories, biographies, and the collected works of British divines of all eras.[67]

Briggs increased the collection during his term as Librarian and afterwards to approximately 12,000 titles.[68] It was said to be third in size only to the British Museum and the Bodleian Library in the inclusion of titles listed in Dexter's Bibliography of Congregationalism.[69]

Briggs's Last Two Years as Librarian

Other events were taking place in the Library at this time. The fall of 1881, for example, was the time of the receipt of approximately 1,000 volumes from the library of former President William Adams.[70]

Charles R. Gillett was, on May 1, 1883, nominated for election as Librarian at a salary of $1,500.[71] The Faculty Library Committee nominated him at a salary of "not less than $2,000" during the same month;[72] but he was employed at the lower figure by the Board at their meeting on May 7 with the appointment to begin November 1.[73] It was understood that Briggs would retain his professorship.

His librarianship closed with 50,000 volumes, 44,000 pamphlets, and 165 manuscripts in the collection,[74] which represented an increase of 20,000 volumes during the seven years of his career in that office,[75] an enrollment of 124 students,[76] and an increase in the permanent funds of the school in the amount of approximately $750,000. This increase is shown in the following chart of the additions to the endowment between November 1, 1873 and late 1883 or early 1884:

Endowments

James Brown	1873	$300.000
For Elocution	1880	10.000
Henry M. Flagler (Elocutn)		40.000
E. D. Morgan legacy	1884	200.000

New Buildings

Frederick Marquand	1775-76	35.000
E. D. Morgan	1881	50.000
E. D. Morgan		100.000
H. R. Bishop	1881	10.000
Dr. Hastings' Friend		10.000
John T. Terry		10.000
Misses Jaffrey & Freeman	1881	1.000
Frederick Marquand	1882	25.000
Wm. E. Dodge	1882-83	10.000
Henry Day	1882-83	5.000
Russell Sage	1882-83	5.000
F. P. Schoals, legacy	1882-83	6.000
Stokes, legacy	1883	2.000
Roosevelt	1883	1.000
H. G. Marquand	1883	5.000
Wm. E. Dodge		5.000
John Crosby Brown		5.000
Charles Butler		10.000
Henry Ivison		3.000
D. Willis James		100.000
Morris K. Jesup		50.000
John Taylor Johnston		1.000

Library

E. D. Morgan	1880	50.000

Fellowships

Philadelphia	1876-77	10.000
F. P. Schoals	1876-77	10.000

Scholarships

Mrs. E. C. Griggs	1876	2.000
Fairchild	1876	2.500
Otis Allen	1881	3.000
Hartley	1881	3.000
Kerr	1881	2.000
Hills	1883	5.000
Miss Constable	1883	4.000

Total		$1.090.500 77

The esteem of the Board for Briggs's librarianship was reflected in a resolution adopted at the time of his final report, which included the announcement that 5,000 volumes had been received from the library of the late Edwin F. Hatfield:

> The Board of Directors of Union Theological Seminary in view of the retirement of Prof. Charles A. Briggs from the charge of the Seminary library desires to place on record its high appreciation of his services in that department. By his patient industry, the collection has been thoroughly classified and catalogued; valuable donations have been secured both for the Library and Museum through his agency, and important and judicious purchases have been made under his direction.
>
> The Board would hereby convey to Prof. Briggs its recognition of his energy, good judgment and practical skill in the management of the Library, and would tender to him its hearty thanks therefor.[78]

The faculty expressed their gratitude for his librarianship, further, at a celebration commemorating twenty-five years of his connection with the school:

> . . . Finding the library of the Seminary in need of rearrangement you gave seven years of hard and trying toil to that work, not always allowing yourself the needed summer vacation, and resigning the task only when the present Librarian had been prepared to take it up. . . .[79]

One of his students said of him:

> How well we remember, some of us, that stalwart figure with the high voice and the stiff gray beard. . . . To his imperialistic mind the Seminary was more than a training school for the ministry. It was to be a Christian university in which all branches of theological learning should find a place and scholars from every part of Christendom flock to study under its graduate faculty. Even the Pope of Rome was not exempt from Briggs' paternal care, and some of us can remember his mingled sense of surprise and disappointment when after an interview in which he had explained to the Holy Father the proper way to secure the reunion of Christendom he found that well-meaning but misguided man still unconvinced. We may smile at his faith in

the power of scholarship to bring healing to the
world; but something he gave us we would not will-
ingly let go. To those who have studied under Dr.
Briggs and the scholars whom he has trained . . .
lack of thoroughness is not an intellectual failing.
It is a moral fault. We cannot help this feeling.
It is bred in our bones. We have drunk it in from
the mother who has nurtured us. We owe it to ourselves; we owe it to our fellowmen . . . to learn all
that we can learn, that we may be able to do all that
we can do.[80]

FOOTNOTES

[1]Minutes of the Faculty of Union Theological Seminary in the City of New York, February 14, 1877.

[2]Minutes of the Board of Directors of Union Theological Seminary in the City of New York, March 13, 1877.

[3]George Lewis Prentiss, The Union Theological Seminary in the City of New York: Its Design and Another Decade of Its History, with a Sketch of the Life and Public Services of Charles Butler, LL.D. (Asbury Park, N. J.: M., W., & C. Pennypacker, 1899), p. 312.

[4]Ibid.

[5]Ibid.

[6]Union Theological Seminary, General Catalogue of Union Theological Seminary in the City of New York, 1836-1897 (New York: Union Theological Seminary, 1898), p. 121.

[7]Prentiss, op. cit., pp. 312-13.

[8]Union Theological Seminary, op. cit., p. 121.

[9]Prentiss, op. cit., p. 313.

[10]Union Theological Seminary, op. cit., p. 121.

[11]Directors, op. cit., March 5, 1877.

[12]Ibid., April 3, 1876.

[13]Ibid., July 9, 1877.

[14]Ibid., May 8, 1876.

[15]Ibid.

[16]Ibid., March 13, 1877.

[17]"Report by Dr. Briggs, May 7, 1877," "Extracts from Source Materials Used in Preparing a History of Union Theological Seminary," ed. by Charles Ripley Gillett [New York, 1937] (Typewritten), p. 64-A.

[18]Ibid.

[19] Ibid.

[20] Ibid.

[21] Ibid.

[22] Ibid.

[23] Minutes of the Finance Committee of Union Theological Seminary in the City of New York, May 14, 1877.

[24] Ibid.

[25] Finance Committee, op. cit., September 3, 1877.

[26] Ibid., May 14, 1877.

[27] Minutes of the Alumni Association of Union Theological Seminary in the City of New York, May 7, 1877.

[28] Charles Ripley Gillett, "Detailed History of the Union Theological Seminary in the City of New York [New York, 1937] (Typewritten), p. 1106.

[29] Ibid., p. 1135.

[30] Charles Ripley Gillett, "The Library of the Union Theological Seminary, Its Proper Position, Its Present Condition, Its Pressing Needs, April 1899" (Typewritten), p. 421.

[31] Gillett, "Detailed History," p. 1106.

[32] Prentiss, op. cit., p. 356.

[33] Finance Committee, op. cit., March 4, 1878.

[34] Directors, op. cit., March 12, 1878.

[35] Alumni, op. cit., May 7, 1878.

[36] Directors, op. cit., May 5, 1879.

[37] Alumni, op. cit., May 6, 1879.

[38] Faculty, op. cit., May 20, 1879.

[39] Ibid., September 17, 1879.

[40] Henry Sloane Coffin, A Half Century of Union Theological Seminary, 1896-1945, An Informal History (New York: Charles Scribner's Sons, 1954), p. 75.

[41] Faculty, op. cit., September 24, 1879.

[42]Faculty, op. cit., March 25, 1880.

[43]Directors, op. cit., April 5, 1880.

[44]Charles R. Gillett, "Reminiscences of Dr. William Adams," in Union Theological Seminary, "In Memoriam William Adams, D.D., LL.D., Union Theological Seminary, 1873-1880" (Typewritten), p. 26.

[45]Union Theological Seminary, Catalogue of the Officers and Students of the Union Theological Seminary in the City of New York, 1880-81 (New York: Wm. C. Martin, 1881), p. 5.

[46]Finance Committee, op. cit., May 3, 1880.

[47]"Librarian's Report, May 10, 1880," "Archives," "Extracts," ed. by Gillett, p. 65-A.

[48]Directors, op. cit., May 10, 1880.

[49]Alumni, op. cit., May 11, 1880.

[50]Directors, op. cit., September 2, 1880.

[51]Ibid., November 9, 1880.

[52]Ibid., January 11, 1881.

[53]"Hastings, Thomas Samuel," The National Cyclopedia of American Biography, VII (New York: James T. White & Company, 1897), 317-18.

[54]Directors, op. cit., March 8, 1881.

[55]Ibid., April 11, 1881.

[56]Ibid.

[57]Finance Committee, op. cit., April 21, 1881.

[58]Directors, op. cit., May 26, 1881.

[59]Minutes of the Building Committee of Union Theological Seminary in the City of New York, June 3, 1881.

[60]Ibid., June 20, 1881.

[61]Ibid., September 15, 1881.

[62]Ibid., May 15, 1882.

[63]Ibid.

[64]Ibid., May 24, 1882.

[65]Ibid., July 25, 1882.

[66]Union Theological Seminary, Library, Catalogue of the McAlpin Collection of British History and Theology, comp. and ed. by Charles Ripley Gillett (New York: Union Theological Seminary, 1927), I, v.

[67]Prentiss, op. cit., pp. 354-55.

[68]Union Theological Seminary, Library, Catalogue of the McAlpin Collection [etc.], I, v.

[69]Prentiss, op. cit., pp. 354-55.

[70]Directors, op. cit., November 8, 1881.

[71]Minutes of the Executive Committee of Union Theological Seminary in the City of New York, May 1, 1883.

[72]Gillett, "Detailed History," p. 1169.

[73]Directors, op. cit., May 7, 1883.

[74]Union Theological Seminary, Catalogue of the Officers and Students of the Union Theological Seminary in the City of New York, 1883-84 (New York: Wm. C. Martin, 1884).

[75]Ibid., 1877-78 and 1883-84.

[76]Ibid., 1883-84.

[77]"Increase in the Seminary's Permanent Funds Since Nov. 1, 1873," "Archives," "Extracts," ed. by Gillett, p. 67.

[78]Directors, op. cit., November 13, 1883.

[79]Union Theological Seminary, "Union Theological Seminary, 1874-1899, Address Presented by the Faculty to The Reverend Charles Augustus Briggs, D.D. . . . to Commemorate the Twenty-Fifth Anniversary of His Connection with the Institution, January 19th, 1899" [New York? 1899], pp. 6-7.

[80]William Adams Browns, "A Century in Retrospect," Union Theological Seminary, One Hundredth Anniversary, 1836-1936 (New York: Union Theological Seminary, 1936), pp. 28-29.

Chapter V

THE LIBRARIANSHIP OF CHARLES
RIPLEY GILLETT, 1883-1908

Charles Augustus Briggs said in his first library
report in 1877 that the principal needs of the Library of
Union Theological Seminary were for an endowment in the amount
of $50,000 and for a full-time Librarian. Governor E. D.
Morgan provided the permanent funds, and the first full-time
librarianship of the school was provided by Charles Ripley
Gillett.

The Background of Gillett for Librarianship

Gillett's life revolved about Union Seminary. He was
the son of E. H. Gillett, Professor of Political Science at
New York University, who was also part-time Librarian at Union
during the illness of Henry B. Smith and one of the leading
benefactors of its collection. Charles studied civil engin-
eering at the University where his father taught until 1877.
Young Gillett entered Union in this year and became an Assistant in the Library. He was an outstanding student and was
chosen as the Fellow of his class for 1880-81. Upon the
completion of this year, he was granted funds by the school
to study in Berlin for two years.[1]

The First Year of His Administration

Two months after Gillett began as Librarian, David H. McAlpin sent a check to the school for $10,500, the interest on $5,000 of which was designated for the collection on the history and theology of Great Britain which bore the McAlpin name, with the stipulation that the materials purchased should be similar to those which already had been acquired. The maintenance of the Gillett Collection was the cause for which the interest on the second $5,000 of this amount was to be used. The other $500 were for purchases for the McAlpin Collection made this year.[2]

The report of the Librarian at the end of this first academic year indicated that 6,829 volumes and 5,381 pamphlets had been received from the library of Edwin F. Hatfield.[3] Fifteen years later, Gillett noted that the Hatfield Collection, which was said to be especially strong in Americana and periodicals, was the "richest gift ever made to the Seminary Library." Many of the Hatfield books were incorporated into the Gillett Library, while others were placed in the general collection.[4] Unfortunately, no record of the contents of the Hatfield Library was found.

The Completion of the New Buildings

Plans were being made, in the meantime, for the completion of the new buildings on Park Avenue. A great deal of work was done in the process of moving. The shelves were read with missing books being put in their proper places, and the catalog was "compared to detect errors and to supply any omissions." The moving began during the last week in July, 1884, when one room in the new Library was ready. The Librarian said that "The old system of arrangement was necessarily retained, but modified so that the library could be immediately available." Thus, 60,000 volumes were moved three miles and made ready for use by the time school opened in the fall.[5]

The new buildings were occupied on September 19, 1884, having been constructed at a cost of $687,937.83, including the cost of the grounds.[6] They were dedicated on Tuesday, December 9, 1884.[7] They consisted of four structures, a chapel, a library, a lecture hall, and a dormitory, which together surrounded a quadrangle. The Building Committee consisted of Ezra M. Kingsley, Roswell D. Hitchcock, Erskine N. White, David H. McAlpin, John Crosby Brown, D. Willis James, and Henry Day.[8] The service of dedication was held in Adams Chapel with the Rev. John Hall reading the scripture and giving the prayer and with President Hitchcock delivering the address. The statement in the report on the events of the day that "There is no finer group of buildings in the City" was probably not justified; but, on the other hand, the claim revealed the pride of the institution in its new facilities.[9]

The Early Administration of Gillett

Professor Briggs offered the following February to sell the Library copies of records of the Assembly of Scotland related to the church there as well as copies of letters in the Woodrow manuscripts. The price was to be the cost paid by him for having the duplicates made. The Faculty accepted this

proposition and recommended to the Librarian that he complete
the arrangement with Briggs for the acquisition of the materials.[10]

Gillett, at this time, projected a complete rearrangement of the Library according to a uniform plan for all divisions.
Each case was to have its own number in this proposed scheme,
the two cardinal requirements of which were to be "uniformity
and consistency." He also hoped to complete the subject catalog in a short time.[11]

He justified the closed-stack policy which had been
inaugurated in the new building by insisting that the staff
was willing to escort students working on special subjects to
the stacks, that the reference collection was operated on an
open-stack basis for six hours each day, that reference materials
could be checked out overnight, and that an additional $720 per
year would be required to have the stacks opened.[12]

He said that the average daily attendance in the Library
was twenty-five to forty, which represented an increase over
that in the old building, although the outside lay readers were
not so numerous because of the proximity to the Astor Library.[13]

Gifts received during this period included 300 volumes
given by the family of the late Rev. Edward D. Smith and a
number of books of "considerable value" from the Rev. J.
Glentworth Butler. The Library was also selected as the de-
pository for a "rare and valuable" manuscript of the Syriac
New Testament belonging to the Protestant Syrian College at
Beirut and the manuscripts of Henry B. Smith, which had been

From HARPER'S WEEKLY, Feb. 9th, 1884.—Copyright 1884, by Harper & Brothers.

UNION THEOLOGICAL SEMINARY, LENOX HILL, PARK AVENUE.

Figure 2^{14}

sent by his widow to be placed with those from the collection of Edward Robinson.[15]

Gillett spent this summer in working on the rearrangement of the collection "according to topics." This subject index corresponded with the classification scheme. While making the index, the cards and the books were compared to detect errors in the catalog.[16]

The Library had increased use during this period. The reference room was, for example, nearly filled with students every afternoon except Saturday. The report for the year showed, moreover, that forty-four per cent of the works circulated had been from the reference collection, from which the books could be taken from the building overnight. The circulation from the general collection was broken down by the following percentages:

Dogmatics	17
Practical Theology	15.5
History	14
Philosophy and Literature	8.5
Philology	10
Exegetical Theology	7
British History	7
Periodical Literature	7
Apologetics	5
Miscellaneous (Patristic Writings, Missions, American History, and Pamphlets)	11 [17]

The Alumni Association asked this year that the funds heretofore devoted to the reference collection be assigned to the Henry B. Smith Memorial Library of Philosophy,[18] and this transfer of funds was authorized on November 9, 1886.[19]

The cataloging of the general collection was proceeding in the meantime. During the academic year 1886-87 the minutes

of ecclesiastical bodies, a part of the American history
collection, were cataloged; the periodical literature and reports of various organizations were rearranged and recataloged;
the hymnology and bibliography collections were rearranged for
cataloging; and the pamphlets were rearranged.[20]

Gifts during this era included 71 volumes in the field
of political and social science given by Colonel Elliott F.
Sheppard and 68 volumes and 32 pamphlets on the immaculate
conception contributed by Charles W. Hassler of Englewood,
New Jersey.[21] He later contributed more books on this subject,
so that the material donated by him on this theme was over 100
volumes.[22]

A problem, which was to plague the Librarian until the
end of his office, was revealed in his report for this year.
Most of the book budget was being provided from the Henry B.
Smith Memorial Library Fund endowment and the McAlpin Funds,
both of which were designated for special types of materials.
Gillett was, in fact, forced to spend most of his funds for
current purchases for periodicals and other continuations. The
Library was becoming deficient, therefore, in currently-
published materials. He estimated, therefore, that $1,000 more
were needed for these books. He said that the volumes available
in English literature, philology, and missions were especially
weak and that serious gaps were evident in the materials available in the fields of history, dogmatics, and exegesis.[23]
This report was read to the Board because Gillett was at the
time in Berlin pursuing studies in the field of Egyptology
while on a brief leave of absence.[24]

Some major realignments in the Faculty, which were
brought about by the death of President Hitchcock, were made
at this time. Thomas Hastings was elected President.[25] Philip
Schaff was transferred to the Professorship of Ecclesiastical
History made vacant by Hitchcock's death, leaving open the Chair
of Sacred Literature.[26] Marvin Richardson Vincent was selected
to fill this position.[27] He had graduated from Columbia in
1854 and had taught in the Columbia Grammar School and the Troy
Methodist University before becoming Acting Pastor of the
Pacific Street Methodist Episcopal Church in Brooklyn in 1862.
He was subsequently ordained by the Presbytery of Troy and became the Pastor of the First Presbyterian Church in that city
in 1863. He served there for ten years and then became Pastor
of the Church of the Covenant in New York, from which post he
was called to the position in Union. His books included The
Age of Hildebrand, A History of Textual Criticism of the New
Testament, A Critical and Exegetical Commentary on the Epistle
to the Philippians and to Philemon, and Word Studies in the
New Testament, which was published in four volumes. The latter
work was a study of the vocabulary of the Greek New Testament
and has been widely used by students of the English Bible.[28]
His name is well-known in the field of Biblical studies, in
which he is regarded as one of the most important New Testament
scholars of the nineteenth century. He undoubtedly assisted
in the development of the collection in this field as he, for
one thing, acquired tools necessary for his own writing and
research. His books reveal that he depended on the latest

American, English, and Continental research in his area of interest.

The school was "Presbyterian, but liberal" at this time and had close relationships with the Congregational Church; but it was far from being an interdenominational institution. The election of a member of the Board was, for example, termed invalid because he was a member of the Reformed Church.[29]

The curriculum during this period was focused on the Old Testament, perhaps because of the dynamism of Professor Briggs. This was a period of intense debate throughout Christendom as the methods of historical criticism were applied to the study of the Bible. Entrants to the Seminary were expected to know Latin and to have had at least three years of Greek. Juniors were required to take six hours of Hebrew grammar and translation each week.[30] This heavy emphasis on Biblical studies had a strong influence on the materials used from the Library at this time, with twenty-four per cent of the total circulation and forty-five per cent of the reference circulation being accounted for by exegetical books for the Bible.[31] Gifts, such as Elliott F. Sheppard's presentation of Tischendorf's Monumenta sacra inedita and a facsimile of the Vatican Codex,[32] were especially welcome at this time because of this emphasis in the curriculum.

The subject index to the alphabetical author card catalog was completed this fall. The students' appreciation of this index was revealed in the circulation report, which showed that the weekly average, after the index was made

available for use, rose above the weekly average previous to
that time by an increase of fifty-five per cent.[33] During the
previous year, over one-half of the books circulated was from
the reference library; with the introduction of the subject
index, seventy-one per cent of the materials taken from the
library was from the general collection.[34]

The announcement was made to the Faculty in the first
semester of the next academic year that Henry Day of the Board
of Directors had purchased the hymnological collection of the
Rev. Frederic M. Bird for $2,000 and was giving the materials
to the Library.[35] Day was a graduate of Yale College and had
been admitted to the New York bar in 1845. It was said of him
at his death that "he had drawn more wills, involving millions
perhaps, than any other lawyer in New York City." He was a
Director and the Counsel of the Equitable Life Insurance Company,
the Mercantile Trust Company, and the Lawyers' Title Insurance
Company.[36]

The Bird collection included approximately 5,000 volumes
with such works as the Herrnhut Gesangbuch of 1741, the French
Psalm books of Marot and Beza published in Geneva in 1607, a
line of Latin hymnals including the Poemata sacra of L. Torrentius
in 1594, the Enchiridion scholasticorum of F. Le Tort in 1586,
Lyricorum libri from 1645, Jacob Balde's Sylvae lyricae from
1646, in addition to George Buchanan's Poemata quae extant
from 1687 and Psalmorum Davidis paraphrasis poetica from 1725.[37]
The collection was a notable contribution to the materials on
hymnology already presented from the collections of Edward

Robinson, Edwin F. Hatfield, Roswell D. Hitchcock, Lowell Mason, and Thomas Hastings.[38]

A catalog of these materials was prepared, and a count in the hymnological collection revealed the sources from which the materials were received:

From the original collection of the library   646 vols.
Day Gift of the "Bird Collection"   3252
Hatfield Gift   582
Hitchcock Gift   79
Mason Gift, in the Dept. of Psalmody   52
Hastings Gift   29
        Total   4679 [39]

The Executive Committee appointed a subcommittee during this fall to clarify the relationships of the Faculty to the administration and development of the Library.[40] The Faculty appointed a similar committee to meet with a committee of the Board.[41] The laws of the Seminary concerning the Library were thereafter changed to provide for a committee of the Board and of the Faculty to confer about the Library, to designate the books which could not be taken from the building, and to make decisions on the selection of materials.[42]

The stacks were located on the second floor at this time; and for the first five years of occupancy, it was necessary for students to request books and then to pick them up following one of four deliveries made each day. This was changed, however, by 1889, when immediate deliveries had been arranged.[43] This change resulted in an increase of sixty-one per cent in the circulation figures, which totaled 2,757 for 1889-90.[44]

The cirriculum of an educational institution has some effect on the materials in its library, and this was true at

Union during this period. Juniors studied in their first
semester theological bibliography and methodology, Hebrew,
Greek, exegesis, mission work, Biblical theology, apologetics,
and music. The exegesis courses included both higher and
lower criticism of the Old and New Testaments. The lives of
Christ studied included those by Schürer, Robinson, Neander,
Edersheim, Andrews, and Farrar. The middle class studied
exegesis, church history, theology, homiletics, ethics, and
music. Authors whose works were read in the church history
course included Neander, Schaff, Conybeare, Lewin, and Farrar.
The seniors studied exegesis, Biblical theology, church history,
homiletics, and pastoral theology. Church histories read during
this year included those by Gieseler, Neander, Hagenbach, Winer,
and Schaff. Approximately one-third of the courses offered in
the Seminary were, therefore, in the field of Biblical studies.[45]
This curriculum influenced the use of the Library and brought
about the heavy demand for exegetical works.

Two other related developments influenced the selection
for and use of the Library. One was the introduction of seminars with more opportunity for independent study.[46] The
other was the establishment of the Hitchcock Prize in church
history, which was awarded to the senior who had attained the
highest excellence in this field and who had submitted a paper
on an assigned topic.[47] The preparation of these papers,
along with the increased reliance on independent research,
made necessary the improvement of the resources of the collection as well as the establishment of the policy of keeping
the building open during the summer.[48]

Relationships with Columbia
and New York Universities

Another important decision made during this period
affecting the Library was one to enter closer relationships
with New York and Columbia Universities. The first mention
in the records of this proposal was in the announcement of the
appointment by Charles Butler, President of Union's Board, of
a committee to consult with a committee of New York University
about a union of the two institutions. This announcement was
made at the same time that he told the Board that he intended
to endow the Edward Robinson Chair of Biblical Theology in
the amount of $100,000.[49]

Progress in the direction of greater cooperation between
the two schools was indicated in a letter from Butler to the
joint committee of the Seminary and the University, in which
the basis of their cooperation was explicated. The plans included that New York University would confer the bachelor of
divinity degree candidates approved by Union's Board and Faculty
and the doctor of divinity degree to Alumni on the same basis
of recommendation. They further stipulated that students from
the Seminary would be entitled to the use of the Library and
that these students would be admitted to graduate courses
without fee and to undergraduate classes with the consent of
the professor involved. The Seminary was, in return, to admit
seniors and graduate students from the University to the use
of its Library. Graduate students were to be admitted, moreover, if qualified, to classes in Union. These provisions
were called "Terms of Voluntary Agreement"[50] and were adopted
by Union's Directors on May 6, 1890.[51]

A letter was received during this month from President
Low of Columbia, in which he wrote that the Trustees of that
institution had resolved

> . . . That permission be granted to such persons
> as may be nominated to that privilege by the deans
> of the General and Union Theological Seminaries . . .
> to attend the lectures delivered by the School of
> Political Science on Political economy and sociology,
> and the lectures in the School of Arts on the Semitic
> languages, philosophy and ethics, without the payment
> of fees.[52]

Plans were completed in the following weeks providing
that, in addition to these stipulations, Columbia would accept
Union's courses toward the doctor of philosophy degree in the
minor subjects, with these to be approved and examinations to
be conducted on them by Columbia. A member of the Seminary
Faculty was asked, further, to sit with the Council at Columbia
as an advisory member. The Seminary was, in return, to admit
recommended seniors and graduate students from Columbia and to
recognize courses taken there for Seminary credit. The two
institutions were to enjoy reciprocal library privileges.[53]
Most of these provisions were announced in Union's catalog for
1890-91.[54] The Faculty there decided, however, that work in
the two Universities was not to interfere with the regular
Seminary program and that a minimum grade of eighty per cent
would be required for transfer of credit from those institutions.[55]
The lecture hours at Union were soon consolidated in the fore-
noon to permit attendance at the two Universities in the afternoon.[56] The use of the Seminary's facilities by the students
from the Universities caused the Faculty to establish a category

called "special students," who were excluded from Seminary scholarship funds and housing in the school.[57]

The Briggs Heresy Trials

All developments in the Seminary were, however, made pale by the excitement created by the trials of Charles Augustus Briggs for heresy during this period. He was transferred by the Directors on November 11, 1890 from the Professorship of Hebrew and the Cognate Languages to fill the newly-created Robinson Chair of Biblical Theology.[58] Briggs's inaugural address on January 20, 1891 was given during a period when the Presbyterian Church was disrupted by the suspicion that the use of historical and literary principles in the study of the scriptures was heretical, and Briggs's speech seemed to indicate sympathy for this new approach.[59]

The General Assembly, exercising powers assumed to have been acquired by the agreement of 1870 with Union, disapproved of the transfer.[60] Union's Board insisted that the agreement did not give the Assembly any powers in disapproving the transfer of a professor from one chair to another and was valid only in connection with original appointments to the Faculty.[61] Briggs was subsequently tried for heresy before the Presbytery of New York and acquitted. Yet the matter was carried to the General Assembly, where he was declared guilty of heresy and suspended from the ministry. Union's board, thereupon, sought legal advice and were told that by their charter they could not share with another body the government of the institution and that they had, in fact, been unfaithful

to the purpose of the founders in submitting in any way to
"ecclesiastical domination." The resolution of 1870 was then
rescinded, the arrangement with the General Assembly terminated,
and the Seminary restored to its independent status.[62] Briggs
was retained as Professor of Biblical Theology at Union and
became a priest in the Protestant Episcopal Church a few years
later.[63] John Crosby Brown, W. E. Dodge, D. Willis James, and
M. K. Jessup contributed $175,000 to the endowment fund to
show their approval of the Board's action.[64]

Union Seminary was on its way to becoming an interdenominational institution. Evidence of this development was
seen in the revised constitution published the next year. This
required that the Directors be members of "some evangelical
church," not the "Presbyterian Church" as before.[65] The
decision to cancel the relationships with the General Assembly,
with the accompanying interdenominationalism which was to
develop at Union, were important for the development of the
Library, for it was to become less a Presbyterian-oriented
collection and more interdenominational in scope.

Growth during the Gay Nineties

Announcement was made at this time that the Curriculum
Committee of the Faculty had approved an "exercise" to be conducted by the Librarian in the bibliography and history of
theological literature. This class was to be open to all
levels of students.[66]

Descriptions of Union's special collections appeared
in Notes on Special Collections in American Libraries edited

by William Coolidge Lane and Charles Knowles Bolton at this
time. In addition to outlining the contents of the collections
of the Van Ess Library, the hymnology collection, and the books
on the immaculate conception, Gillett, who wrote the Union
article for this work, said that the McAlpin Collection of
British Divines amounted to 10,000 volumes; the collection of
Westminster Divines and the Puritans of the seventeenth century
totaled about 5,000 titles; and the Deistic, Dissenting, and
Unitarian controversial works amounted to over 1,200 volumes.
He said that the materials on American Theology and History
included "a very large collection of pamphlets" from the
libraries of his father, Hatfield, Marsh, Sprague, Field, and
others. The Henry B. Smith Memorial Library of Philosophy was
said to include approximately 1,500 volumes. Gillett said,
further, that the Seminary had about 10,000 volumes of theological and literary periodicals, with over 100 current titles
being received.[67]

A substantial contribution to the institution was made
this year through the gift of $40,000, half of which was des-
ignated as the William Hayes Fogg Library Fund and half of
which was for scholarships, from Mrs. Elizabeth Fogg. A bust
of Fogg was also included in the gift with the expectation
that it would be placed in the Library. The income from this
Fund was to be spent for bibliographical materials, including
maps.[68]

Fogg was one of the oldest and most widely-known
merchants in New York. He was born in Berwick, Maine on

December 29, 1818. The son of a farmer, he moved to Boston, where he established the firm of Bennock, Fogg and Shannon, which dealt in dry goods and notions. The venture was not successful; and he later went into business with his brother, James, a commission merchant, as agents for an elder brother, Hiram, who was in business in Shanghai, China. The firm was transferred by 1852 to New York, where it was known as the William H. Fogg Co. The organization was dissolved in 1875, when Hiram died; but the business was continued under the name of The China and Japan Trading Company with William Fogg as President. The company, which dealt in general merchandise, tea, and silk, had branches in Yokohama, Kobe-Osaca, and Nagasaki, in Japan, as well as in London. Fogg was also a Director of the Park Bank, the Atlantic Mutual Insurance Company, the Equitable Life Assurance Company, and the Mercantile Trust Company.[69]

He died on March 24, 1884; and the funeral was held at All Souls' Unitarian Church with Roswell Hitchcock, a life-long friend, assisting.[70] His widow contributed the money for the establishment of the William Hayes Fogg Art Museum at Harvard University, as well as to such causes as the Union Library.

The school also received a legacy at this time from the estate of Daniel B. Fayerweather,[71] by which $116,500 was realized.[72] He was a leather merchant who entered the firm of the New York house of Hoyt Brothers in 1854 as a clerk, and he emerged as a senior partner of the largest leather firm

in the United States, Fayerweather and Ladew, which specialized
in belts and soleleather. His will left from $50,000 to $300,000
to a score of American educational institutions, with no re-
strictions as to use.[73] One wag suggested at this time that
the good fortune of the Seminary lay between fog and fair
weather. [74]

The constitution was revised during this era; and the
new edition, published in 1893, while retaining the first three
provisions for the Library of the 1886 document, added three
more. First, the Faculty was charged with the responsibility
of deciding what materials should not be allowed to circulate.
Second, the Library Committee of the Faculty, with the approval
of the Directors, was to advise with the Library on the selection of materials. Third, the Faculty was authorized to make
rules governing the use of the Library, subject to the approval
of the Executive Committee.[75]

Several Faculty changes occurred this fall as the result
of the retirements of Philip Schaff and William Shedd. Arthur
Cushman McGiffert was called, for example, from the Chair of
Church History in Lane Theological Seminary in Cincinnati to
fill the Professorship of Church History. He was a graduate
of Western Reserve and Union and had studied further at Marburg,
Berlin, Paris, and Rome. He had been a pupil, for instance,
with Adolf Harnack, whom he was said to resemble in theological
stance and manner of lecturing. The latter was noteworthy for
its crispness, incisiveness, and clarity. He contributed a
volume on Eusebius to the <u>Nicene and Post-Nicene Fathers</u>, in

which he reconstructed the library of Eusebius. McGiffert's
History of Christianity in the Apostolic Age was published in
1899, and in this work he applied historical methods to the
study of the New Testament. Church people in this country
were not accustomed to this, and the Presbytery of Pittsburg
asked the General Assembly to condemn the book. This request
was denied, but agitation continued until McGiffert withdrew
from the Presbyterian Church and became a Congregationalist.[76]

One of his students remembered him as a fascinating
lecturer who was logical and modest. Another alumnus remembered
him for his grasp of the history of Christian thought, which
he later embodied in a two-volume work on the subject. He
forced the students to read many of the Fathers and to report
their ideas accurately. Another graduate criticized him for
being too systematic and interpreting Paul, Luther, the prophets,
and other religious figures as too orderly and thus missing the
dynamic quality of their thought. Still another student noted
that his sympathies were usually with the heretics. He seems
to have taught those who studied with him to be skeptical of
almost everything in the Christian tradition.[77]

Some scholars during this period were willing to apply
the historical approach to the Old Testament but not to the
New. One of these was Charles Augustus Briggs, who was offended
by McGiffert's treatment of Jesus' career. Briggs was on the
point, during one era, of registering a complaint with the
Directorate; but some of the Faculty convinced him that it
would be inappropriate, if a "heretic" whom the Seminary had

supported, should become the accuser of a former student and colleague. Briggs became such a defender of the doctrine of the Virgin Birth, in the process, that he was asked to speak at meetings of conservatives on this subject.[78] McGiffert played an important role in the development of the church history collection by recommending not only source materials but scientific and historical studies of the Christian tradition which were published during his years at Union.

William Adams Brown was chosen to fill the vacancy in Systematic Theology which was created by the retirement of Professor Shedd. He was a graduate of Yale and of the Seminary. He had been the travelling fellow of his class and had spent two years in German universities. He was the grandson of two important figures in Union's history, William Adams and James Brown. He served on the Board of Home Missions of the Presbyterian Church, on which he was a leader in planning for the unification of Protestants in coping with urban populations. He became Secretary of the General Wartime Commission of the Churches during the First World War and was a member of the Corporation of Yale.[79]

One of his books was The Christian Hope, which deals with the Christian outlook on the world's future as well as immortality. His writings reveal a straightforwardness and fullness, which sometimes made his lectures wearisome. In contrast to this tediousness, his work entitled Beliefs That Matter is a summary of Christian doctrines. This was a period when Systematic Theology was not a high point in the education

of most Union students, and Brown's weakness in speaking did
not add to the young ministers' enthusiasm for the subject.
Yet, Norman Thomas, a graduate of the Seminary, said that this
professor was the one whom he remembered as being the most
helpful of those with whom he had studied. One student even
said that his squeaky voice drew students to him. Brown taught
them to think in a systematic and experience-centered manner.[80]
His contributions to the growth of the Library in the field
of his specialization were important through his recommendations
for contemporary materials and through his gifts.

Charles Prospero Fagnani began teaching Hebrew and
Old Testament at Union during this era. He was the son of a
famous portrait painter for whom many of the royalty of Europe
during the era of Louis Napoleon had sat. His son was educated
in Paris, the College of the City of New York, the Law School
of Columbia, and Union. He was said to be an interesting
teacher who had a fine sense of humor. The conventional were
sometimes shocked by the latter quality. He, for example,
said once to a group of elderly women at a dull prayer meeting
at Madison Avenue Presbyterian Church, "Mothers in Israel,
listen to me, and you will learn something--an unusual experience for most of you." On another occasion, when an elder
had prayed following his remarks, he rose and stated, "Mr. So-
and-So has 'unprayed' all I said." One student said that
"His beginning Hebrew classes were unforgettable--the classes,
not the Hebrew." He was short, wore a mustache and goatee,
and sometimes entered the classroom with the stem of a rose

between his teeth.[81] He was unquestionably colorful, but his contribution to the development of the Library probably did not match his eccentricity.

Gillett was appointed at this time as an Instructor in Propaedeutics[82] to continue the class in theological bibliography begun by Schaff.[83] Perhaps the addition of this responsibility was one reason for increasing Gillett's salary to $2,250.[84] The Librarian of the University of Michigan was making $2,700 at this time.[85]

The curriculum of the Seminary was changed during this era. Three lectures had been given daily in the school until 1894; in that year the number was increased to four. An elective system, which allowed specialization, was inaugurated at the same time. The curriculum was, therefore, divided into required ("in particular years or terms"), variable ("as to year or class, although required for graduation"), and elective courses. A certain percentage of the latter could be taken at Columbia and at New York Universities.[86] The latter school was, in exchange, willing to give credit for work done at Union toward a degree in the amount of classwork equal to one major and one minor or to two minors.[87]

Further liberalization during this period was seen in the increase of the number of seminars for special research;[88] the proposal to introduce representatives of other denominations for lectures;[89] arrangements with Columbia for tutorial instruction for qualified students and instruction for deficient ones;[90] and the admission of women.[91] The first of the latter was Emilie Grace Briggs, who was permitted to attend classes as a "special student and a candidate for a certificate."[92]

These and other developments led to the growth of the Library, especially with $64,000 of permanent endowment designated for it. Among the additions were a copy of the Holmes and Parsons' edition of the Septuagint text of the Old Testament in five folio volumes[93] and the publications of the New York Historical Society, which had been secured through the purchase of a share in their publication fund.[94]

More changes were made in the curriculum during this period. An honors course for graduates and undergraduates, for instance, was established. This course had a wider range of electives and higher standards than did the regular schedule; it was, further, designed to lead to the bachelor of divinity degree[95] from New York University.[96] Requirements for the degree were to include a bachelor of arts degree or its equivalent, marks of at least eighty per cent during three years of study beyond the first bachelor's degree, "special searching examinations," and a thesis demonstrating ability to do original work.[97]

Proposals were also made for the appointment of three teaching fellows in Hebrew, Greek, and church history; two tutors to aid students deficient in Latin, Greek, logic, philosophy, and history; a new professor; and five lecture series to be given between 1896 and 1898.[98] Additional income in the amount of $7,500 a year would have been required to have implemented this plan.[99] Estimated receipts and expenditures

for the year were $72,000 each, which did not include $9,000
in student aid which was to be provided from "outside"
sources.[100]

Changes were occurring in the Library also, one of
the most drastic of which was the employment of a woman as a
cataloger. When Gillett suggested that she be appointed, the
plan was met with mild disapproval and was accepted only after
an interview between President Hastings and the woman, Miss
Euphemia K. Corwin.[101]

Other alterations were taking place in the circulation.
The Library was being more heavily used, in part because of
the increased number of papers being assigned by professors,
in part by the increased use of its resources being made by
ministers and laymen, and in part through the referral of
readers from the New York Public Library, Columbia University,
and New York University.[102]

The receipts of the Library amounted at the time to
approximately $4,580; from this many expenditures had to be
paid. Salaries accounted for $2,850, including $600 for two
Assistants. Of the remaining $1,730, $580 were designated
for special collections. Two hundred fifty dollars of this
were for the McAlpin Collection, $250 for the Gillett Collec-
tion, and $80 for the Henry B. Smith Memorial Library of
Philosophy. This left a balance of $1,1150; and $838 of this
were designated for bindings, insurance, supplies, and continuations. This left $317 for the selection of books with a
free choice.[103]

The calendar year 1897 began with the resignation of President Hastings and the selection of Charles Cuthbert Hall, long-time Pastor of First Presbyterian Church in Brooklyn, to replace him and to serve as Professor of Pastoral Theology, Church Polity, and Missions. Hall was an extroverted man who was a champion of academic freedom. He was highly personable and was, further, greatly appreciated by the student body and the employees of the school. One of his weaknesses, however, was his seeming inability to evaluate people objectively and to understand their faults. One of the contributions which he made to the school was to help restore its reputation following an era when it had been torn by ecclesiastical strife. Henry Sloane Coffin, for example, records this anecdote:

> . . . Shortly after my ordination I happened to occupy a seat in a railway train with an Episcopal bishop from the West. We entered into conversation, and he asked of what Seminary I was an alumnus. When I told him, he turned and faced me and looking into my eyes said emotion:
>
> "My dear fellow, like my friend Dr. Cuthbert Hall, you have far too kind a face to be a higher critic."[104]

Hall's graciousness and his evangelical preaching helped to change the image of the Seminary in the popular mind.

On two occasions he went to Asia on the Barrows Lectureship. He proved to be quite sympathetic there to non-Christians, and this gave him a large hearing. Unfortunately, he returned from the second trip an ailing man who lived only a few months.[105] His recommendations for books reflected his interest in the more pragmatic aspects of theological education.

Professor Prentiss retired at the time of Hall's
appointment, and soon after James Everett Frame was appointed
Instructor in the New Testament. He had B.A. and M.A. degrees
from Harvard and his theological degree from Union. He was a
meticulous scholar whose academic excellence is revealed in
his book on Thessalonians in the International Critical
Commentary. One of his emphases was on the importance of the
proper method in Biblical study rather than on conclusions
which he had drawn. One student, who later became the president of a great university, said that he gave students the
feeling that they had been brought to the "very edge of critical study of the New Testament." Another student remembered
him as small in stature, unobtrusive in manner, and shy in
social relationships. Still another recalled his "almost
pathological passion for accuracy to the last detail."[106] His
contributions to the development of the Library were primarily
in the area of contemporary Biblical studies.

The announcement was made at this time that the relationship between Union and New York University which had
begun in 1890 had been declared void by the Council of the
University. It thus ceased to be a binding instrument, but
the interchange of library and lecture privileges was continued
as a matter of academic courtesy.[107]

The Librarian requested this fall that a permanent
Assistant in the Library be employed.[108] The Executive Committee authorized the appointment of a woman assistant for
$750 per year.[109] The person employed was the first Union

librarian to have attended library school. This appointment
may have been in part responsible for plans this winter to
abandon the fixed location system borrowed from the Astor
Library and to prepare "a comprehensive scheme for the classification of theological libraries." This was to be a scheme
whereby "any subject or the same phase of a subject will stand
together, where they may be consulted with the least possible
loss of time."[110] The influence of the "library trained"
assistant may have been in part responsible for Gillett's
suggestion, too, that the stacks be opened.[111]

The attention of the Directors was called by the
Faculty during this fall to the opportunity of purchasing the
collection of the late Dr. Isaac H. Hall.[112] David McAlpin
gave $5,000 soon afterwards with the stipulation that the
materials be purchased by President Hall, Professor Briggs,
and himself.[113] Part of this amount was used for the purchase
of the Hall Library, which included 754 texts of the New Testament in Greek.[114]

A general catalog published during this period showed
that 2,955 students had studied at Union in the period 1837 to
1897, of whom 1,836 were graduates of the regular course.
Approximately 860 were dead, leaving about 2,100 alumni. Of
the total, 57 had become physicians, 97 lawyers, and 38 business
men. The Presbyterian Church had received 1,318 of those who
were ordained. Other Presbyterian bodies had received 110,
and the Reformed Churches had ordained 98, making almost 62
per cent of the Alumni in denominations of the Reformed

tradition. The Congregational Church received 691 of them,
with 101 in other denominations having congregational government. In addition, 21 Lutherans, 59 Episcopalians, 61 Method-
ists, and 6 Moravians had also graduated. Union also had
educated in this period 84 teachers for theological seminaries,
72 college presidents, 196 college professors, 105 principals
of academies or superintendents of education, and 124 school
teachers.[115]

A description of the Library at the close of the
nineteenth century was given by Gillett in Prentiss' book
The Union Theological Seminary in the City of New York: Its
Design and Another Decade. He claimed that the aggregate
titles and volumes of the school amounted to 115,000, which
made it the largest library of a theological seminary in the
United States and tenth in size in the list of collections of
educational institutions.[116]

The Gillett Collection of American Theology and History
was described as containing secular and ecclesiastical histories
with many biographies. Large and valuable collections of minutes and proceedings, as well as early theological works from
New England, were said to be in its materials. The pamphlets
in this collection, which were contributed by Gillett, Samuel
Hanson Cox, William B. Spragg, and John Marsh, were still in
the manilla paper covers in which they had been encased by
E. H. Gillett. The pamphlets had been increased through
acquisitions from the libraries of Henry B. Smith, William
Adams, and Edwin F. Hatfield.[117] The collection on hymnology
was said to be the largest in the nation.[118]

The general collection was divided into four divisions
which corresponded to a classification scheme at the time:
exegetical, historical, systematic, and practical theology.
The collection was especially strong in patristics and the
history of doctrine as well as in the area of Reformation,
and European history. Systematic theology was represented by
works on "symbolics, polemics, irenics, apologetics, the
systems of the various confessions, and monographs on the
separate doctrines." Controversies and their resulting literary works were classified with the historical period to
which they were related. The department of theology was represented by works on personal religion and the work of the pastor. The collection also included material on "homiletics
and sermonic literature, the doctrine of the church, the sacraments, missions, and applied Christianity."[119]

The situation the Librarian was in at this time, with
the designation of nearly all of the book funds for special
collections and continuations, was not helped by the announcement of the Ely Foundation this spring that any surplus from
the interest on the Lectureship Fund could be used for the
purchase of books for the Library "in the general line of the
lectureship."[120]

Plans for an Enlarged Library

Despite the fact that it had probably the best theological collection in the nation, the Seminary was never satisfied
with its Library nor, for that matter, with its program. The
Faculty approved a report on enlargement on April 26, 1899.

This report insisted that work beyond the bachelor of divinity
degree was demanded in theological education and that Union
was the seminary best "qualified to give it." They thought
also that the professors as well as the students should be
free from ecclesiastical control and regretted that, with the
existing form of subscription to the Westminster Confession
and the Presbyterian form of polity, this was not possible.
Instructors, they said, should be chosen, not by denominational
loyalties, but solely on their aptness to teach. The instruction of the school, they said, should include subjects required
by several denominations. They also asked for associate professorships in Old Testament, church history, New Testament,
and Biblical texts and versions as well as for instructorships
in New Testament, church history, and Old Testament. Lectureships were requested for comparative theology, ecclesiology
and liturgics, modern church history, education of Christian
teachers, and modern social problems.[121]

All of these improvements would have influenced the
selection of materials for the Library; but specific proposals
for the development there were made in a report entitled, "The
Library of the Union Theological Seminary: Its Proper Position,
Its Present Condition, Its Pressing Needs" by the Librarian.[122]

The Library was said in this report to be the theological department of a system of libraries in the city of New
York and adjacent area. This position was said to have been
realized by the fame of the institution as well as by the
intrinsic value of its collection. The reliance of the New
York Public Library on Union's holdings was demonstrated by

the fact that the former's meager theological collection was
placed at the farthest distance from the delivery desk and by
the relegation of the subject of religion to a "distant part
of its classification." Columbia had not developed its holdings
in this field, principally because of its comity with Union.
The fame of the Seminary's Library was also demonstrated in
the large number of inquiries from all parts of the nation
which were addressed to the Librarian each year.[123]

The Collection of British History and Theology was
said by this time to include nearly all of the most famous
British Divines of the eighteenth and nineteenth centuries.
The materials on the Deistic, Trinitarian, and Non-Conformist
controversies were said to be almost complete. The Van Ess
materials on the church fathers had in the succeeding years
since its purchase been supplemented by the two great series
of Migne's Patrology in Greek and Latin.[124] It was regretted,
however, that these materials were not heavily used and did
not excuse the institution from acquiring more current materials
for which there was greater demand. The richness of the hymnology section made possible through the generosity of Henry Day
was also recognized; yet little provision had been made for
expanding since the initial gift. Serious gaps, especially
for current materials, were also recognized in the general
collection and in the reference collection.[125] The periodical
collection included approximately 750 titles, some of which
were incomplete. About 125 current periodicals were preserved
each year.[126]

159

The selection policies current at the time were summarized in these statements:

> It is of the nature of a truism to say that
> our library ought to contain every book which the
> professors need in their investigations; every book
> to which the students are referred in the class-
> room; every book which the seeker after theological
> information might sanely expect to find. This does
> not mean, however, that it should contain all the
> books that bear a religious or theological stamp.
> There is much theological rubbish just as there is
> much literary trash. But what it does mean is that
> every book that can pass the test of usefulness,
> every book which brings a distinct addition to the
> theological thinking of the age, every book which
> is a contribution to our historical knowledge, every
> book that can endure the application of enlightened
> and scholarly scrutiny, should find a permanent
> lodgment upon our shelves.[127]

> . . . The development of a library takes time
> and money, and a complete library cannot be ordered
> over night. It requires study, consultation, selection,
> caution, and a wide range of knowledge. It must be
> built upon plans which embrace the future as well as
> the present, and regard must also be made to the
> shortcomings of the past.[128]

The Librarian said that the collection needed to be
reclassified according to the "relative location" system.
Although he claimed that the books were classified according
to an "excellent scheme" developed by Charles A. Briggs,
Gillett recognized that it did not provide adequate opportunities for expansion and that delaying the reclassification would
only make matters worse. This rearrangement would also make,
he said, the catalog uniform with other large libraries and
would allow him to apply a uniform system in the formation of
the catalog.[129] The existing catalog contained approximately
fifteen styles of handwriting and about the same number of
eclectic systems of rules. He estimated that the reorganization

of the Library could be accomplished by six people, with some
extra help, in two years at a cost of $10,000. Yet, because
he said that it would have to be done during the summer or by
slow degrees during the academic year, he thought that it
might be four years before the work could be finished. He
recommended that the reclassification be accomplished before
the 10,000 titles in the McAlpin Collection were cataloged.[130]

He also wanted an elevator powered by electricity
instead of the one in existence which was operated by a "strong
and heavy man." Electric lights were needed, too, throughout
the Library, for under the existing conditions, most of the
books were not available after four or five o'clock in the
afternoon.[131]

Approximately $15,000 were needed, he said, to supply
current books for which funds had not been available previously.
Some of the areas of greatest need were said to be those of
English literature, English grammar and rhetoric, missions,
ethics, philosophy and history of religion, and music.[132] Yet
the principal need of the Library was for adequate endowment
of the general Library fund. The existing permanent funds for
the Library consisted of the Morgan Endowment in the amount of
$50,000, the Fogg Memorial of $20,000, the McAlpin and Gillett
Funds, in the amount of $5,000 each, and the Henry B. Smith
Memorial. The income from all this amounted to about $4,580,
which, after the salaries and fixed charges were paid, left
nothing for general purchases. Gillett estimated that approximately $3,000-$4,000 would be required to meet this need.[133]

He suggested that $10,000 of the Morgan Fund be des-
ignated for the reference library, leaving the remaining $40,000
as a part of a general fund for administration. He said that
the Fogg Fund of $20,000 could be added to this or designated
for general purchases. The McAlpin and Gillett Funds of $5,000
each were deemed sufficient for their purposes. The Henry B.
Smith Fund, which amounted to $1,800, he reported, should be
raised to $5,000.[134]

Gillett claimed that the exegetical department should
receive $20,000, the historical department $10,000 according
to this plan. He noted, further, that $5,000 should be
designated for each of the following areas: Reformation
literature, dogmatic theology and ethics, apologetics and
history of religions, homiletics and missions, canon law and
liturgics, and hymnology. Practical theology, he thought,
should receive $18,000; and $10,000 should, he claimed, be
added to a fund for the acquisition of manuscripts and other
rare materials. The periodical department, he said, should
receive $10,000.[135]

These suggestions, along with many others, were submitted to the Directors on May 16.[136] They were adopted on
November 14 as a blueprint for the development of the school
in the years ahead.[137]

New Faculty Members for the New Century

The Faculty was enriched during the new century by
the addition of several scholars. They included Thomas Cumming

Hall, George William Knox, Julius A. Bewer, Hugh Black, and
Harold Tryon.

Hall, a graduate of Princeton University and Union,
had held pastorates in Omaha and Chicago before returning to
the Seminary as Professor of Christian Ethics. He had, during
his ministries, supported left-wing social movements. His
views on the subject of such causes is shown in his book
entitled Social Solutions. Although he was frequently eloquent,
the lack of arrangement in the material presented in his lectures limited his ability as a teacher.[138] His nominations
for Library materials probably reflected his interest in the
social gospel.

George William Knox, who had attended Hamilton College
and Auburn Seminary and who had filled the Chair of Philosophy
and Ethics in the Imperial University in Tokyo, was named
Professor of the Philosophy and History of Religion. He was
a slight man who had a limp. His scholarship is reflected in
his article on "Christianity" in the eleventh edition of the
Encyclopaedia Britannica as well as in his series of Taylor
Lectures at Yale on The Direct and Fundamental Proofs of the
Christian Religion. He had a rare ability to make abstract
philosophical principles vital to his students. Fosdick quoted
him as saying to a class, "Be very careful how you baptize
the modern belief in progress into the Christian faith." Another student was said to have written on an examination in
one of Knox's classes, "I believe in God; but not for the
reasons suggested in this course."[139] He made many suggestions

for the purchase of contemporary materials for the philosophy
and history of religion sections in the Library.

Julius A. Bewer, a graduate of the Gymnasium at
Düsseldorf and Union, had studied also at Basel, Halle, and
Berlin. He was called from a professorship at Oberlin to be
Assistant Professor of Biblical Philology. He later filled
the Davenport Chair of Hebrew and Cognate Languages. His book
entitled The Literature of the Old Testament in its Historical
Development was a standard in its field for many years. His
teaching was outstanding for his thorough knowledge of the
message of the prophets and for his interest in his students'
personal problems.[140] As one of the nation's leading authorities on the Old Testament, he was a vital force in the
development of the Library in that field. His knowledge of
German materials was especially advantageous for the selection
of books from the Continent.

Hugh Black came to Union as a Professor of Preaching
from the Free St. George's Church in Edinburgh. He had established a reputation in that city as an outstanding speaker and
as an author of several popular books. Friendship, Listening
to God, The Adventure of Being Man, and Christ or Caesar were
among his published works. He was enthusiastic about preaching
and inspired his students to take the work of sermon preparation quite seriously.[141] His addition to the Faculty contributed to the growth of sermon materials in the Library.

Harold Harrison Tryon, an Instructor in New Testament
and Church History, was educated at the University of

Pennsylvania, Union, Berlin, Heidelberg, and the American
School for Oriental Research in Jerusalem. He was said to
be an efficient, modest teacher. One of his Greek students
said of him, "He not only taught us Greek painlessly; a dozen
of us liked our work with him so well that we formed a special
class to read Plato in his apartment." He was noted for his
thoroughness, with each class period being used to the full.[142]
He undoubtedly contributed to the growth of the New Testament
studies in the Library.

The Library in the New Century

Negotiations were made at the beginning of the new
century for the sale of the property acquired on St. Nicholas
Avenue, which had been purchased for the Seminary before it
was moved to Park Avenue. The city of New York finally purchased the lots for a park at the price of $269,560.59,[143]
with the net profit of $24,568.95 being added to the professo-
rial endowment funds.[144]

Although no accessions lists are available for this
period, the selection of materials for the general collection
was correlated with the curriculum, which was divided into
the four major areas of theological study: Biblical, historical,
systematic, and practical. The Biblical department was sep-
arated into sections on introduction, philology and exegesis,
and theology. The courses in introduction included a general
introduction to the Bible and surveys of the Old and New
Testaments. Thirteen courses were offered in Hebrew and one
course was given in Biblical Aramaic. Fourteen classes were

given in Greek. The field of Biblical theology included
studies of the doctrines of God and redemption, a Biblical
history of religion, two courses on the life of Jesus, a
survey of the apostolic church, and a seminar on the theology
of St. Paul. The church history courses were divided among
the primitive and early Catholic church, the western Catholic
church and the Reformation, the history of doctrine, English
church history, history of the Roman Catholic Church since
the Reformation, and a seminar on the origin and history of
the Apostles' Creed.[145]

The courses in theology were divided among apologetics,
systematic theology, ethics, the philosophy of religion, and
comparative religions. The practical theology classes consisted of units on homiletics, pastoral theology, catechetics,
church polity, missions, the sacraments, liturgics, the
spiritual life of the minister, and the practical study of
the English Bible. Vocal culture, exercises in sacred music,
and physical education completed the curriculum.[146] Bibliographical materials were needed for these courses.

The Library received at this time a large number of
volumes relating to Zwingli and the Reformation at Zurich from
Samuel Macauley Jackson.[147] The donor had been a student at
Union in 1871-73 and had done further study at the Universities
of Leipzig and Berlin. He used personal resources to aid
scholars in the production of their works, such as the New
Schaff-Herzog Encyclopedia of Religious Knowledge.[148]

Jackson wrote <u>Huldreich Zwingli, the Reformer of
German Switzerland</u> and planned to finance the publication of
a translation of Zwingli's works in six volumes, four of which
actually appeared.[149] He brought together, in the process, a
large collection of materials by and about Zwingli; and these
were given to Union with the reservation that he would have
the privilege to use them at his discretion. They were
accepted by the Directors on these terms on November 13, 1900.[150]
This contribution was said by William Adams Brown[151] and in
<u>Special Collections in Libraries in the United States</u> by
W. Dawson Johnston and Isadore G. Mudge, to be "an almost
exhaustive collection" relating to Zwingli.[152]

David Hunter McAlpin, "the chief benefactor" of the
Library for "upwards of thirty years" died in this era. The
Directors, in a minute expressing their bereavement, recognized
his gifts for the purchase of books on the Deistic controversies
and British theology in the eighteenth century for his Pastor,
E. H. Gillett. These books, as it has been noted, ultimately
came into the possession of the Seminary. The Directors also
paid tribute to McAlpin's generosity, through which the school
had acquired thousands of books and tracts on British history
and theology. They, moreover, expressed their appreciation
for his endowment of the Gillett and McAlpin Collections, other
generous sums given for these materials as well as those for
the general collection, and his purchase of the Henry B. Smith
Library for the school.[153] McAlpin's children continued to
contribute funds for materials for the Collection bearing his

name. One year after his death, for example, $1,000 were
given for this purpose.[154]

The Librarian's report this spring showed that the
special McAlpin gift of $6,500 made three years earlier had
been depleted. This led Gillett to assert,

> Perhaps no more pathetically cogent reason can be
> given to prove the need of an increase in the income
> of the library, unless it is found in the fact that
> the professor in one department has found the pecu-
> niary resources of the library so limited that he
> has procured an annual donation which is to be spent
> along lines of his own choosing.[155]

Some estimate of the nature of the purchases made
during this period may be gained through these copies of two
letters discovered in the Union Library:

Sept. 9, 1901

G. P. Putnam's Sons, 27 W. 23d St. City

Dear Sirs:--

Please procure for us the following volumes.
If they can be found in stock in this city, do not
import them, but send directly,

Edgar: The genius of Protestantism. Edinb.
  Oliphant etc. 1900
Harnack. What is Christianity?
Candlish: The Christian salvation. Clarke. 1900.
Whittaker: The Neo-Platonists. Cambridge. 1901.
Richmond: An essay on personality as a philosophic
  principle. London: Edwin Arnold. 1900.
Royce: The conception of immortality. Boston:
  Houghton & M.
Kuyper: The work of the Holy Spirit.

Yours truly

Librarian.[156]

Sep. 9, 1901.

G. E. Stechert. 9 E. 16th St.

    Dear Sirs:--

        Please import for us the following
volumes:

    Ruyssen: Les grandes [sic] philosophes: Kant.
        Paris: Alcan. 1900.
    Jalaguier. De l'Eglise. Paris: Fischbacher.
        1899 or 1900.

                        Yours truly[157]

    The next calendar year began with the announcement

that 1,800 volumes had been received from the Library of the

late Professor Schaff. Approximately one-half of these were

duplicates, which were sent to the Seminary at Lancaster,

Pennsylvania.[158]

    The Faculty appealed at this time to the Board for

$3,000 as a norm for Library expenditures.[159] The Professors,

further, requested that this amount be appropriated from the

income from the Ely Lectureship Fund, provided that the donor

would consent to this use of the interest.[160] This decision

was approved by the Directors on May 13.[161] The Chairman of

the Board, on informing Gillett that the money had been

appropriated, asked him to make it "go as long and as far as

possible." The former Librarian, Briggs, however, advised

his successor to spend it all at once and then to demand more.

This suggestion was brought about by what Briggs considered

to be the "cheese-paring and parsimonious treatment" given

the Library.[162]

An analysis of the Library budget from May 1, 1883
to May 1, 1902 showed that the E. D. Morgan Fund had produced
approximately $5,536.85 in interest and that all of the per-
manent accounts showed a credit balance, except the McAlpin.
The overdrafts from this account had been made by Briggs.[163]

Conflict between Gillett and Briggs

Gillett seemed to be pleased to report that he had
kept within his bounds financially and that the only over-
spending had been done by the former Librarian. This was but
one bit of evidence, parallels of which were found in many
places in the records, of the conflict between the two men.
Briggs was undoubtedly a strong personality who was somewhat
difficult to work with administratively. He had emerged from
the heresy trials as the leader of the historical and critical
approach to Biblical scholarship in the nation; and his reputation was growing through his authorship of many books, including
volumes for the International Critical Commentary set. He was,
further, elevated by a new appointment in the Seminary. This
was accomplished by his transfer from the Edward Robinson
Professorship of Biblical Theology to the graduate Faculty at
the salary of $5,000 a year,[164] which was twice what new
appointees to the Faculty during this era were paid.[165]

The professional jealousy directed against Briggs was
probably further increased by the fact that his father was
Chairman of the Finance Committee of the Board of Directors.[166]
Evidence of Professor Briggs's influence in this body may have
been indicated by the provision made by the Directors for the

appointment of two new professors without subscription to the
Westminster Confession and with the stipulation, for the first
time in Union's history, that these new men, as Faculty members,
were not required to belong to the Presbyterian Church.[167]
Another bit of evidence of Briggs's lack of conformity was to
be seen in a minority report which he issued as a member of a
Committee on Curriculum Revision, on which he, McGiffert, and
Knox were serving.[168]

The conflict between Briggs and Gillett came to a
climax in the spring, when the Faculty's Library Committee,
influenced by Briggs, made these recommendations "to the
librarian":

It is recommended in the first place that at
least four members of each periodical be retained
in the upper room of the library before removal to
the basement.

2ndly. That the newly published books purchased
by the librarian during the term, or the summer before the term, be placed on vacant shelves in the
museum until the expiration of the term.

3rdly. That the shelves in the librarian's
room be specially devoted to bibliography and all
important works on that subject be kept open to the
inspection of the faculty.

4thly. That all shelves be provided with supports
of wood or metal so that the books may stand upright
in their places.

5th. That books shall not be left lying out of
place in the library. If temporary removal is necessary, they should be kept in the store-room until
they can be replaced. That the library should be
kept constantly in good order, so that it may not
be criticized as disorderly or slovenly; and finally

That $500. of the extraordinary fund be appro-
priated for the purchase of books in systematic
theology, apologetics and related subjects under
the direction of W. A. Brown; and that $500. be

appropriated for the purchase of books in liturgics, canon law &c. by Prof. Briggs; and that $1.500 be spent by the librarian under the advice of the different professors, and that the librarian be requested to secure lists from the several professors of the books needed in their several departments.[169]

Another list of suggestions was made the following day to the Faculty in the following form:

1st. That as soon as possible an extra assistant librarian be appointed, who shall give the greater portion of his time to the perfecting of the catalogue and the systematic filling of the gaps in the library.

2nd. That a special appropriation be made for binding and repairs, in order that valuable works may be rescued from the peril of decay and injury to which they are now exposed.

3rd. That the attention of the Board be called to the danger to which the library is now exposed from the present wooden floor of the basement, and that as soon as possible steps be taken for the removal of the floor and the wooden shelves in the basement and the substitution therefor of concrete flooring and steel shelves.

Pending these needed improvements the library committee recommends that the faculty request the Board to make provision for extra assistance in the care and cleaning of the library-- provided that it can be done without injustice to the general administration expense of the Seminary.[170]

While many of these suggestions were commendable, the censorious and curt manner in which they were expressed would have repelled almost any sensitive Librarian. Gillett was especially hurt because the "recommendations" were adopted by the Committee in his absence and without his consultation. He felt that Briggs would have rendered more valuable assistance to the Library through persuading his father to increase the appropriations for it than by sponsoring these resolutions. Gillett excused himself for the criticisms of his administration by pointing out that he was, during this period,

> devoting all of his time, both day and night, to
> the work of his office, while encumbered with a
> multitude of details and a great many duties un-
> noted and unappreciated by the members of the
> faculty.[171]

He claimed that the only effect of the recommendations was
to be found in the provision of the Finance Committee for the
employment of a person to clean the books at the wages of $30
a month, which was to be paid out of the general income and
expense account.[172]

Gillett was probably quite involved during this time,
for he was doing nearly all of the cataloging and classification
in the Library in addition to serving as its administrator.
He was also available in his office for reference assistance,
although students were employed to oversee this department.
He was assisted by one person in cataloging the McAlpin
Collection and at various times by other people who did rou-
tine cataloging under his supervision.[173]

Gillett's annual report must have been made this year
with some misgivings about the appreciation for his work. It
showed that approximately 600 people other than students and
Faculty members in the Seminary had used the collection; this
represented a doubling of this usage during the year.[174]

Expenditures had been charged against the following
funds:

Wm. H. Fogg Memorial Fund	$1007.99
McAlpin Special Gift of $5000 (Balance)	131.30
McAlpin Fund (Westminster)	806.67
Gillett Fund (American History etc.)	154.03
H. B. Smith Memorial: Philosophy	76.45
Brown Special Fund	23.63

```
Director's Special Appropriation (Books)        218.44
Director's Special Appropriation
  (Administration)                              283.51
E. D. Morgan Library Fund (Administration)      3836.14 175
```

The name of the reference library was changed at the meeting
at which this report was given to the "H. B. Smith Memorial:
Philosophy."[176]

Gillett was probably further chagrined to learn that
in a gift for the Library from the heirs of David H. McAlpin
in the amount of $9,000, provisions were made that the selec-
tion of the materials from this Fund and the preparation of
the catalog for it were to be under the supervision of Briggs.
The terms of the agreement, which was accepted by the Seminary,
were as follows:

AGREEMENT as to the arranging, editing, printing
and publishing a catalog of the McAlpin Library of
Theology of Great Britain.

This agreement made this eleventh day of February
1904, between Edwin McAlpin, William W. McAlpin,
George L. McAlpin, David H. McAlpin, Jr., Charles W.
McAlpin and Adelaide McAlpin Pyle, the children of
the late David H. McAlpin, deceased, parties of the
first part and the Union Theological Seminary in the
City of New York, duly incorporated under the laws
of the State of New York, party of the second part,
witnesseth:

First: that for and in consideration of the sum
of one dollar duly received by the parties of the
first part from the party of the second part, the
receipt of which is hereby acknowledged, and in consideration of the promises hereinafter made by the
party of the second part to the parties of the first
part, the parties of the first part agree, each for
himself or herself, and his or her executors and
administrators, but not for the others, to pay to
the said Union Theological Seminary the sum of ($250.)
two hundred and fifty dollars each on the fifteenth
day of February of each year for six successive years,
amounting in all to fifteen hundred dollars ($1.500)
to be paid by each of the parties of the first part,
his or her executors or administrators.

Second: the party of the second part agrees
that if any additional sum remains after the expenditures for the arranging, editing and printing
and publishing of said catalogue, it shall be expended in the purchase of new books on the theology
of Great Britain to be included in said library.
The said party of the second part also agrees that
said library shall always be known as designated as
the McAlpin Library of the Theology of Great Britain.

Fourth: the party of the second part also
agrees that the said cataloguing shall be completed
within six years from the date hereof, unless it
shall be retarded by some unavoidable obstacle, in
which event it shall be completed as soon thereafter
as possible.

Fifth: the party of the second part also agrees
that the said work of arranging, editing, printing
and publishing a catalogue of the McAlpin Library of
the theology of Great Britain, and the distribution
of said catalogue when published, shall be done under
the supervision of Prof. Charles A. Briggs, or in
the event of the death of the said Prof. Charles A.
Briggs, under the supervision of some person to be
selected by mutual agreement.[177]

Briggs and Gillett became entangled immediately in a

quarrel about the scope of the catalog. Briggs advocated a

list of books and tracts with shortened title entries, while

Gillett wanted a work which would include "occasional colla-

tions," paginations, size of the pages in centimetres, and

annotations on sources of information. Charles W. McAlpin

agreed with the latter plan,[178] but the first volume of the

set was not published until 1927.

Two Major Decisions of 1904

Two other major events in the development of the Sem-

inary occurred in this year. The first was involved with a

promise of Willis James to give the institution $1,000,000 on

several conditions, one of which was that the school was to

be moved to a new location and the second of which was that the names of existing buildings were to be preserved.[179] The sum of $69,250 of this money was given during the calendar year.[180] This gift, which ultimately nearly doubled the original amount promised, exceeded the $1,400,000 in the professorship endowments extant at this time.[181]

The second development was the revocation of the required pledge for new members of the Faculty to support the Westminster Confession and Presbyterian polity. The new declaration was:

> I promise to maintain the principles and purposes
> of this Institution, as set forth in the Preamble
> adopted by the founders on the 18th of Jany [sic]
> 1836, and in the charter granted by the Legislature
> of the State of New York on the 27th of March 1839, and
> accepted by the Board of Directors on the 20th of
> December 1839.[182]

Elihu Root wrote an opinion of this decision to the effect that

> The provisions of the constitution relating to
> the subscription of the directors and the professors
> to the Westminster Confession of Faith, and all pro-
> visions relating to that subject were of this tem-
> porary character; they were subject to be changed at
> any time by the board and formed no part of the
> object of the institution.
>
> The only limitation prescribed by the charter
> was in the words "Theological Seminary." Qualifica-
> tions for membership might be changed as the direc-
> tors saw fit. The limitations of the power of the
> directors are found in the nature of the institution
> and in the preamble, not at all in the "constitution"
> which formed actually a section of the by-laws, and
> was liable to alteration.
>
> Donations and endowments were to be considered
> as intended for the general purposes of the institu-
> tion unless the donors had specified the object in
> view and embodied it in a contract.[183]

The position was clarified soon after by an amendment to the constitution, requiring only that members of the Faculty be affiliated with some "evangelical body."[184] The stipulation that students had to be members of some Christian church before admission was also soon abandoned.[185] These were the last major steps in severing official relationships with the Presbyterian Church and in the establishment of the school as an interdenominational institution. The ramifications of these decisions for the Library were manifold.

Library Developments during an Era of Liberalization

The heaviest responsibilities in the Library at this time were those connected with the cataloging of the backlog. Approximately 800 volumes in the Hall Collection of New Testaments in Greek, which required the work of a specialist to classify them, were uncataloged. Another 6,000 in the McAlpin Westminster Collection, approximately 15,000 pamphlets, and 600 volumes in German on the philosophy of Kant, which had recently been contracted for, were in the same state. The Librarian said in his report in 1904 that it would require the work of the entire staff for an entire year, exclusive of any other labor, to catalog these materials.[186] He did not have time to do this himself, because he was teaching a course in theological bibliography twice weekly in the first term as well as serving as Secretary of the Faculty and Registrar throughout the year.[187]

The decision made earlier in the year to broaden the sectarian requirements for the Faculty began to be supported

immediately. Mrs. William Earl Dodge, for instance, was so
pleased with this decision that she promised to contribute
$120,000 to endow a Chair of Applied Christianity.[188] She
was the wife of a partner in the firm of Phelps, Dodge & Co.,
which, as has been noted, dealt in copper and iron.[189] Similar
approval was indicated in the desire of Morris Ketchum Jesup
to endow a Graduate Professorship of Preaching. Jesup, who
had made a fortune in banking, had retired in 1884 and had
spent his retirement contributing to many philanthropic organizations. He gave, for example, $2,000,000 to The American
Museum of Natural History and helped to finance Peary's dis-
covery of the North Pole. He also contributed the Maria
Dewitt Jesup Hospital to the Syrian Protestant College at
Beirut and made large contributions to Hampton, Tuskegee,
Yale, Harvard, Williams, and Princeton.[190]

The battle over the historical and literary approach
to the Old and the New Testaments had been won at this time
by the liberals at the Seminary. The emphasis had, in fact,
shifted at Union from the debates which had occupied the 1890's
in that area to an interest in religion among savage tribes
and cults which had existed in the Graeco-Roman world during
the first few centuries of the existence of Christianity.
Henry Sloane Coffin, who began hearing sermons at Union in
1904, said that it was common for the students at this time
to illustrate Biblical passages by allusions to customs of
primitive people or the myths of the first century.[191] This
shift in interest was sure to affect the selection for the
collection.

The Library during a Period
of Planning to Relocate

This growth in the curriculum was matched by development in the facilities. Willis James contributed $1,030,000
for this purpose in 1905,[192] and the present site on Morningside Heights near Columbia University was selected. Thirty-
six lots bounded by 120th, 122nd, Broadway, and Claremont were
purchased, leaving $500,000 for the construction of the build-
ings. The north end of the structure was planned for income-
producing purposes.[193] The deed for the site was conveyed to
the school on February 3, 1905.[194] A committee of the Faculty
was appointed immediately to consider the needs of the institution in connection with the new buildings.[195]

The committee brought its report to the meeting of the
professors on April 12. They recommended that the architecture
should be "congruous with but distinct" from that of Columbia.
The chapel was to be twice the size of the Park Avenue building.
The Library was to be the chief academic building, with a
reference room twice the size of the old one and with administrative offices adjoining. Stack space for 200,000 volumes
and room for expansion were requested. At least six seminar
rooms with other rooms for private study and a museum were
also suggested. Classrooms, offices, studies for twenty professors, a robing room, a directors' room, dormitories for
150 men, a social room, guest rooms, a refectory, an infirmary,
a gymnasium, a president's house, and duplex apartments for
professors were also proposed. All of this was to be connected
with corridors, and the quadrangle suggested for the middle

was requested to be as large as possible.[196] Anyone who has
visited the Seminary since its construction will recognize
that the Faculty got in its new set of buildings almost everything for which it asked.

The Librarian's lot was improving too. He was, for
one thing, appointed to the Faculty. His predecessors had
held that distinction through their professorial appointments.
Since the fall of 1883 the additions had totaled 13,686 volumes
and 767 pamphlets by purchase, 21,470 volumes and 13,728
pamphlets by gift, making an aggregate of 35,156 volumes and
14,495 pamphlets. Because of the large amount of work to be
accomplished before moving into the new facilities, Gillett
asked to be relieved of some of his clerical responsibilities
but planned to continue in his roles as Secretary of the Faculty,
Instructor, and Librarian.[197] An appropriation of $500 was
authorized to employ an Assistant for him as Registrar, to
do the detail work in this office.

Plans progressed, in the meanwhile, for the construction of the new facilities. The Committee on Site and Buildings
met on October 6, 1905 and decided to call the building for
instruction and administration "Jesup Hall," with the "fire-
proof" Library to be named for Governor Morgan. Plans were
made at this time to name the chapel for former President
William Adams.[198]

Four architects were asked to compete with an honorarium
in each case, but the competition was left open to others.
The successful competitor was to be in charge of the

construction.[199] Announcement was made at this time that
Jesup Hall and the dormitories could not be constructed for
$500,000; but additional gifts of $325,000 were announced.[200]

Plans were completed on April 19 for printing a program about the competition. The announcement was to include
a promise of $800 to the invited architects and to each of
the four next high in order of merit. Three people were chosen
as a jury.[201] The additional sum of $200,000 was contributed
for the project by Willis James on May 22.[202]

The increased funds available influenced the development of the Library in several ways. The Staff was, for
example, increased to four students, one Chief Assistant, one
Reference and Circulation Assistant, and one Bibliographer,
who was engaged in making lists of desiderata. A Copyist,
whose work was to prepare catalog cards, was also employed by
the hour.[203] Materials were being added so quickly to the
cramped space that the scheme of classification by fixed
location was breaking down. The Librarian was working on a
relative scheme to overcome this limitation.[204]

Professor Briggs announced at this time that a special
program was being inaugurated for graduate students. The
courses in the curriculum included those on the system of
theological study, the history of the study of theology, the
history of theological literature, comparative symbolics,
irenics, the history of creeds, the history of Christian
institutions, the history of worship, and church polity. The
methods utilized in these classes included seminars and private

tutorial instruction in Briggs's office.[205] The introduction
of new courses into the curriculum and the promotion of more
opportunities for individual research had many implications
for the selection for and usage of the Library.

The collection was also benefited at this time by an
Alumni Library Endowment Fund established by the Alumni Club
in November, 1906, to increase the money available for the
purchase of books. Ten thousand dollars were received within
a brief time, and this yielded approximately $500 a year for
the development of the book collection.[206]

The Completion of Plans for the New Buildings

The fall was also a busy time for the development of
plans for the new buildings, including the new Library facilities. Thirty-five sets of plans for the proposed structures
were submitted by October 6.[207] The jury, consisting of
Walter Cook, Robert S. Peabody, and Warren P. Laird, announced
their award to Allen & Collens of Boston, who had submitted
the plan numbered "thirteen." This plan had also been selected
independently by the Board and the Faculty.[208]

A meeting of the Building Committee with Messrs. Allen
& Collens was arranged for January 17, 1907. Suggestions from
the Faculty and the Janitor were relayed to them at this
time.[209] An additional gift of $200,000 for the chapel from
James must have encouraged those involved in this planning.[210]
Yet, a note of frustration was introduced into these developments when James died in the fall.[211]

His donations were, however, mostly in hand at this time, and plans for construction proceeded. Architectural sketches were made for the entire project, but it was understood that all of the buildings would not be constructed at once.[212] Ten bids were received, but all were rejected because they were too high, and the architects were asked to make a restudy to reduce the costs. A decision was reached at this time to place the dormitory on Broadway.[213] It was decided also to build the Library, dormitory, administration building and President's house but to delay the construction of the chapel.[214]

The funds available for building amounted to $881,000. The Directors, therefore, authorized the committee to proceed, provided that the cost did not exceed this amount by more than $100,000, which James had thought could be taken temporarily from the sale of the site on Park Avenue.[215] Twelve bids were received on May 25, the lowest of which was for $912,400. The plans were, accordingly, revamped to reduce the costs.[216] Bids were finally accepted on June 2 for the construction of the buildings for $855,000.[217] The plans for the new buildings were by this time nearly complete, and a program for the laying of the cornerstone was projected.[218]

The End of an Era

It was planned that the money from the sale of the buildings on Park Avenue, which were estimated to be worth $250,000, would be used as endowment for the Library. An

annual appropriation of $4,000 was made at the same time for
the Library until the recataloging was completed.[219]

Another important decision reached at the meeting of
the Directors in which these plans were made was the one
creating the office of Registrar. His duties were

> to supervise the students' election of courses; to
> advise with them and keep a record of their work;
> to keep a record of the alumni and to endeavor to
> promote cordial relations between the Seminary and
> the alumni-body; to have general charge of the
> publications and printing of the Seminary; and if
> so designated to act as secretary of the faculty.[220]

Gillett was appointed to this post, which under these conditions
was more than the clerical position which it had been previously.[221] It was understood that he would be replaced as
Librarian.

Soon after, President Cuthbert Hall died.[222] The
Alumni immediately decided to create the Charles Cuthbert Hall
Memorial Library of Christian Missions through raising $5,000
for this purpose.[223]

Gillett's Final Report as Librarian

Gillett's twenty-fifth and final annual Library report
was submitted to the Directors on May 12, 1908. It showed
that the Staff consisted of a General Assistant, a Reference
Assistant, four student Assistants, and a "corps of cataloguers."
One of the latter was assigned the task of preparing the catalog of the McAlpin books under the supervision of Briggs.
Nearly all of the titles had been copied by this date, but the
preparation of the indexes and other addenda remained to be

184

done. The number of titles in the collection at this time
was approximately 10,000.[224]

Gillett was still spending a great deal of time in
the development of a scheme of classification based on the
subject index which he had prepared for the Library.[225] This
system was the foundation on which the Union Theological Seminary Classification Scheme developed a few years later under
the guidance of Julia Pettee.[226] Of this early plan, Gillett
said:

> It is expected that in this way the entire resources
> of the library will be made available to students,
> and to other scholars engaged upon special studies
> in which exhaustive aids are of immense importance.
> This scheme of classification will also furnish an
> outline by which the re-classification of the library
> may be effected when sufficient space is obtained in
> the new building.[227]

Gillett, who, according to the Directors, had "devoted
the best twenty-five years of his life to the Library,"[228]
retired as Librarian on August 1, 1908.[229] He served the
institution in succeeding years not only as Registrar but also
as Dean of Students and Alumni Secretary, retaining the latter
office until his death at the age of ninety-two in 1948.[230]
His full-time service to the institution stretched from his
appointment as Librarian in 1883 until his retirement forty-
six years later. His part-time appointments began in 1877 as
a student assistant in the library and continued after his
retirement for nineteen years for a total of twenty-three
years. These sixty-nine years are one of the longest periods
of professional service to one institution in the history of
American education.

FOOTNOTES

[1]Union Theological Seminary, General Catalogue of Union Theological Seminary in the City of New York, 1836-1897, comp. by Charles Ripley Gillett ([New York: Union Theological Seminary], 1898), p. 205.

[2]Minutes of the Board of Directors of Union Theological Seminary in the City of New York, January 8, 1884.

[3]Charles Ripley Gillett, "Report of the Librarian of Union Theological Seminary to the Directors of the Seminary for the Year, May 1, 1884 to May 1, 1885."

[4]Charles Ripley Gillett, "The Library, General Catalogue, and the Alumni," in George Lewis Prentiss, The Union Theological Seminary in the City of New York: Its Design and Another Decade of Its History, with a Sketch of the Life and Public Service of Charles Butler, LL.D. (Asbury Park, New Jersey: M., W., & C. Pennypacker, 1899), p. 357.

[5]Gillett, "Report of the Librarian . . . May 1, 1884 to May 1, 1885."

[6]Directors, op. cit., November 11, 1884.

[7]Minutes of the Faculty of Union Theological Seminary in the City of New York, note following minutes of December 3, 1884.

[8]Union Theological Seminary, Services in Adams Chapel at the Dedication of the New Buildings of the Union Theological Seminary, 1200 Park Avenue, New York City, December 9, 1884 (New York: Printing House of William C. Martin, 1885), pp. 4-5.

[9]Ibid.

[10]Faculty, op. cit., February 25, 1885.

[11]Gillett, "Report of the Librarian . . . May 1, 1884 to May 1, 1885," p. 2.

[12]Ibid., pp. 2-3.

[13]Ibid., p. 3.

[14]Union Theological Seminary, <u>Services in Adams Chapel at the Dedication of the New Buildings of the Union Theological Seminary, 1200 Park Avenue, New York City, December 9, 1884</u> (New York: Printing House of William C. Martin, 1885).

[15]Ibid.

[16]Charles Ripley Gillett, "Report of the Librarian of Union Theological Seminary, for the Year May 1, 1885 to May 1, 1886," p. 1.

[17]Ibid., p. 2.

[18]Directors, <u>op. cit.</u>, May 11, 1886.

[19]Ibid., November 9, 1886.

[20]Charles Ripley Gillett, "Report of the Librarian of Union Theological Seminary, to the Board of Directors, for the Year Ending on May 10th 1887," p. 1.

[21]Ibid., pp. 2-3.

[22]William Coolidge Lane and Charles Knowles Bolton, <u>Notes on Special Collections in American Libraries</u> ("Library of Harvard University, Bibliographical Contributions," edited by Justin Winsor, No. 45, Cambridge, Mass.: Issued by the Library of Harvard University, 1892), p. 49.

[23]Gillett, "Report of the Librarian . . . May 10th 1887," pp. 3-4.

[24]Ibid., p. 1.

[25]Ibid., May 8, 1888.

[26]Directors, <u>op. cit.</u>, July 20, 1887.

[27]Ibid., September 22, 1887.

[28]James Everett Frame, "Vincent, Marvin Richardson," <u>Dictionary of American Biography</u>, ed. Dumas Malone, XIX (New York: Charles Scribner's Sons, 1937), pp. 279-80.

[29]Ibid., November 22, 1887.

[30]Henry Sloane Coffin, <u>A Half Century of Union Theological Seminary, 1896-1945, An Informal History</u> (New York: Charles Scribner's Sons, 1954), p. 181.

[31]Charles Ripley Gillett, "Report of the Librarian of Union Theological Seminary to the Board of Directors, May 8th 1888," pp. 3-4.

[32]Directors, op. cit., November 8, 1887.

[33]Gillett, "Report of the Librarian . . . , May 8th 1888," p. 2.

[34]Ibid., p. 3.

[35]Faculty, op. cit., November 21, 1888.

[36]George Lewis Prentiss, The Union Theological Seminary in the City of New York: Historical and Biographical Sketches of Its First Fifty Years (New York: Anson D. F. Randolph and Co., 1889), p. 392.

[37]W. H. Allison, "Theological Libraries," in The New Schaff-Herzog Encyclopedia of Religious Knowledge, edited by Samuel MacAuley Jackson et al., XI (New York: Funk and Wagnalls Company, 1911), p. 340.

[38]Charles Ripley Gillett, "Report of the Librarian of Union Theological Seminary for the Year 1889-90," p. 2.

[39]Ibid.

[40]Minutes of the Executive Committee of Union Theological Seminary in the City of New York, November 8, 1888.

[41]Faculty, op. cit., November 14, 1884.

[42]Directors, op. cit., November 18, 1888.

[43]Charles Ripley Gillett, "Detailed History of the Union Theological Seminary in the City of New York" [New York, 1937] (Typewritten), p. 1149.

[44]Gillett, "Report of the Librarian . . . 1889-90," pp. 1, 3.

[45]Prentiss, op. cit., p. 88.

[46]Faculty, op. cit., February 18, 1889.

[47]Union Theological Seminary, Catalogue of the Officers and Students of the Union Theological Seminary in the City of New York, 1889-90 (New York: Wm. C. Martin, 1889).

[48]Charles Ripley Gillett, "Report of the Librarian of UTS for the Year, May 1, 1891 to May 1, 1892, p. 1.

[49]Directors, op. cit., March 11, 1890.

[50] Charles Butler, Letter to the Joint Committee of the Union Theological Seminary and to the University of the City of New York, April 1, 1890 in "Extracts from Source Materials Used in Preparing a History of Union Theological Seminary," ed. by Charles Ripley Gillett [New York, 1937] (Typewritten), pp. 70-71.

[51] Directors, op. cit., May 6, 1890.

[52] Minutes of the Executive Committee of Union Theological Seminary in the City of New York, April 22, 1890.

[53] Faculty, op. cit., February 4, 1891.

[54] Union Theological Seminary, Catalogue of the Officers and Students of the Union Theological Seminary in the City of New York, 1890-91 (New York: Wm. C. Martin, 1891).

[55] Faculty, op. cit., October 22, 1890.

[56] Ibid., May 6, 1891.

[57] Ibid., October 7, 1891.

[58] Directors, op. cit., November 11, 1890.

[59] Coffin, op. cit., p. 18.

[60] Ibid.

[61] Directors, op. cit., October 16, 1891.

[62] Ibid., October 13, 1892.

[63] Prentiss, The Union Theological Seminary . . . : Its Design and Another Decade . . . , p. 334.

[64] John Crosby Brown et al., Letter, November 11, 1892, "Extracts," ed. by Gillett, p. 73.

[65] Union Theological Seminary, Constitution and Laws of the Union Theological Seminary in the City of New York, Founded on the 18th of January, A. D. 1836, As Revised and Amended A. D. 1847 (New York: Wm. C. Martin, 1893).

[66] Charles Ripley Gillett, "Report of the Librarian of Union Theological Seminary for the Year, May 1, 1891 to May 1, 1892," pp. 3-4.

[67] Lane and Bolton, op. cit., pp. 48-49.

[68] Gillett, "The Library . . . ," Prentiss, The Union Theological Seminary . . . : Its Design . . . , p. 357.

[69]The New-York Times, March 25, 1884.

[70]Ibid.

[71]Minutes of the Finance Committee of Union Theological Seminary in the City of New York, December 20, 1890.

[72]Ibid., May 7, 1908.

[73]William Bristol Shaw, "Fayerweather, Daniel Burton," Dictionary of American Biography, ed. Allen Johnson and Dumas Malone, VI (New York: Charles Scribner's Sons, 1937), p. 306.

[74]Gillett, "Detailed History . . . ," p. 308.

[75]Union Theological Seminary, Constitution . . . , 1893, p. 18.

[76]Coffin, op. cit., pp. 34-37.

[77]Ibid., pp. 37-39.

[78]Ibid., pp. 39-40.

[79]Ibid., pp. 26-27.

[80]Ibid., pp. 28-31.

[81]Ibid., pp. 32-34.

[82]Union Theological Seminary, General Catalogue . . . , 1892, p. 205.

[83]Charles Ripley Gillett, "Librarian's Report to the Board of Directors of Union Theological Seminary for the Year 1893-94," p. 3.

[84]Directors, op. cit., December 12, 1892.

[85]Michigan. University, Regents' Proceedings, 1891-96, p. 109.

[86]Prentiss, The Union Theological Seminary . . . : Its Design . . . , pp. 341-42.

[87]Faculty, op. cit., December 11, 1895.

[88]Prentiss, The Union Theological Seminary . . . : Its Design . . . , pp. 341-42.

[89]Directors, op. cit., June 4, 1895.

[90]Faculty, op. cit., October 9, 1895.

[91] Ibid., October 14, 1896.

[92] Ibid., December 4, 1895.

[93] Charles Ripley Gillett, "Report of the Librarian of Union Theological Seminary to the Board of Directors for the Year Ending May 14, 1895," p. 303.

[94] "Certificate for One Share of the Publication Fund of the N. Y. Historical Society, "Extracts . . . ," ed. by Gillett, p. 73.

[95] Directors, op. cit., March 10, 1895.

[96] Ibid., May 19, 1896.

[97] Faculty, op. cit., October 14, 1896.

[98] Directors, op. cit., March 10, 1896.

[99] Finance Committee, op. cit., March 20, 1896.

[100] Ibid., May 7, 1896.

[101] Gillett, "Detailed History . . . ," p. 1150.

[102] Charles Ripley Gillett, "Report of the Librarian, 1896-97, Union Theological Seminary," p. 1.

[103] Ibid.

[104] Coffin, op. cit., pp. 21-24.

[105] Ibid., pp. 25-26.

[106] Ibid., pp. 45-48.

[107] Directors, op. cit., February 9, 1897.

[108] Faculty, op. cit., September 29, 1897.

[109] Executive Committee, op. cit., October 25, 1897.

[110] Charles Ripley Gillett, "Library, Union Theological Seminary, New York, May 17, 1898, Librarian's Report," p. 2.

[111] Ibid., pp. 2-3.

[112] Faculty, op. cit., October 27, 1897.

[113] Directors, op. cit., January 11, 1898.

[114] Charles Ripley Gillett, "Report of the Librarian of Union Theological Seminary, New York, May 16, 1899."

[115]Union Theological Seminary, General Catalogue . . . ,
(1898).

[116]Prentiss, The Union Theological Seminary . . . :
Its Design . . . , p. 352.

[117]Ibid., pp. 355-56.

[118]Ibid., p. 358.

[119]Ibid., pp. 358-59.

[120]"Extracts . . . ," ed. by Gillett, May 26, 1899.

[121]Faculty, op. cit., April 26, 1899.

[122]Charles Ripley Gillett, "The Library of the Union
Theological Seminary, Its Proper Position, Its Present Condition, Its Pressing Needs, April 1899," (Typewritten).

[123]Ibid., Section 4.

[124]Ibid., Sections 5-7.

[125]Ibid., Sections 7-9.

[126]Ibid., Section 9.

[127]Ibid., p. 11.

[128]Ibid., Sections 13-14.

[129]Ibid., Section 19.

[130]Ibid., Section 21.

[131]Ibid., Section 23.

[132]Ibid., Section 25.

[133]Ibid., Section 26.

[134]Ibid.

[135]Ibid.

[136]Directors, op. cit., May 16, 1899.

[137]Ibid., November 14, 1899.

[138]Coffin, op. cit., pp. 41-42.

[139]Ibid., pp. 42-45.

[140]Ibid., pp. 49-50.

[141]Ibid., pp. 53-56.

[142]Ibid., pp. 84-87.

[143]Directors, op. cit., May 15, 1900.

[144]Ibid., June 22, 1906.

[145]Ibid., pp. 29-32.

[146]Ibid., pp. 32-35.

[147]Faculty, op. cit., October 10, 1900.

[148]Francis A. Christie, "Jackson, Samuel Macauley," Dictionary of American Biography, ed. Allen Johnson and Dumas Malone, IX (New York: Charles Scribner's Sons, 1937), pp 553-55.

[149]Ibid.

[150]Directors, op. cit., November 13, 1900.

[151]William Adams Brown, "Union (New York)" in "Theological Seminaries," The New Schaff-Herzog Encyclopedia of Religious Knowledge, . . . XI . . . , p. 377.

[152]W. Dawson Johnston and Isadore G. Mudge, Special Collections in Libraries in the United States (U. S. Bureau of Education Bulletin, 1912, No. 23, Washington: U. S. Government Printing Office, 1912), p. 17.

[153]Directors, op. cit., March 12, 1901.

[154]"Extracts . . . ," ed. by Gillett, April 21, 1902, p. 77-A.

[155]Charles Ripley Gillett, "[Librarian's Report], May 14th, 1901," p. 2.

[156]Charles Ripley Gillett, Letter to G. P. Putnam's Sons, 27 W. 23d, New York, N. Y., September 9, 1901.

[157]_____, Letter to G. E. Stechert, 9 E. 16th St., [New York, N. Y.], September 9, 1901.

[158]Directors, op. cit., January 14, 1902.

[159]Ibid.

[160]Finance Committee, op. cit., April 4, 1902.

[161]Directors, op. cit., May 13, 1902.

[162]Gillett, "Detailed History . . . ," p. 1154.

[163]"Analysis of Income and Expense Accounts of Library Funds, May 1, 1883 to May 2, 1902," "Extracts . . . ," ed. by Gillett, p. 77.

[164]Finance Committee, op. cit., May 8, 1903.

[165]Directors, op. cit., November 14, 1905.

[166]Gillett, "Detailed History . . . ," p. 1156.

[167]Executive Committee, op. cit., January 13, 1903.

[168]Faculty, op. cit., February 4, 1903.

[169]Ibid., May 14, 1903.

[170]Ibid., May 15, 1903.

[171]Gillett, "Detailed History . . . ," p. 1156.

[172]Ibid.

[173]Ibid., p. 1171.

[174]Charles Ripley Gillett, "Report of the Librarian, Union Theological Seminary, May 19th, 1903."

[175]Ibid.

[176]Directors, op. cit., May 19, 1903.

[177]Gillett, "Detailed History . . . ," p. 1125.

[178]Ibid.

[179]Letter from Willis James, January 18, 1904, "Extracts . . . ," ed. by Gillett, p. 11A.

[180]Gillett, "Detailed History . . . ," p. 310.

[181]Minutes of the Alumni Association of Union Theological Seminary in the City of New York, May 16, 1905.

[182]Directors, op. cit., June 14, 1904.

[183]Opinion by Elihu Root, "Extracts . . . ," ed. by Gillett, p. 78.

[184]Executive Committee, op. cit., October 24, 1905.

[185]Faculty, op. cit., October 3, 1906.

[186]Gillett, "Report of the Librarian . . . , May 10, 1904," p. 1.

[187]Directors, op. cit., May 10, 1904.

[188]Directors, op. cit., November 15, 1904.

[189]William B. Shaw, "Dodge, William Earl," Dictionary of American Biography, ed. Allen Johnson and Dumas Malone, V (New York: Charles Scribner's Sons, 1937), pp. 152-53.

[190]William B. Shaw, "Jesup, Morris Ketchum," Dictionary of American Biography, ed. Dumas Malone, X (New York: Charles Scribner's Sons, 1937), pp. 61-62.

[191]Coffin, op. cit., p. 183.

[192]Gillett, "Detailed History . . . ," p. 310.

[193]Directors, op. cit., January 26, 1905.

[194]Coffin, op. cit., p. 73.

[195]Faculty, op. cit., February 8, 1905.

[196]Ibid., April 12, 1902.

[197]Charles Ripley Gillett, "Report of the Librarian of Union Theological Seminary to the Board of Directors, May 16, 1905," p. 1.

[198]Minutes of the Committee on Site and Buildings of Union Theological Seminary in the City of New York, October 6, 1905.

[199]Directors, op. cit., January 4, 1906.

[200]Ibid., March 13, 1906.

[201]Committee on Site and Buildings, op. cit., April 19, 1906.

[202]Gillett, "Detailed History . . . ," p. 310.

[203]Charles Ripley Gillett, "Librarian's Report: May 15, 1906, to the Board of Directors of Union Theological Seminary."

[204]Ibid.

[205]Union Theological Seminary, Catalogue of the Officers and Students of the Union Theological Seminary in the City of New York, 1906-07 (New York: Union Theological Seminary, 1906), insert between pp. 46 and 47.

[206]Union Theological Seminary, Statement of the Most Important Facts and Dates Connected with the History of the Union Theological Seminary from the Election of President Charles Cuthbert Hall, D.D., LL.D. to the Laying of the Corner Stone of the New Buildings on Morningside Heights, Prepared by William Adams Brown, Ph.d., D.D., for the Board of Directors (New York: Irving Press, 1909), p. 19.

[207]Committee on Site and Buildings, op. cit., October 6, 1906.

[208]Ibid., December 12, 1906.

[209]Ibid., January 17, 1907.

[210]Directors, op. cit., May 14, 1907.

[211]Ibid., September 24, 1907.

[212]Ibid., November 12, 1907.

[213]Committee on Site and Buildings, op. cit., December 10, 1907.

[214]Faculty, op. cit., January 8, 1908.

[215]Directors, op. cit., May 12, 1908.

[216]Committee on Site and Buildings, op. cit., May 25, 1908.

[217]Ibid., June 2, 1908.

[218]Directors, op. cit., May 12, 1908.

[219]Ibid., January 14, 1908.

[220]Ibid.

[221]Ibid., January 19, 1910.

[222]Faculty, op. cit., March 25, 1908.

[223]Alumni Association, op. cit., May 12, 1908.

[224]Charles Ripley Gillett, "Librarian's Report, May 12, 1908, to the Board of Directors, Union Theological Seminary."

[225]Gillett, "Librarian's Report, May 12, 1908. . . ."

[226]William W. Rockwell, "Librarian's Report, May 17, 1910, to the Board of Directors of Union Theological Seminary," p. 2.

[227]*Ibid.*

[228]Directors, *op. cit.*, January 19, 1910.

[229]William W. Rockwell, "Librarian's Report, May 18, 1909, to the Board of Directors, Union Theological Seminary," p. 1.

[230]Coffin, *op. cit.*, p. 56.

Chapter VI

THE ACTING LIBRARIANSHIP OF WILLIAM

WALKER ROCKWELL, 1908-13

The Pre-Union Background of Rockwell

Charles Ripley Gillett was succeeded by William Walker
Rockwell, who became Acting Librarian of Union in 1908.[1] He
had been born in Pittsfield, Massachusetts on October 4, 1874
and had been educated at Harvard College and Andover Theological Seminary. He had been the Traveling Fellow from Andover
in 1900-02 and had earned the Licentiate of Theology degree
from the University of Marburg in 1903.[2]

Following a year as an Instructor in Andover Theolog-
ical Seminary, he was appointed as Assistant Professor of
Church History at Union in 1905. He was called to this post
to assist Arthur Cushman McGiffert, whose health was failing.[3]
Three years later he was given the responsibility for the
Library while retaining his professorial post.

Events of the Early Years

The school received a new President, Francis Brown,
in the fall.[4] George Knox had been serving in this office
since the death of President Hall in March.[5]

Shortly before the new President was inaugurated,
an offer was received from Mrs. Daniel Willis James to

contribute $300,000 for a chapel as a memorial to her husband.[6]
This proposal was accepted by the Directors; and, at the same
time, authority was given by them to build an apartment house
for professors at a cost not to exceed $200,000. The funds
for this were to be taken from the sale of the buildings on
Park Avenue.[7]

Bids for the new buildings in the amount of $859,905
were submitted to the Directors on November 12;[8] and the corner
stone was laid on November 17.[9]

George Albert Coe, the first non-Presbyterian elected
to a chair in the school, was nominated by the Directors at
the beginning of the new year.[10] A Methodist, he came to
New York from Northwestern University, where he had been a
Professor of Philosophy. He had already published two books,
The Spiritual Life and The Religion of a Mature Mind, in which
insights from psychology were applied to the religious life.
Other books by him included A Social Theory of Religious
Education and What is Religious Education? A pioneer in the
field of religious education, he made a great distinction between "transmissive" and "creative education." He had a strong
social conscience and sought to encourage independent thinking
among his students.[11] This was a heyday for religious education, and Coe made many recommendations for purchases of
secular and theological materials for the improvement of
Union's holdings on this subject. his books are also, of
course, important contributions in this field of study.

The Directors, at the suggestion of the Library Committee, approved the appointment of a Chief Cataloger at the

same time because of the prospective move to the new site.[12]
The Finance Committee set the salary for this position at
$1,500.[13] This appears to have been a good salary, for the
Head Cataloger at the University of Michigan was only making
a salary of $925 at this time.[14] The Board was told during
this era that the endowment of the Library amounted to
$87,240.27, with an income of $2,970, of which $1,125 was
designated for the purchase of books. Announcement was also
made that, following the sale of the Park Avenue property,
$250,000 would be added to the Library's endowment.[15]

A few days later the Directors were told that Mrs.
Daniel Willis James planned to build a gymnasium on Claremont
Avenue at 120th Street and that she and Arthur Curtiss James
were giving $550,000 for endowments.[16] He was a railroad
financier who was to become Union's most generous benefactor.[17]

Rockwell announced at the end of the academic year
that Julia Pettee of the Vassar College Library would begin
work at Union as Chief Cataloger on June 1, 1909. She was
educated at Mount Holyoke, the Library School of Pratt Institute, and Vassar. After serving at the latter school for ten
years as a cataloger, she was approached by the Librarian of
the Rochester Theological Seminary with an invitation to
classify the 30,000 books belonging to that institution. She
agreed to begin this assignment during the following summer
vacation. Her background in theology was meager; and before
she began at Rochester, she visited such seminaries as Andover,
Hartford, and Mount Airey to orient herself on problems faced

by theological librarians. It took her two summers and a
semester to complete the reclassification of the Rochester
Library.[18] She was, according to Rockwell,

> evidently the most skilful [sic] and experienced
> woman who could be found to guide our Library
> through its pressing problems of unification and
> revision of the catalogue.[19]

The Acting Librarian also announced that Mrs. R. Hall
McCormick, daughter of Henry Day, had promised $5,000 for the
purchase of materials on hymnology, liturgies, and church
music, in memory of her father. This gift was to be used for
enlarging the Collection of Hymnology which bore his name.[20]
The Library also received a number of volumes on Dutch theology
and history from Mrs. Van Helden, widow of the Dutch consul in
Philadelphia and 500 volumes from the collection of the late
Professor Prentiss.[21]

The Park Avenue property was sold to Arthur Curtiss
James for $475,000 at this time,[22] and Rockwell reported that
the move of the collection to Morningside Heights was being
completed. He also noted that a Library of Religious and
Moral Education was being instituted. It was made up of materials contributed by publishers.[23] This collection was
developed to supplement the curriculum which was at this time
expanded to include classes on the psychology of religion,
mental hygiene, and the psychology of mysticism.[24]

The New Buildings

The buildings were opened for instruction on September
28 of this year and dedicated on November 27-29.[25] The

architecture was English Perpendicular Gothic. Occupying a
double block bounded by Broadway, Claremont, 120th and 122nd
Streets, the buildings formed a rectangle, enclosing a quadrangle. A tower at the corner of Broadway and 120th Street
contained the main entrance hall, rising three stories. A
circular stairway led to the upper floors of the Library.[26]

The library building occupied the Broadway side from
the tower to the Library Tower opposite 121st Street. The
first floor had two rooms which were devoted to a museum and
the exhibition of rare books. Several seminar rooms were on
the second and fourth floors; and the third floor was the
location of the Reference Library, 100 feet by 40 feet, with
an oak-beamed ceiling. Offices for the librarians adjoined
this. The stacks were beneath the Reference Library and contained five levels. The complex also included an administration building, a chapel, a President's house, an apartment
house for faculty members, and a students' dormitory. The
construction was of native stone taken from the site.[27]

The final statement on the costs of these buildings
was made on November 10, 1911 by the Building Committee:

Total contributions	$2,026,000.00
Appropriations from other Seminary Funds	351,236.38
Interest on bank balances	64,300.59
Total receipts	2,441,536.97
Payments for land and legal fees	879,616.03
Buildings and commissions	1,561,920.94
Only outstanding bills	
Allen & Collens	311.14
E. J. Robinson & Co.	2,000.00 [28]

New Buildings, Broadway and 120th Street.
Figure 329

The New Classification System

As the collection was moved into its new quarters,
it became apparent that the fixed location system used in the
old building was obsolete. Miss Pettee, therefore, set out
to prepare a new classification scheme for the nation's leading theological library.

She rejected the existing standard classifications
for general collections becuase of their inadequacies for a
theological institution. Dewey, she thought, had inadequate
divisions for a large theological library. The Cutter scheme,
she said, was unacceptable for such a collection because of
its lack of coordination of subjects within the field.[30]

She set out, therefore, to prepare a scheme which
was based on several sources. She had worked out, for example,
a system for the classification of the Rochester Theological
Seminary Library; and this was coordinated with a subject
catalog which had been prepared by Charles R. Gillett at
Union.[31]

The primary classification scheme upon which her
system was built was that proposed by Professor Münsterberg
for the Congress of Arts and Sciences meeting at St. Louis
in 1904. He had divided knowledge into four main divisions:
historical sciences, normative sciences, physical and mental
sciences, and practical sciences. She made a minor change in
the order, however, placing normative sciences after the physical and mental sciences.[32]

The resulting system followed the traditional theological departments, exegetical, historical, systematic, and

practical, in their regular order. By broadening the scheme,
however, she was able to provide within it all fields of
knowledge. The Biblical section, for example, was expanded
to include many types of literature; and secular history was
entered with church history.[33]

The scheme was constructed on the principle that all
subjects can be categorized from the point of view of theology.
Knowledge was divided, thus, into the following areas:

    Historical Sciences
        A   Bibliography, Library science
             Encyclopedias and general reference works
        B   Philology and literature
        C   Whole Bible
        D   Old Testament
        E   Judaism, Apocryphal literature
        F   New Testament
        G   Patristics and Christian literature
        H   History
        I   History of Christianity
        J   History of doctrine
        K   History of separate denominations
        L-M History by country; church history and political
             history
        N   History of missions
        O   History of religions
    Experimental Sciences Dealing with the Material Universe
        and Mental Phenomena
        P   Philosophy, Aesthetics, Ethics
        R   Theory of religion
    Practical Sciences
        S   Social institutions and activities
        T   Education
        U-X Specifically religious institutions and activities
        Y   Fine arts and practical arts
        Z   Special or miscellaneous collections[34]

New Faculty Appointments

Several significant additions were made to the Faculty
at this time. Harry Emerson Fosdick, for example, was appointed
Instructor in Homiletics. His first books, _The Manhood of the
Master_ and _The Meaning of Prayer_ had good sales; but he was

known foremost at Union for his excellent teaching. He was said to be courteous in his criticisms of sermons and helpful in showing the men how their attempts could be improved. As the foremost preacher of the country, he had unusual empathy with the neophytes he taught.[35]

He was later named Morris K. Jesup Professor of the English Bible, and his lectures given in this position were so well received that the school had to issue tickets to control the size of the classes. The core of this course was published in The Modern Use of the Bible. He soon after became a special preacher at First Presbyterian Church, where a storm arose over a sermon he preached on "Can the Fundamentalists Win?" Complaints were registered with the Presbytery of New York and the General Assembly; and Fosdick, a Baptist, was told that if he were to continue in the pulpit of that congregation, he would have to accept the creeds of Presbyterianism. Because he was unable to do this, he resigned. Following a year in Palestine, which was summarized in his book entitled A Pilgrimage to Palestine, he became the Pastor of the Park Avenue Baptist Church, which later became the Riverside Church. Although he subsequently resigned the Jesup Chair, he continued to teach at Union in the field of homiletics.[36]

Fosdick was as able as any man of the twentieth century to make the kernel of the Christian faith understandable and meaningful to his generation. His books are outstanding for their clarity and popularization of the best in

critical scholarship. His ability in these directions was
one of the reasons that he has also been one of the most
controversial figures in American Christianity. His ideas
had been taught by others at such places as Harvard and Union
in the cloistered theological circles in a language which was
not understandable to laymen. He had the rare ability to
take the best of these ideas and interpret them in a manner
that ordinary folk could grasp. This was one of the reasons
he came to be labelled as a heretic in fundamentalist circles.
If his position was heretical, the real deviants were the
German scholars and the faculty members at such places as
Union from whom he borrowed.

His contributions to the development of the Library
included not only judicious recommendations in his fields of
responsibility but also thousands of gifts from his own collection of books, which was one of the largest owned by any
clergyman in America.

Another new faculty member was G. A. Johnston Ross,
who was called from a chair in the Presbyterian College in
Montreal. He had previously held pastorates at the Bridge
of Allan in Scotland, in London, in Cambridge, England, and
in Bryn Mawr in the United States. During his tenure at the
Seminary, it undoubtedly had the strongest homiletics teaching
in the nation with Black, Ross, Fosdick, and Coffin in command.
Ross's published works include several books on preaching and
many volumes of sermons.[37] Along with his colleagues in the

department of preaching, he made numerous suggestions for the
improvement of the collection in this area.

Clarence Dickinson was appointed Musical Director at
this time.[38] A graduate of Northwestern University, he studied
further in Berlin and Paris. In the early part of his career
he served as Organist and Choirmaster of St. James Church in
Chicago and founded the Musical Arts Society of that city.
While serving at Union, he was also Organist and Choirmaster
at Brick Presbyterian Church for fifty-one years and held a
similar post at Temple Beth-El for twenty years. He composed
and edited more than 500 choral works, and his books include
Technique and Art of Organ Playing and Excursion in Musical
History.[39] As the long-time Director of the School of Sacred
Music, he was influential in the development of the collection
in this field. His recommendations for Library acquisitions
included both retrospective and contemporary materials to
supplement the curriculum of the School. His affability, as
well as his scholarship and musical ability, made him a valued
member of the Seminary community. It is difficult to think
of him without remembering also his vivacious, talented wife
who also taught sacred music at Union. Generations of students
remember this couple as the most competent team in the field.

Another appointee was Robert Ernest Hume, who, upon
the death of George William Knox, was asked to fill the
Marcellus Hartley Professorship of the Philosophy and History
of Religion. Hume had B.A., M.A., and Ph.D. degrees from Yale
and a B.D. from Union. Born in India, he had taught in the

theological seminary at Ahmednagar. His fame in theological circles came in part through his translation of The Thirteen Principal Upanishads and his World's Living Religions.[40] As an authority in the field of comparative religions, his service to the Library in the selection of materials was invaluable.

A fifth newcomer was Daniel Johnson Fleming, who had degrees from Wooster, Columbia, and Chicago. He was appointed first as Director of the Department of Foreign Service and later as Professor of Missions. He had earlier been a Professor of Science in the Forman Christian College in Lahore, India, for eight years. Some of his books, such as Devolution in Mission Administration, Village Education in India, and Sharing with Other Faiths, deal with problems faced by missionaries. Others deal with ethical issues and include Ventures in Simpler Living and Ethical Issues Confronting World Christians. Still others, such as Heritage of Beauty, Each with His Own Brush, and Christian Symbols in a World Community, deal with aesthetics.[41] He undoubtedly made many fine recommendations for materials on the contemporary missionary movements.

The Close of Rockwell's Acting Librarianship

A Graduate Faculty, whose purpose was to supervise the programs of doctoral students, was appointed at this time. Yet only one student was successful in earning the "Doctor of Divinity" degree.[42]

Announcement was made at the same time that Mrs. Cleveland H. Dodge was giving $110,000 for the endowment of the Charles A. Briggs Graduate Professorship of Christian

Institutions.[43] Her husband, the son of William Earl Dodge,
was Chairman of the Board of Phelps, Dodge & Company of copper
mining fame.[44]

Miss Emily O. Butler also notified the Board that she
intended to give $120,000 to endow the Charles Butler Pro-
fessorship of Theological Encyclopedia and Symbolics and
$80,000 for the professorial retirement fund. The chair was
named for her father, who had owned large interests in the
Michigan Southern, the Rock Island, and the Chicago and Northwestern Railroads and who was one of the founders of Union.[45]

The last major change in the Faculty in 1913 was the
resignation of William Walker Rockwell as Acting Librarian.
In that year he re-assumed his full-time responsibilities as
Associate Professor of Church History and was replaced as the
administrator in the Library by Henry Preserved Smith.[46]

FOOTNOTES

[1]Union Theological Seminary, Catalogue, 1908-09 (New York: Union Theological Seminary, 1908) p. 6.

[2]Who's Who in New York (New York: Lewis Historical Company, Inc., 1947), p. 886.

[3]Henry Sloane Coffin, A Half Century of Union Theological Seminary, 1896-1945, An Informal History (New York: Charles Scribner's Sons, 1954), p. 52.

[4]Union Theological Seminary, Catalogue, 1908-09 (New York: Union Theological Seminary, 1908), p. 35.

[5]Minutes of the Faculty of Union Theological Seminary in the City of New York, April 1, 1908.

[6]Minutes of the Committee on Site and Buildings of Union Theological Seminary in the City of New York, 1905-11, September 21, 1908.

[7]Minutes of the Board of Directors of Union Theological Seminary in the City of New York, November 9, 1908.

[8]Ibid., November 10, 1908.

[9]Union Theological Seminary, The Laying of the Corner-Stone of the New Buildings of the Union Theological Seminary and the Inauguration of the Reverend Professor Francis Brown as President of the Faculty (New York: Union Theological Seminary, 1908), p. 1.

[10]Directors, op. cit., January 12, 1909.

[11]Coffin, op. cit., pp. 87-88.

[12]Directors, op. cit., January 12, 1909.

[13]Minutes of the Finance Committee of Union Theological Seminary in the City of New York, March 5, 1909.

[14]Michigan. University. Regents' Proceedings, 1906-10, p. 558.

[15]Directors, op. cit., March 9, 1909.

[16]Ibid., March 12, 1909.

[17]_Time_, August 14, 1964, p. 36.

[18]Josephine E. Raeppel, "Julia Pettee," _ALA Bulletin_, XLVII (October, 1953), 417-19.

[19]Union Theological Seminary. Library, Report, May 18, 1909, p. 2.

[20]_Ibid._, p. 3.

[21]_Ibid._, p. 4.

[22]Finance Committee, _op. cit._, September 9, 1909.

[23]Union Theological Seminary. Library, Report, May 17, 1910, p. 4.

[24]Union Theological Seminary, _Catalogue, 1909-10_, p. 28.

[25]Union Theological Seminary, _The Dedication of the New Buildings of the Union Theological Seminary_ (New York: Union Theological Seminary, 1910), p. 1.

[26]_Ibid._, p. 10.

[27]_Ibid._

[28]Committee on Site and Buildings, _op. cit._, November 10, 1911.

[29]Union Theological Seminary. _Catalogue, 1909-10_ (New York: Union Theological Seminary, 1910), p. 26.

[30]"A Classification for a Theological Library," _The Library Journal_ (December 1911), p. 611.

[31]_Ibid._

[32]_Ibid._, pp. 613-14.

[33]_Ibid._, p. 614.

[34]_Ibid._, pp. 623-24.

[35]Coffin, _op. cit._, pp. 90-91.

[36]_Ibid._, pp. 91-92.

[37]_Ibid._, pp. 93-94.

[38]Finance Committee, _op. cit._, November 8, 1912.

[39]<u>Who's Who in Music</u> (New York: Hafner Publishing Company, 1962), p. 59.

[40]Coffin, <u>op. cit.</u>, p. 97.

[41]<u>Ibid.</u>, pp. 97-98.

[42]Directors, <u>op. cit.</u>, May 14, 1912.

[43]<u>Ibid.</u>, January 29, 1913.

[44]"Dodge, Cleveland H.," <u>The National Cyclopaedia of American Biography</u>, XXVI (New York: James T. White, 1937), p. 407.

[45]David Seville Muzzey, "Butler, Charles," <u>Dictionary of American Biography</u>, III (New York: Charles Scribner's Sons, 1937), pp. 359-60.

[46]Coffin, <u>op. cit.</u>, p. 53.

Chapter VII

THE LIBRARIANSHIP OF HENRY
PRESERVED SMITH, 1913-25

The Pre-Union Background of Smith

Henry Preserved Smith graduated from Amherst College
in 1869 and entered Lane Theological Seminary, to which his
father was a generous donor. He graduated in 1872 and spent
the academic year 1874-75 at the University of Berlin. He
returned to Lane where he taught church history one year and
Hebrew the next. He was ordained in 1875 by the Presbytery
of Dayton and then returned to Germany for another year at
the University of Leipzig.[1]

He came back to Lane as Professor of Hebrew and Old
Testament and remained in that office from 1877 to 1893. He
came to believe during this period that the Bible was not
infallible and refused to join a party in the Presbytery of
Cincinnati which favored the condemnation of Charles A. Briggs.
Smith was consequently soon tried for heresy himself. As a
result, he was forced to leave Lane, was suspended from the
ministry of the Presbyterian Church, and was without regular
employment for five years, during which he wrote books.[2]

He then became a Congregationalist and returned to
Amherst as Pastor of the college church and Professor of

Biblical Literature. He served from 1907 to 1913 as Professor
of the History of Religions in Meadville Theological Seminary,
a Unitarian school in Pennsylvania.[3]

His books included <u>Old Testament History</u> and <u>The
Religion of Israel</u>. In some of his essays, published shortly
before his appointment at Union, he called the Christ of the
Fourth Gospel fictitious. He said that many parts of the
Bible were unhistorical.[4]

His appointment was announced during a period when
the General Assembly of the Presbyterian Church was investi-
gating Union's doctrinal, ecclesiastical, and financial
affairs. He was appointed as a member of Union's staff at a
salary of $4,000.[5] This was the same amount that William W.
Bishop was making as Librarian of the University of Michigan.[6]
Although Smith was not to be a member of the Faculty, his
election was considered by Presbyterian leaders to be "likely
to provoke further controversy.[7]

Events of the Early Years

One of the first major actions in Smith's administration was the purchase of part of the library of Charles Briggs,
who had died in the preceding year. This was made possible
through an appropriation of $1,000 from the Board.[8]

Briggs had spent thirty years adding to the collection
begun in the 1860's by Ezra Hall Gillett. The McAlpin Collection was said to contain 12,000 volumes at the time of Briggs's
death. His papers included a list of 2,000 desiderata for
the Collection; and when this was made known to the heirs of

McAlpin, they gave the money to enable Charles Ripley Gillett
to visit Great Britain in search of some of these. He succeeded in securing 500 titles from Briggs's list as well as
nearly 3,000 books and tracts not suggested by Briggs. Many
of these lacked an imprint, being chiefly the productions of
unlicensed or secret presses.[9]

Another encouragement to the new Librarian was provided
by the approval by the Board of the James Library Endowment
Fund in the amount of $250,000 from the sale of the Park Avenue
site. It was announced at this time that a gift of $250,000
of undesignated funds for the Seminary had been received from
Mrs. Stephen V. Harkness and Edward S. Harkness,[10] a Director
of the Southern Pacific Company and the New York Central
Lines.[11] Edward gave $100,000,000 away during his lifetime,
including $25,000,000 to Harvard and Yale. His contributions
to Union totaled $1,250,000.[12]

Another indirect influence on the development of the
Library occurred at this time with the inauguration of a summer
session,[13] which has become one of the most important of such
programs in the field of theological education. Courses taught
by Union professors were offered in the Columbia summer school
for many years. The thousands of attending clergymen, many
of whom have not been graduates of Union, have been heavy users
of the Library during the intervening years; and the collection
has been developed in part to meet their needs.

Union's Faculty had some changes during this period,
including the appointment of the Reverend Frederick John

Foakes Jackson, Dean of Jesus College in Cambridge, as the
Charles A. Briggs Graduate Professor of Christian Institutions.
Foakes Jackson was a mature scholar who was a specialist in
New Testament and church history. He wrote many books before
and after his arrival at Union. He was said to be genial and
witty in the best Anglican tradition. Students also appreciated
his ability to make difficult topics clear and appealing.[14]
He must have made many suggestions for Library purchases for
contemporary materials in his fields of specialization, because
he was in the forefront of scholarship in those areas.

After Francis Brown, the President, died, during the
fall of 1916,[15] McGiffert was appointed Acting President and
subsequently was inaugurated as President.[16] Brown had spent
a high percentage of his time in securing the $2,160,000 which
John D. Rockefeller had insisted be raised before his $250,000
would be contributed; but, although most of the money had been
obtained before Brown's death, the campaign was not concluded
until the following year. The pressure of the financial drive
was said to have been a contributing cause of his death.[17]
The Librarian was asked to assume Brown's duties as Davenport
Professor of Hebrew and the Cognate Languages[18] in addition
to retaining the responsibilities for the Library.

Agitation had existed for several years for the
establishment of a master's degree in theology. Permission
was given in 1917 by the Regents of New York for conferring
this degree.[19] Requirements for the degree included a year
of study beyond the Bachelor of Divinity degree, a working
knowledge of French or German, and a thesis.[20]

The World War I Era

World War I was beginning to have an influence on developments at the Seminary by this time. The Faculty was informed, for example, on October 3, 1917 that twenty-seven students and four members of the Faculty had volunteered for military service.[21] The dormitories of the Seminary were used commonly to house soldiers, 27,189, for example, being cared for in this manner during a two-year period.[22]

The Library did not, of course, remain unaffected by the War. The vast amount of literature on the conflict presented, for example, a problem to the Librarian, who limited his selection only to those materials which were directly related to the religious phases of the strife. The German publications, which had previously been considered to be essential for a theological collection, were cut off. The Library received in September, 1916 a notice that a parcel of mail from Berlin was being held in London; and the suggestion was made that application for its release be forwarded to the American Consul General in London. This application was made with an affidavit stating that the material was for educational purposes. The Consul General, in his reply, stated that "Theological works are not regarded as coming within the category of those to which free transit is accorded." The Librarian of Congress endorsed the second application for the materials, but it was becoming apparent that no more German literature would reach the Seminary until the cessation of hostilities. Even the importation of English books was difficult because of the submarine peril.[23]

Among the materials, however, which the Library was
able to acquire from the Day Fund during the academic year
1916-17 were Kircher's _Mesurgia Universalis_ (Rome 1650),
Haberl's _Magister Choralis_, _Paléographie Musicale_ in seven
volumes, Proske's _Musica Divina_, and Latrobe's _Music of the
Church_. The holdings in church history were increased through
the acquisition of forty-three numbers of _Görres Gesellschaft_,
the _Monumenta Societatis Jesus_ in forty-eight volumes, and
three volumes of the _Analecta Franciscana_.[24]

Other sets in the year's list included:

```
Archief voor Nederlandsche Kerkgeschiedniss (14 volumes)
Church Quarterly Review (17 volumes)
Horae Semiticae (7 parts)
International Journal of Ethics (13 volumes)
The Monist (13 volumes)
London Theological Review (7 volumes)
Proceedings of the Society of Psychology Research
    (8 volumes)
Transactions of the Scottish Ecclesiological Society
    (7 volumes)
Sermons by various authors on the death of President
    Lincoln (70 numbers)[25]
```

Among the holdings of the Library at this time were

. . . a nearly complete file of the reports of the
Society for the Propagation of the Gospel in Foreign
Parts from 1702 to 1845, the Ausführliche Berichte from
1718-1760, and other original imprints of the Danish
missionaries in India under Ziegenbalg, . . . a complete file of the Reports of the Board of Foreign
Missions of the Presbyterian Church U. S. A. and of
the American Bible Society. Many other reports, such
as that of the Baptist Missionary Society and American
Baptist Missionary Societies, lack only a comparatively few numbers.

The Minutes of Presbyterian, Congregational, Baptist,
Methodist, . . . Lutheran, Moravian, the Disciples,
New Jerusalem, Protestant Episcopal and Reformed
ecclesiastical bodies . . .

were also available at Union.[26]

Four new faculty members began their duties at this time. The first was Harry F. Ward, who was called to the Chair in Christian Ethics in the spring of 1918 from Boston University. A Methodist, he had been a minister of several churches in the stockyards district of Chicago. A holder of radical social views and a disciple of the Russian Revolution, he wrote Our Economic Morality and the Ethic of Jesus and In Place of Profit. More complaints were registered against him than against all other members of the faculty combined. Despite these criticisms the Board invited him to continue for three years past his retirement. One student called him a "wild Indian" but recognized that "his provocativeness had place in a heavily endowed institution dedicated to preparing men to work in the usually conservative American Churches."[27] Many of the books in Union's holdings on socialism were placed there at the nomination of this professor.

The second new professor was Eugene W. Lyman, who was asked to fill the Marcellus Hartley Professorship of the Philosophy of Religion. He was educated at Amherst, Yale Divinity School, Halle, Berlin, and Marburg. He served as Professor of Philosophy at Carleton, Professor of Systematic Theology and the Philosophy of Religion at the Congregational College in Montreal, Professor of Christian Theology at Bangor Theological Seminary, and as a teacher at Oberlin. He taught by the discussion method and relied upon carefully prepared reading lists with assignments which led the students to select sections of sources on the topics considered. A thorough liberal, he stressed the development of personality, social progress, and cosmic evolution. His books include <u>The Experience of God in Modern Life</u>, <u>The Meaning of Selfhood and Faith in Immortality</u>, and <u>The Meaning and Truth of Religion</u>.[28] Believing that students should be exposed to all sides of a theological question, he helped the Library to gather not only books which expressed his liberalism but also those which held contradictory points of view.

The third new teacher was Ernest Findlay Scott, who was appointed Edward Robinson Professor of Biblical Theology. He was educated at Glasgow University, Balliol College, Oxford, and the United Presbyterian College, Edinburgh. He had, prior to coming to Union, been a teacher at the Theological College of Queen's University in Kingston, Ontario and had published <u>The Fourth Gospel</u> and <u>The Kingdom and the Messiah</u>. His lecturing was noteworthy for its clarity, humor, and provocative nature. His book entitled <u>The Literature of the New Testament</u> was based on his introductory course. Other books included <u>The Validity of the Gospel Record</u>, <u>The Ethical Teachings of Jesus</u>, <u>The Epistle to the Hebrews</u>, <u>The Book of Revelation</u>, and <u>The Varieties of New Testament Religion</u>. More of his books were chosen as primary Selections of The Religious Book Club than was true of any other author.[29]

A paper on "The Eschatological Element in the Consciousness of Jesus" was read in one of his seminars, and the student comment following it was laudatory. Scott, contrary to his usual practice, tore the paper to shreds. The author rejoined, "But Dr. Scott, I thought I was basing my paper principally on your own <u>The Kingdom and the Messiah</u>." Scott's reply was, "Yes, but I've changed my mind since then." An omnivorous reader, his interests ranged widely. He learned Spanish, for example, in order to read Ortega and Unamuno.[30] As a man of books, he must have been of great assistance to the Librarian in the development of contemporary materials in the field of New Testament, as well as in many other areas in which he was interested.

The fourth was Arthur L. Swift, who became Director of Field Work in 1918. His education was received at Williams College, Union, and Columbia, the latter of which awarded him the doctorate. He later became a Professor of Applied Christianity. He served as the editor of <u>Religion Today</u> and wrote <u>New Frontiers of Religion</u> and <u>Make Your Agency More Effective</u>. His primary contribution at Union was made, however, in his long tenure as Director of Field Work. He, in this capacity, watched generations of fledgling ministers try their wings and sail forth expectantly, often to drop to the ground. They frequently sought his counsel when they failed, as well as his encouragement when they succeeded. As an intensely pragmatic man, his contributions to the development of the collection were made through his suggestions for books on the parish ministry and on the relationship of the church to its community. He attempted to keep the materials for the students as current as possible in these areas. He is remembered in theological education as the dean of directors of field work.

Three changes important for the development of the
school were made at this time. The first was the introduction
of the first tuition fee in the amount of $150 per year.[31]
The second was the cancellation of the Hebrew requirement for
the Bachelor of Divinity degree;[32] and the third was the
elimination of the Graduate Faculty, with the provision for
the supervision of graduate students being placed in the hands
of a committee of the regular Faculty.[33]

Approximately 1,100 pieces of war literature were received at this time from the General War Time Commission of
the Churches. The end of World War I resulted also in the
shipment of nearly complete files of the reports of the British
and Foreign Bible Society. Another interesting acquisition
was the note books of the Reverend Solomon Stoddard, predecessor
of Jonathan Edwards in the pastorate of Northhampton, from
one of Stoddard's descendants, Charles Augustus Stoddard, a
Union Alumnus.[34]

Post-War Developments

The Library began a new service at this time through
the supervision of the formation of a collection for the Union
School of Religion, a settlement-house school of religious
education in New York. The expenses for this collection were
paid from a special appropriation, but the cataloging was done
by the Library staff.[35]

The following representative acquisitions were made
for the various collections of the Library during 1921-22:

McAlpin Collection

Bainbridge; Seasonable Reflections, 1689.
Behmen; The Way to Christ Discovered, 1648.
Brabourne; Defence of the King's Authority, 1660.
Bridges; Defence of the Government in the Church of
England, 1587.
Clarke; England's Remembrance, 1677.
Conference Betweene the Pope, The Emperour and the
King of Spain, 1642.
Cotton; Serious Considerations for Repressing the
Increase of Jesuites, 1641.
Crisp; Christ Made Sin, 1692.
Jones; Nonconformity not inconsistent with Loyalty,
1684.
A Lively Portrait of our New Cavaliers, called
Presbyterians, 1661.
Perkins; A Reformed Catholike, 1634.

Gillett Collection

Adams; The Founding of New England, 1921.
Journals of the Diocese of Alabama, four numbers.
Barratt; History of Old Saint Paul's Church,
Philadelphia, 1917.
Belden; History of the Cayuga Baptist Association,
1851.
Campbell; The Southern Highlander and his Homeland.
Daly; Catholic Problems in Western Canada, 1921.
Hooper; History of Saint Peter's Church, Albany, 1900.
Leyden Documents Relating to the Pilgrim Fathers, 1920.
History of Old Saint David's Church, Radnor, Pa., 1907.
Savaète; Voix Canadiennes, eleven volumes concerning
the Catholic Church in Canada.
Smith; The Mennonites, 1920.

Day Collection

Androutsos; Validity of English Ordinations, 1909.
Augustine; Commentary on the New Code of Canon Law,
1921.
Bacuez; Major Orders (also Minor Orders by the same
author), 1913.
Bailey; Ordinum Sacrorum in Ecclesia Englica Defensio,
1870.
Baumstark; Festbrevier und Kirchenjahr der Syrischen
Jakobiten, 1910.
Chabot; Synodicon Orientale, 1902.
Doelger; Das Sacrament der Firmung, 1906.
Field; The English Liturgies of 1549 and 1661.
Gardner; History of Sacrament, 1920.
Grohmann; Aethiopische Marienhymnen, 1919.
Leadbeater; The Science of the Sacrament, 1920.
Missale Chaldaicum, 1594.
The Priest in Absolution, 1869.

Charles Cuthbert Hall Collection of Mission

Literature

Amado; Memorias de las Missiones Catolicas en el Tonkin, 1846.
Arms; History of the William Taylor Self-supporting Mission in South America, 1921.
Baker; Story of the Women's Foreign Missionary Society of the M. E. Church.
Brewster; A Modern Pentecost in South China, 1909.
The Christian Movement in the Japanese Empire, 1921.
Centenary Volume of the Church Missionary Society.
Clarkson; India and the Gospel, 1850.
Corfe; The Anglican Church in Corea, 1905.
Gamble; Peking; a Social Survey, 1921.
Gollock; Introduction to Missionary Service, 1921.
Ware; Christian Missions in the Teleugu Country, 1912.
Wylie; The Gospel in Burma, 1859.

Henry B. Smith Collection of Philosophy

Fuller; The Science of Ourselves, 1921.
Hobhouse; Mind in Evolution, 1915.
Kishinami; The Development of Philosophy in Japan, 1915.
Robinson; Mind in the Making, 1921.
Sorley; History of English Philosophy, 1920.
Woodworth; Psychology, 1921.

General Collection

Babson; The Future of the Churches, 1921.
Bouquet; Is Christianity the Final Religion? 1921.
Bryce; Modern Democracy, 1921.
Campbell; Christianity and International Morality, 1921.
Carter; Spiritualism; its Present Day Meaning, 1920.
Davies; The Church and the Plain Man, 1919.
Glover; The Free Churches and Reunion, 1921.
Herman; Christianity in the New Age, 1919.
Spencer; The Social Function of the Church, 1921.
Vogt; Church Cooperation in Community Life, 1921.
Woods; Lambeth and Reunion, 1920.[36]

Harrison Sackett Elliott was appointed Assistant Professor of Religious Education at this time to replace George Albert Coe, who resigned on November 14, 1922.[37] The new professor had degrees from Ohio Wesleyan, Drew Theological Seminary, and Columbia. He had been a secretary under the

International Committee of the Y. M. C. A. and had been a
teacher at Drew. His books included The Why and How of Group
Discussion, The Process of Group Thinking, Group Discussion
in Religious Education, and Can Religious Education be Christian?
His influence in promoting the discussion method was indicated
by a reference of one of his students to "The Scotch and other
uneducated professors," which was a critique of all who taught
by other methods than those advocated by Elliott. Henry
Sloane Coffin officiated at the ceremony in which this professor was married. Prior to the service, Coffin remarked
that he had been thinking of where the group participated in
the ceremony and said that he could think of only one point,
that at which any present were asked if they knew any just
reason why the couple should not be united in marriage. After
a pause, Elliott remarked, "I think we can leave the group
out."[38] Elliott contributed to the development of the Library
by recommending materials in the field of religious education
with emphasis upon those dealing with group dynamics.

The doctorate which had been offered by the Seminary
up to this time had not proved popular, partially because the
requirements for it were too rigid. These were relaxed by
the Faculty,[39] and the name of the degree was changed to
"Theologiae Doctor (Th.D.)."[40] The degrees of Master of Arts
and Doctor of Philosophy in various fields of religion were
also offered by Columbia University, with much of the work
being taken at Union.[41]

The Frederick Ferris Thompson Collection

The most important event of this era for the Library was the announcement that Mrs. Mary Clarke Thompson had given fifteen manuscripts and eighty-eight printed books, which had been collected by her husband, the late Frederick Ferris Thompson, and herself.[42] Her husband had helped to found the National Currency Bank, the First National Bank of Detroit, the Columbia Bank of Chatham, New York, and the First National Bank of New York. She was the daughter of Myron H. Clarke, Governor of New York in 1857, when she and Thompson were married.[43]

The gifts included:

Biblia. Vel. (XIIIth c.), 489 ff. (17 x 13 cm.). Written in France. Illum. initials. . . .

Black stamp, ca. 1880, of Count Ladislas Bielinski; L. S. Olschki, Inv., n. 22011; obtained from L. Rosenthal by Frederick Ferris Thompson . . .

Biblia. Vel. (XIIIth c.), 530 ff. (19 x 12 cm.). Probably written in England. Illum. initials. . . .

Biblia. Vel. (XIIIth c.), 384 ff. (19 x 14 cm.). Probably written in France. Illum. initials. . . .

Prefixed is an initial E (with St. Luke) from a liturgical ms.; n. 26 in an old collection; obtained from L. Rosenthal . . .

Horae, in Flemish. Vel. (ca. 1480), 153 ff. (16 x 12 cm.). 21 miniat. Illum. borders. . . .

Belonged (early XIXth c.) to Hermann Hinrich Theysken, aus Osten Walde. . . .

Horae. Vel. (ca. 1460), 80 ff. (19 x 15 cm.). Sarum use (Probably written in England).

Early obits of the Clyfford and Culpeper families. . . .

Horae. Vel. (ca. 1450), 148 ff. (20 x 14 cm.). Said
to have been written at Mons. 12 miniat. . . .

Sale by Sotheby (London, 25 Feb. 1901, n. 871) to
Maggs . . .

Graduale. Vel. (ca. 1540), 272 ff. (17 x 11 cm.).
Written in France. 1 miniat. Musical notation.

Made by Soeur Marie de Fortia for her aunt, Soeur
Geneviève de Courtin; belonged ca. 1650 to Goyet, ca.
1800 to Janvier Delaunay and last to Maggs . . .

Petrus de Riga, Aurora. Vel. (XIVth c.), 157 ff.
(24 x 14 cm.). Written in Italy. . . .

Coll. of Count D. Boutourlin, Florence (Cat., 1831,
n. 37); his sale (Paris, 25 Nov. 1839, I, n. 18) to
Techener; Joseph Barrois coll. (no. 70) sold in 1849
to the Earl of Ashburnham; his sale (London, 1901,
no. 468) to Maggs . . .[44]

Other items included a copy of the Indian Bible of

John Eliot printed in 1663, a copy of a German Bible printed

at Nuremberg in 1483, and Latin Bibles printed in 1475, 1495,

and 1498. Association volumes in the gift were those marked

with the arms of Charles I and James I in addition to one with

Cromwell's arms. A Hebrew Bible and a Greek Bible once owned

by Elizabeth Barrett Browning were also in the collection.

The conditions of the gift were that the materials should be

kept together and designated "The Frederick Ferris Thompson

Collection."[45]

The John D. Rockefeller, Jr. Promise

The Seminary was pleased to receive a notice from

John D. Rockefeller, Jr. at this time that he would give

$1,083,834 to the school if a total of $4,000,000 were raised

in a special campaign.[46] A gift of $1,250,000 toward the

campaign from Edward Harkness was also announced.[47]

Mrs. Andrew Carnegie contributed $100,000 toward the
drive and, in doing so, congratulated the school on the interdenominational nature of its program and the high quality of
clergymen whom it was educating.[48] Another contribution in
the amount of $300,000 was received from Miss Emily Ogden
Butler in memory of her father, Charles Butler.[49]

The total of the contributions to the campaign stood
at $3,479,612 by the end of the year. The funds acquired were
to be used to create an endowment fund of $1,850,000 and for
the purchase of additional land, a refectory, a home for
missionaries on furlough, a professorial retirement fund, the
endowment of foreign fellowships,[50] a tower on 120th Street,
and a social hall.[51]

The McAlpin Collection

A report on the McAlpin Collection by Charles Ripley
Gillett appeared in The Union Theological Seminary Bulletin
during this year. He wrote that Briggs had searched the
antiquarian catalogs and second-hand book shops of Great
Britain thoroughly and that he had acquired an almost complete
collection of the books written by the men who made up the
Westminster Assembly of Divines. Union has, for example, as
the result of Briggs's efforts, seven of the first editions
of the Confession of Faith listed by Warfield in his bibliography on the subject. Yet Briggs was not able to limit his
attention to the Westminster period. The McAlpin Collection
under his direction had come to include books on the era preceding the civil wars and of the Commonwealth, as well as

those in the remaining part of the seventeenth century.
Briggs had also bought materials from the beginning of the
Puritan movement, including literature which signalized the
revolution against "bloody Queen Mary." In the Elizabethan
literature collected were the two "Admonitions to the
Parliament" by John Field and Thomas Wilcox and by Thomas
Cartwright. Most of the tracts of "Martin-Marprelate" were
also acquired.[52]

The Collection had become strong in materials about
the Presbyterian form of ecclesiastical government advocated
during the reign of Elizabeth as it had in books about the
discussion of the royal succession after her reign. By 1924
the Collection also included over 800 titles published before
1600 on religious subjects. These included laws enacted by
Parliament in regard to ecclesiastical affairs.[53]

The McAlpins had also bought a large number of books
from the reigns of James VI of Scotland and I of England as
well as from that of Charles I. The latter reign was especially
well-known for religious controversies which resulted in many
books. The Collection was especially rich in the writings of
four men who were persecuted by William Laud, Bishop of London
and afterward Archbishop of Canterbury. These men were
William Prynne, a London barrister; John Lilburn, who dis-
tributed books by Prynne; John Bastwick, a physician of London;
and Henry Burton, a London preacher. The books were written
in opposition to the alleged Catholic attempt to supplant the
established church. Three of these men were said to have had

their ears cut off, and all were banished by the court of
Star Chamber. The volumes in the Collection from this period
of 1600 to 1640 totaled over 3,000 books and tracts.[54]

Yet the period 1640 to 1660 was best represented in
the Collection. The literature included from this period
contained books and tracts from the secret presses as well as
those dealing with religious controversies. Another area of
strength was that of sermon materials, with almost complete
holdings of the sermons preached before Parliament and those
delivered on the anniversary of the King's death.[55]

The religious literature springing from the final
years of the reign of Charles II and the brief reign of
James II were heavily anti-papal. The last three decades of
the century were heavily represented by materials by and
about the Dissenters, matters of doctrine and practice, and
the beginning of the Deistic controversy.[56]

Smith's Last Six Months as Librarian

Smith submitted his resignation during this period;
and it was accepted on November 11, 1924 to take effect June 30,
1925, with a $4,800 annual retirement allowance provided.
William Walker Rockwell was nominated at the same time to become Librarian[57] with the salary of a professor.[58]

The following spring the Hymn Society of America requested that it be permitted to deposit 1,800 books in the
Library. The Society promised to pay the expenses for cataloging these materials, with the understanding that they would
be accessible to the constituents of the Seminary.[59]

A gift of 166 volumes "in large measure of seventeenth century literature" from the library of Walter William Law was received at this time.[60] Law was a partner in the W. J. Sloane firm, which dealt in rugs and carpets and which at one time was the sole distributor for large industries such as Mohawk Carpet Mills.[61] Still other gifts included fifteen volumes of Buddhist sacred books and commentaries in the Pali language, contributed by the Siamese legation in Washington as a gift from the King of Siam and the Prince and Princess of Chandaburi.[62]

The campaign to raise $4,000,000 for buildings and endowments was completed at this time,[63] with $100,000 of this amount being given by the McAlpin family to establish the McAlpin Library Foundation in honor of David Hunter McAlpin.[64] The total amount was the largest fund ever raised in a campaign by a theological seminary.[65]

Smith retired during this era of the Seminary's history and died a year and a half later, in February, 1927.[66] His predecessor in the Library was his successor there.

FOOTNOTES

[1]William Walker Rockwell, "Henry Preserved Smith," Union Theological Seminary, _Alumni Bulletin_, II (April-May, 1927), p. 138.

[2]_Ibid_.

[3]_Ibid_.

[4]_New York Times_, September 12, 1913, 10:8.

[5]Minutes of the Board of Directors of Union Theological Seminary in the City of New York, May 13, 1913.

[6]Michigan. University. _Regents' Proceedings_, 1914-17, p. 227.

[7]_New York Times_, September 12, 1913, 10:8.

[8]Directors, _op. cit._, January 13, 1914.

[9]Union Theological Seminary. Library, _Catalogue of the McAlpin Collection of British History and Theology_, I, compiled and edited by Charles Ripley Gillett (New York: Union Theological Seminary, 1927), p. vi.

[10]Directors, _op. cit._, January 12, 1915.

[11]"Harkness, Edward Stephen," _Who Was Who in America_, I, 1897-1942 (Chicago: The A. N. Marquis Company, 1942), p. 521.

[12]_New York Times_, January 30, 1940, 1:2, 5:5, 6.

[13]Minutes of the Faculty of Union Theological Seminary in the City of New York, December 13, 1915.

[14]Henry Sloane Coffin, _A Half Century of Union Theological Seminary, 1896-1945, An Informal History_ (New York: Charles Scribner's Sons, 1954), pp. 98-100.

[15]Faculty, _op. cit._, October 15, 1916.

[16]Coffin, _op. cit._, p. 103.

[17]Faculty, _op. cit._, January 9, 1919.

[18]Directors, _op. cit._, March 13, 1917.

[19]Faculty, _op. cit._, October 3, 1917.

[20]_Ibid._, April 12, 1916.

[21]_Ibid._, October 3, 1917.

[22]Directors, _op. cit._, May 13, 1919.

[23]Union Theological Seminary. Library, Report, 1917, pp. 1 ff.

[24]_Ibid._, p. 5.

[25]_Ibid._

[26]Union Theological Seminary. Library, Report in _Union Theological Seminary Bulletin_, I (May, 1918), pp. 32-33.

[27]Coffin, _op. cit._, p. 101.

[28]_Ibid._, pp. 107-10.

[29]_Ibid._, pp. 110-12.

[30]_Ibid._, pp. 112-14.

[31]Faculty, _op. cit._, November 6, 1918.

[32]_Ibid._, March 27, 1918.

[33]_Ibid._, April 17, 1918.

[34]Union Theological Seminary. Library, Report in _Union Theological Seminary Bulletin_, III (July, 1920), pp. 38-40.

[35]_Ibid._, V (July, 1922), p. 47.

[36]_Ibid._, pp. 41-43.

[37]Directors, _op. cit._, November 14, 1922.

[38]Coffin, _op. cit._, pp. 155-58.

[39]Faculty, _op. cit._, April 2, 1923.

[40]Directors, _op. cit._, May 15, 1923.

[41]Union Theological Seminary, _Catalogue_, 1923-24 (New York: Union Theological Seminary, 1923), pp. 61-62.

[42]Union Theological Seminary, Library, Report in *Union Theological Seminary Bulletin*, VI (July, 1923), p. 35.

[43]"Thompson, Frederick F.," *The National Cyclopaedia of American Biography*, VI (New York: James T. White Company, 1929), pp. 140-41.

[44]Seymour De Ricci and W. J. Wilson, *Census of Medieval and Renaissance Manuscripts in the United States and Canada*, II (New York: Kraus Reprint Corporation, 1961), pp. 1646-47.

[45]Union Theological Seminary. Library, Report, April 30, 1923, p. 35.

[46]*New York Times*, May 21, 1924, 1:4.

[47]Directors, *op. cit.*, April 11, 1924.

[48]*New York Times*, November 27, 1924, 18:8.

[49]*Ibid.*, December 25, 1924, 18:8.

[50]*Ibid.*, November 27, 1924, 18:8.

[51]Charles Ripley Gillett, "Detailed History of the Union Theological Seminary in the City of New York" [New York, 1937] (Typewritten.), p. 404.

[52]Charles Ripley Gillett, "The McAlpin Collection," *Union Theological Seminary Bulletin*, VII (January, 1924), pp. 4-5.

[53]*Ibid.*, p. 6.

[54]*Ibid.*, pp. 6-7.

[55]*Ibid.*, pp. 7-10.

[56]*Ibid.*, pp. 13-15.

[57]Directors, *op. cit.*, November 11, 1924.

[58]*Ibid.*, March 11, 1927.

[59]Union Theological Seminary. Library, Report in *Union Theological Seminary Bulletin*, VIII (July, 1925), pp. 33-34.

[60]*Ibid.*

[61]"Law, Walter William," *The National Cyclopaedia of American Biography*, XXXI (New York: James T. White Company), p. 73.

[62] Union Theological Seminary. Library, Report in *Union Theological Seminary Bulletin*, VIII (July, 1925), p. 36.

[63] *New York Times*, May 20, 1924, 1:4.

[64] *Ibid.*, January 4, 1925, II, 1:7.

[65] *Ibid.*, May 20, 1925, 1:4.

[66] Coffin, *op. cit.*, p. 96.

Chapter VIII

THE LIBRARIANSHIP OF WILLIAM
WALKER ROCKWELL, 1925-42

New Faculty Appointees

William Walker Rockwell resumed the responsibilities
in the administration of Union's Library following the twelve-
year period during which Henry Preserved Smith was in charge.
Several other important appointments to the Faculty were made
at this point.

The first was to the office of the President. McGiffert
resigned because of a health condition; and, on the same day,
April 20, 1926, the Directors appointed Henry Sloane Coffin
as the replacement.[1] The new President had been Pastor of
Madison Avenue Presbyterian Church in New York. He had studied
at Yale University, Union Seminary, and New College in Edinburgh.
While serving as a Pastor in New York, he had taught courses
in Practical Theology at Union. Since 1922, he had been one
of the "Successors to the Original Trustees of Yale University";
and about him, James R. Angell, President of that school, subsequently wrote:

> He brought to the Corporation . . . a wide knowledge
> of educational methods and ideals, both here and abroad.
> Few members of the Corporation have ever been the re-
> cipients of so many honorary degrees and these, be it
> said, from institutions of outstanding distinction, not
> only in the United States but also in England in Europe.[2]

His administrative skill was largely responsible for the growth of the school, including its Library, during the twenty years in which he headed the Seminary. He was also a friend to many students, inviting them in small groups to his home for meals and good natured banter. He became in time the Placement Bureau for Union and had a remarkable memory for the weaknesses and strengths of former students. Faculty meetings were presided over so successfully and moved so rapidly that the Secretary was unable to keep accurate minutes and was forced to the practice of preparing in advance an abstract of the record, which could be filled in. His work was done with informality, so that it was easy for students to secure interviews with him; and he was well-known for visiting professors' studies for interviews with them. The following anecdote is illustrative of his personality:

Early one morning a new student from the South arrived at the Seminary and found the main entrance closed. He walked around the corner to what appeared to be a private entrance on Claremont Avenue, dropped his luggage on the doorstep and rang the bell. It was much too early for the President's household to be active. Presently, a figure in shirt-sleeves, perhaps directly from the President's private study on the fifth floor, bounded down the stairs and opened the front door. Identifying the stranger at once as an entering student, he said, "Oh, you belong in the dormitory office," seized one of the student's cases and quickly led him across the quadrangle. As they walked, the student inquired, "Are you the janitor?" "No," was the reply, "but I try to be helpful to the janitor." When they reached the dormitory office, the attendant of many years, Mr. Emanuel Romero, arose in surprise to exclaim, "Why, Dr. Coffin!" The southern lad, with some consternation, protested, "But you didn't tell me you were the President!" "No," was the answer. "You asked me if I was the janitor, and I said I try to be helpful to him."[3]

Although he, as President, helped to build the collection into
one of the important research centers of the second quartile
of the twentieth century, he retained the common touch illustrated by this story and made many recommendations for "how-
to-do-it" books which he thought would be useful for parish
ministers.

Other new Faculty members included A. Bruce Curry,
who had studied at Davidson College, Union Theological Seminary,
Richmond, Princeton Seminary, and New York University. He had
taught at the Biblical Seminary in New York City and at New
York University for twelve years prior to his appointment at
Union. He was named Associate Professor of Practical Theology
and later was appointed to the Jesup Chair in the English
Bible as a replacement for Fosdick. He was highly successful
in helping students to use the English Bible more effectively
in their teaching and preaching. Accepting the finest in
historical criticism, he helped those whom he taught to apply
valid insights from the Scriptures to the solution of contemporary problems.[4] His recommendations for contemporary materials for the Library reflected his dual interests in
popularizing Biblical scholarship and educational techniques.

Another was James Moffatt, who came from the history
chair in the United Free Church College in Glasgow. Educated
at Glasgow University, he had served as Yates Professor of
Greek at Mansfield College, Oxford before taking the history
chair in Glasgow. His books included the Introduction to the
New Testament, two volumes in the Expositor's Greek Testament,

and _The Thrill of Tradition_. He is probably known best, however, for his translation of the Bible. While he was lecturing
at Duke, a headline in the morning newspaper read AUTHOR OF
BIBLE TO LECTURE AT DUKE. A wag clipped it and mounted it on
the Seminary bulletin board with the comment: "We had not
known the eminence of Union's new professor." Moffatt published a volume almost every year that he was at Union and
served until his death in 1944 as Secretary of the Committee
preparing the Revised Standard Version of the Bible. Because
of his great erudition, it was difficult, however, for him to
finish his courses. One of these called "The Great Sequence"
was supposed to cover the history of the Church from the second
through the sixth centuries, but the third was rarely completed.
His students laughingly called it "The Great Sequence which
stopped seeking."[5] His excellent scholarship and knowledge
were responsible for many important titles in the fields of
New Testament and Church History during his service as
McGiffert's successor at Union.

A fourth new appointee was Walter Russell Bowie, a
graduate of Harvard and of the Episcopal Theological Seminary
in Alexandria. He had served as Rector at Greenwood, Virginia,
of St. Paul's in Richmond, as a chaplain in World War I, and
as Rector of Grace Church in New York City. His books include
The Master, _The Story of Jesus_, _Great Men of the Bible_, _The
Story of the Bible_, and _Lift Up Your Hearts_. He was an
Associate Editor of _The Interpreter's Bible_, writing several
of the longer articles. He helped polish the English of the

Revised Standard Version. He was a professor remembered for
his humor, scholarship, and culture. His wife, who was crippled
by illness during their stay at Union, was well-known in the
Seminary for her hospitality, humor, and penetrating comments
on current events.[6] Bowie made many contributions to the
growth of the Library through his recommendations for contemporary materials in the field of preaching.

Another new Faculty member was Henry Pitney Van
Dusen, who was appointed as an Instructor. He had degrees
from Princeton, Union, and Edinburgh, the latter of which has
granted him the doctorate. He rose through the professorial
ranks to become the President of the school in 1945. He was
a Trustee of Princeton, Nanking Theological Seminary, Mill-
brook School, Vassar College, Smith College, and Elizabeth
Morrow School. He held memberships in the United Board
Christian Higher Education in Asia, the Board of Foreign
Missions of the United Presbyterian Church, the American
Theological Society, the Council on Foreign Relations, and
the Board of the National Council of Churches. He was the
President of the Union Settlement Association, a Trustee of
the Rockefeller Foundation, a Director of the Fund for the
Republic, a Fellow of the National Council on Religion in
Higher Education, and the Chairman of the Joint Committee of
the World Council of Churches and the International Missionary
Council. His books include Life's Meaning, Spirit, Son
and Father, One Great Ground of Hope, The Vindication of

241

<u>Liberal Theology</u>, and <u>Christianity on the March</u>. He served
on the editorial boards of <u>Christianity and Crisis</u>,
<u>Christendom</u>, and <u>Ecumenical Review</u>.[7] His contributions to
the development of the collection were tremendous in his
office as President as he had struggled unceasingly for
increased financial support for the Library. He also made
many personal recommendations for acquisitions in the field
of philosophy of religion and systematic theology. Despite
the fact that he brought to the Faculty some of the outstanding neo-orthodox theologians of the nation, his own
position remained that of the liberal evangelical. He
increasingly became disenchanted with the "demythologization"
school of Bultmann and company. No one who studied at Union
during his incumbency can forget the dignity, the brilliance,
and the statesmanship with which he administered the school.
We have always been proud of "Pit" as he was always proud of
Union.

Shortly after his appointment, Reinhold Niebuhr was
named Associate Professor of the Philosophy of Religion. His
formal education was received at Elmhurst College, Eden
Theological Seminary, and Yale Divinity School. He came to
the Seminary from a pastorate in Detroit, where he had worked
since 1915. His many books include <u>Christian Realism and
Political Problems</u>, <u>The Self and the Dramas of History</u>,[8] and
his <u>magnum opus</u>, <u>The Nature and Destiny of Man</u>. Although he
had a national reputation as an author and lecturer, his life
was centered about Union Seminary, where he had lived most of
his adult life. He was one of the most influential thinkers

in the field of Christian ethics in this generation. His insistence that moral decisions are almost never unambiguous has been interpreted meaningfully not only for individuals but also for political groups. His students have known him not so much as a brilliant writer and national figure but as a stimulating and provocative friend. His teaching was not restricted to the classroom but was extended to frequent invitations to his apartment, where exciting "bull sessions" were commonplace. His keen intelligence and forceful manner were sometimes disturbing to an unsuspecting junior, but those who attended the "evenings at the Niebuhrs" know that this was one of the most important and relevant aspects of their theological educations. The conversations were certainly the most discussed factor in the Seminary's life on the following mornings, at least.

Niebuhr was heavily attacked from the right and from the left; but, with all his faults, he was one of the most brilliant Christian intellectuals of the twentieth century. He, too, was a great scholar who recommended many weighty tomes, both retrospective and current, in the fields of ethics, systematic theology, and the philosophy of religion. Neither Union Seminary nor its Library would be what it is today had it not been for "Reinie."

Another Faculty appointee during this era was John C. Bennett. His education was received at Williams, Oxford, and Union. He, like Van Dusen, rose through the profes- sorial ranks to become, in 1964, the President of the Seminary.

He served as Secretary of the Section on the Church and
Economic Order of the Oxford Conference on Life and Work,
Vice Chairman of the Liberal Party in New York State,
President of the American Theological Society, President of
the Society of Christian Social Ethics, and as Co-Editor of
Christianity and Crisis. His books include Social Salvation,
Christian Ethics and Social Policy, Christianity and Communism,
The Christian As a Citizen, Christians and the State, and
Christian Values and Economic Life, the latter of which was a
product of co-authorship.[9]

Bennett was one of the best teachers at Union. His
lecturers were always lucid, well-prepared, and objectively
presented. He has a rare ability to summarize various
theological positions without indicating undue bias toward
any. After such a summary, however, it was common for him to
state the position which was most attractive to him. The
fairness with which he treated the schools of thought and the
questions of students has endeared him to generations of
Alumni. Perhaps his strongest virtue, aside from his
intellectual powers, was his humility. At social occasions
he was frequently found in a corner talking to a shy student
who wanted to become a minister rather than in the cluster of
the great. His inauguration as President, which was executed
in the splendid ecclesiastical tradition, reminded one parti-
cipant, at least, of the coronation of Jesus Christ as
Emperor of Rome. The Alumni were almost unanimously happy at
his election; and this friend of the Library, who recommended
many retrospective and contemporary materials in his field of

specialization for acquisition through the years, continued to be the chief ally of the Librarian in the development of the collection.

New also at the time of Bennett's appointment was Frank Wilbur Herriott, who had degrees from Ottawa University, Union, and Columbia. He had previously been Pastor of a church in Winfield, Kansas, Minister of Religious Education in Central Presbyterian Church in Montclair, New Jersey, and a Chaplain in the Army. His books include A Community Serves Its Youth and Christian Youth in Action.[10] He made many recommendations for contemporary materials in the field of religious education.

Significant Library Acquisitions

The most important gift during Rockwell's first year as Librarian was the payment of the first $20,000 toward the principal of the McAlpin Library Foundation. The total of $100,000 was to be paid in five annual installments, with the income to be used basically for the care and upkeep of the McAlpin Collection and the printing and distribution of the Catalog. Yet, materials for other departments were to be purchased from these funds if these items were not of "recent publication."[11]

Six unpublished autograph letters written during the Reformation were given at this time by Walter S. Hertzog of the class of 1910. An active member of the Christian Churches (Disciples of Christ), he was at the time serving as Professor of Sociology at California Christian College.[12]

The documents contributed included:

Hermann, Graf von Wied, Archbishop of Cologne, Letter signed (31 Dec. 1552), to Wolfgang, Graf von Stolberg, 5 pp.

Charles F. Gunther coll., Chicago.--Obtained (1926) from Westermann, with the five following . . .

Johann Brentz, Autogr. letter signed (Wednesday after Jubilate, 1542), to Chancellor Georg Vogler, 2 pp.

Dr. Gwinner coll., Frankfurt-am-Main; Charles F. Gunther coll., Chicago.

Johann Brentz, Autogr. letter signed (Stuttgart, 20 Oct. 1569), to Claudia, Gräfin von . . . und Witteberg.

N. 32 in a Charavay sale.--Charles F. Gunther coll., Chicago.

Joachim, Markgraf von Brandenburg, Letter signed (Collen ann der Sprew freitags nach Laurenci, 11 Aug. 1553. Date formerly misread 1542), to Hans von Ponickenn.

Albrecht von Brandenburg-Mainz, Cardinal and Elector, End of a letter signed (18 Nov. 1533.)

Nicolaus von Amsdorf, Bishop of Maumburg, Autogr. letter signed (Greitz, 22 Feb. 1542), to Georgius Major, in Latin.[13]

Another unexpected boon came in the middle of February, when the Missionary Research Library of 45,000 volumes, the property of the Boards represented in the Foreign Missions Conference of North America, was forced out of their quarters at 25 Madison Avenue. Union allowed this collection to be housed at the Seminary.[14] The library of Henry Preserved Smith was also given to the school by his children, Professor Preserved Smith of Cornell and Professor Winifred Smith of Vassar. This gift amounted to seventy yards of shelving.[15]

A collection of 2,200 engravings and lithographs of Protestant clergymen was bequeathed to the school at the same time by the Reverend William Nicholas Weir of the class of

1900. He had been since 1912 Pastor of the Church of the Redeemer at Sayre, Pennsylvania. Some of these prints were made in the sixteenth and seventeenth centuries; most were made, however, in the eighteenth and nineteenth.[16]

The purchases during the year included a collection of books, many of which were illustrated with copperplates, relating to Rome and the Papacy from the sixteenth through the eighteenth centuries. Some other books on this subject published during the same period were bought from a Norwegian merchant, Henry Jungmann.[17]

The McAlpin Catalogue

The first volume of the five-volume Catalogue of the McAlpin Collection was published at this time. The year 1700 was set as the cut-off year beyond which no listing was made, although the Collection contained a large number of materials printed beyond that date.[18]

Many copies of the missing title pages had been supplied through a trip by Gillett to England; but he had been, of course, unable to discover all those lacking in the Collection. An example of a successful search involved a Paul's Cross sermon delivered by Thomas White, founder of Sion College, in 1578. The date of delivery seemed to conflict with the calendar. A letter of inquiry printed in Notes and Queries resulted in a reply from the Librarian of the Huntington Library in California. A photostatic copy of six pages, which he sent to Gillett, cleared up all questions of date and authorship.[19]

The separate entries in the _Catalogue_ contained several parts. The author was given, if ascertained, with the authority for the information in footnotes and in the index. Anonymous books were entered in the index under the first important word not an article. Titles were given in full, with line-endings marked by vertical marks. Ornaments, borders, and printers' devices were noted; and imprints were given in full. The _Catalogue_ has become well-known for its full bibliographical notes.[20]

The index included the names and brief statements about each author. This information was followed by the titles of books credited to each. References were also given for other books whose title-pages contained allusions to this writer. Anonymous works were listed in this index under the first important word of the title, not an article, with the name of the author, if known, in brackets.[21]

Library Progress in 1927-28

While this _Catalogue_ was being printed, the John Crosby Brown Tower was being completed, as a memorial to a former President of the Directorate. Aside from its contribution to the architecture of the school, the purpose of the Tower was to hold five tiers of stacks, which would contain 122,720 volumes.[22]

Among the more interesting contributions during the year was a copy of the sixth and last Dutch Bible printed by Jacob van Liesvelt in Antwerp in 1542. The book cost the printer his life because of a note on I Peter 2:5, which

asserted that man should set all his hope on Christ alone.
The copy had formerly been owned by the Bible Hotel, which
was said to be on the site of a residence of Van Liesvelt,
in Amsterdam. One of the Directors also gave $100 to complete
the Library's file of the Jesuit magazine in England, The
Month. He also gave a large number of old pamphlets from the
library of a former Governor of Connecticut, John Cotton
Smith.[23]

Purchases during the year included some materials
from the mid-Victorian book collection of Lord Lindsay, the
Earl of Crawford, through a sale by Hiersemann of Leipzig.
A number of bibliographical tools used by Edward Turnbull,
the former proprietor of the Walpole Galleries, were also
bought at auction.[24]

The Library also received $10,000 at this time from
two members of the Park Avenue Baptist Church, Mr. and Mrs.
Edward Lathrop Ballard and $5,000 from an anonymous alumnus.
Ballard was Chairman of the Executive Committee of the Merchants Fire Assurance Corporation of New York and the Merchants
Indemnity Corporation.[25] The anonymous gift was for the purchase of books on religious education, psychology, and allied
topics. These funds were all invested, with the interest
being designated for book purchases.[26]

Three new collections were begun at Union this year.
The first was the Lending Library for Alumni, which was made
possible through the gift from an anonymous alumnus in the
amount of $5,000.[27]

Another room was designated for the Sacred Music Library, where many of the works from the Day and the Newman Collections were made available.[28] This collection was begun to help in the development of the newly-organized School of Sacred Music, which had been started in 1928 with its own Faculty and curriculum. The latter included courses in the history of sacred music, hymnology, liturgics, plain song, the choir, the church school, voice, organ, and theory. The graduates of the School were awarded the master's degree.[29]

The Missionary Research Library

These two collections were soon eclipsed, however, by plans to form an official connection with the Missionary Research Library, which had been temporarily housed at the Seminary for a brief period. The collection had been begun in 1914 by John R. Mott, who, as Chairman of the Library Committee of the Foreign Missions Conference of North America, secured the financial support of John D. Rockefeller, Jr. for the project.[30] From the time of its founding, the Curator had been C. H. Fahs and the Librarian had been Miss Hollis W. Hering. R. P. Beaver, who succeeded Fahs in 1948, said of them,

> During the next third of a century these two persons formed a team of most unusual competence. Together they built up the magnificent collections and established the pattern of service. They became, without doubt, the world's foremost authorities on Protestant missionary literature. Very few scholarly missionary books were written during these years which had not received some measure of assistance from the curator and librarian of the "MRL" . . .[31]

The collection had grown in fifteen years to include approximately 45,000 books and bound reports and periodicals, in
addition to thousands of pamphlets, making it the largest
and most significant collection of materials on the modern
era of Protestant missions. It was used, not only by students
of missionary problems, but also by scholars in anthropology,
history, and social conditions.[32]

The Beginning of the Depression

The Depression made it difficult for the missionary
boards to pay the expenses of the Library; Union was, therefore, asked to house the collection.[33] The plan was that the
title should remain in the name of the Foreign Missions Conference and that the administration of the Library should be
under the direction of a joint committee made up of five
persons from the Conference and three from the Seminary.
Fahs and Herring were to continue to be in charge.[34] They
were joined soon after by Mrs. Hugh Foster, who remained on
the Seminary Library staff in various capacities for thirty-
two years.[35] The President told the Directors on March 12,
1929 that a session of the joint committee had been held, the
first official connection of the Seminary with the representatives of ecclesiastical bodies since 1892.[36]

The funds for equipping the James Crosby Brown Tower
to receive these books and for their maintenance were provided
by the following gifts:

E. S. Harkness, for endowment	$100,000
J. D. Rockefeller, Jr., for upkeep	50,000
J. D. Rockefeller, Jr., toward building, stacks and elevator	25,000
Arthur Curtiss James, balance of same, about	30,000
	205,000 [37]

The Union School of Religion, a venture begun in 1914
in religious education through which students received practical
experience in applying educational theories, was closed at this
time; and some of the materials from its "Pupils' and Parents'
Library" were incorporated into the Seminary's collection.[38]

The Library was able to retain the services of Julia
Pettee, who was invited during this era by the Library of
Congress to move to Washington to recatalog nearly 200,000
books on religion. They offered her "a very material increase"
in salary and the service of three catalogers as her assistants.
Union's Finance Committee countered with a raise in salary and
a promise to employ more staff for her department to speed up
her life work of reclassifying and recataloging the Library,
so that it could be accomplished "in fifteen instead of thirty-
five years more." She delivered two addresses on cataloging
at the annual meeting of the American Library Association in
1929.[39] She was also mentioned in William Stetson Merrill's
Code for Classifiers in 1928 as having

> performed the task of rearranging the topics treated
> in the Code in classified order, a new arrangement
> that has so commended itself to the author that the
> present edition has been prepared along that line.[40]

The gifts presented at this time included a collection
of Christian Science literature made available through Mrs.
Stella Hadden Alexander and other students of Augusta E. Stetson,

who had come to New York in 1886 at Mrs. Eddy's request and
had, in 1891, established the New York City Christian Science
Institute. The books included some of the most rare early
editions of Science and Health and other works by Mrs. Eddy
as well as long runs of periodicals. Also received from the
New York Public Library was a large lot of theological pamphlets,
many of which were printed in England in the eighteenth century.
The Catholic University of America contributed a number of
theses, and the Historical Library of the American Young Men's
Christian Association gave about twenty-nine yards of material
on religion at this time. The offices of the Stated Clerk of
the Presbytery of New York, moreover, contributed the manuscript
record books of the defunct Presbyterian parishes on Manhattan
Island.[41]

Rockwell, on a trip to Europe at this time, secured
a copy of nearly every service book used by the Greek Orthodox
Church in the Orient and a similar set of works used by the
Armenians who recognized papal jurisdiction. He also bought,
upon returning to America, a lot of books dealing with the
catacombs and other archaeological subjects, collected during
twenty-three years in Rome by Walling Clark, head of the
Methodist work in that city. The rarest item in the lot was
the first volume of De Rossi's Bulletino di Archeologia
Cristiana.[42]

The endowment of the Library was increased this year
through the gift of $10,000 from Mrs. William Sloane, whose
husband had been President of the firm of W. J. Sloane, Inc.

He had also been a Trustee of the United States Trust Company, the Bank for Savings, and the Provident Loan Society.[43]

The effects of the Depression were felt keenly at the Seminary during this period. The budget was, for example, reduced by $117,798; library expenditures and faculty salaries were reduced by ten per cent.[44] The annual Alumni luncheon was cancelled,[45] as were conferences which had become traditional.[46]

The Emergency Employment Committee sent Professor Jacob Hamm Quiring, who for years had been Professor of Old Testament in the Mennonite College and Seminary at Bluffton, Ohio, to work in the Library. He was expert in Hebrew but unacquainted with library work and was, therefore, quite slow. Other clerical help was made available from the same source.[47]

Despite the economic difficulties of this era, some outstanding purchases were made in the academic year 1931-32. They included a set of about twelve volumes of bound Reformation pamphlets published in the sixteenth and seventeenth centuries; a number of items published before 1701, bought in England at the suggestion of Gillett; and the Monumenta Germaniae Historica. The set contained sources, written between 500 and 1500 A.D., for the Germanic peoples. Because a large percentage of mediaeval historians were priests or monks, the work contained a great deal of source material for the study of church history. The set had not been purchased previously because the cost had risen to $6,000; but with the Depression, Union was able to buy the copy owned by the bankrupt

Prince of Stolberg-Wernigerode for $2,300 plus transportation.
Most of the money for this acquisition came from income from
the McAlpin Foundation.[48]

The Library also received a number of books on the
Old Testament and on the teachings of Judaism from an Alumnus
of the class of 1877, Professor George Foot Moore of Harvard.
Upon his death, Union was given the first choice from the
library of this authority in the history of religion.[49]

Recognizing the strength of the Library and the collection of the Hymn Society in the field of hymnology, the
Library of Congress asked at this time for permission to
photostat approximately 10,000 cards, which covered the recataloged books in this field. The cards were sent to Washington, where photostatic copies were filed in the Union Catalogue
of Rare Books in American Libraries.[50]

The Library of Congress also sent the eminent bibliographer, Seymour de Ricci of Paris, to catalog the mediaeval
and sixteenth-century manuscripts of the Seminary. Their
titles were to be included in the Union Catalogue of Mediaeval
Manuscripts in the United States and Cadada, which was financed
by John D. Rockefeller, Jr. An interesting problem encountered
by Rockwell in assisting De Ricci had to do with the identifi-
cation of one of Union's records of a German convent begun in
the fifteenth and completed in the seventeenth century.
De Ricci asked Rockwell to discover the name and location of
the institution.[51]

Rockwell found that the manuscript was like a calendar covering the year, listing days on which the nuns should pray for the souls of various persons. The lists included many bishops of the ancient diocese of Halberstadt, which is northeast of the Hartz Mountains in Germany. Rockwell further discovered that only five of the convents in that diocese had survived the Reformation. Only two of these belonged to the Benedictine Order, which was indicated by the priority of the saints of that Order in the calendar. The number was, therefore, narrowed to two. The Union Librarian used a 200-year-old encyclopedia to conclude that the lost convent was that of Hadmersleben. He wrote a letter in German to a Catholic priest there and received a letter saying that this was the correct solution.[52]

The school year 1932-33 was the greatest in the history of the Seminary for the cataloging of its manuscripts, which by this time had reached a total of 865. One of the interesting examples of this type of literature purchased during the year was an ancient Syriac document, which Rockwell bought from a wholesale druggist in Brooklyn named Dr. Charles A. Rahayel for $100. The Union Librarian immediately consulted Professor Burkitt of the University of Cambridge, one of the foremost Orientalists of modern times, who expressed the opinion that the date in the manuscript was in error and that it should have been about 1200 A. D. He further thought that the document was the second half of a service book written by a Syriac scribe of the Jacobite sect.[53]

Rockwell also bought three Armenian manuscripts during these years from George Lamsa, a Syrian living in New York. Professor Robert Casey of the University of Cincinnati, a New Testament scholar educated at Harvard, who had specialized in the ancient languages of the Near East used by Christians, told Rockwell that one manuscript contained about two or three New Testament fragments, another contained a portion of the Gospels, and another was part of a liturgical psalter.[54]

Gifts during the year included a Latin missal printed at Mainz in 1497, in its original binding, from Frederick William Schaefer, a former student in the Seminary, who had subsequently lived in Zurich, Switzerland. The Swedenborg Foundation also presented a nearly complete set of facsimiles of the manuscripts of Emmanuel Swedenborg. The R. R. Bowker Company, as usual, contributed many review copies in the field of religion.[55]

Faculty Appointments

While acquiring these valuable bibliographical materials, the Seminary was fortunate also in the acquisition of a refugee professor, Paulus Johannes Tillich, who had refused to take an oath of submission to Hitler. He had, for this reason, been deposed from the Philosophical Chair at Frankfurt am Main.[56] His education was received at Berlin, Tübingen, Halle, and Breslau. He had been previously **Privatdozent** of Theology at Berlin, as well as Professor of Theology at Marburg, Dresden, and Leipzig. His books include The Religious Situation, The Interpretation of History, The Protestant Era, The Shaking

of the Foundations, Systematic Theology, The Courage to Be,
Love, Power and Justice, The New Being, Biblical Religion and
the Search for Ultimate Reality, Dynamics of Faith, Theology
of Culture, Christianity and the Encounter of the World Religions, and The Eternal Now.[57]

He was appointed in 1933 as a Lecturer on Philosophical
Theology at Union, with each professor contributing five per
cent of his own salary for the new man's salary. His name was
suggested to Union from a list of refugee professors sent to
Columbia University. He, in subsequent years, became one
of the most important figures in the field of religion. His
ideas have been widely circulated in intellectual circles outside orthodox Christianity. As a teacher, he was difficult
to follow because of his heavy German accent and his abstract
thought. Those who sought him for personal counseling, however,
report him to have been sympathetic and helpful. He forced
the students who took his courses to use the Library frequently;
and his recommendations for contemporary materials were often
scholarly, philosophical, and Continental. He relied not only
on theological authors but also on other scholars as he attempted
to bridge the gap between the ecclesiastical tradition and
secular society.

The thirties also saw the appointment of Cyril Richardson
to the department of church history. Born in London, he came
to this country in 1931. His education was received at the
University of Saskatchewan, Emmanuel College, Union, and
Göttingen. He was ordained to the ministry of the Protestant

Episcopal Church in 1934. His books include The Christianity
of Ignatius of Antioch, The Church through the Centuries,
The Sacrament of Reunion, The Eucharist in Zwingli and Cranmer,
and The Doctrine of the Trinity. He is the editor of The
Pocket Bible and Early Christian Fathers and has collaborated
in the preparation of The Church and Mental Health, The
Christology of the Later Fathers, and An Augustine Manual.[58]
He was one of the best friends of the Library on the Union
Faculty. His recommendations for retrospective and contemporary materials in the field of church history were
numerous. He, in addition, served as the archivist of the
school and was, in this position, responsible for the preservation of many of the school's records which might otherwise
have been destroyed.

Another appointee who came to Union shortly after
Richardson was John Knox, who had degrees from Randolph-Macon,
Emory, and Chicago. Ordained to the Methodist Church's min-
istry, he had served pastorates in Baltimore and Bethesda,
Maryland. He had also been Assistant Professor of Bible at
Emory, Minister of Fisk University, Managing Editor of
Christendom, an Editor of Christian Century, Associate Pro-
fessor of New Testament at Hartford Theological Seminary, and
Associate Professor of Homiletics and New Testament at Chicago.
At the age of 62, he was ordained to the ministry of the
Episcopal Church. His books include He Whom a Dream Hath
Possessed, Philemon Among the Letters of Paul, The Man Christ
Jesus, Marcion and the New Testament, Christ the Lord, The

Fourth Gospel and the Later Epistles, On the Meaning of Christ, Chapters in a Life of Paul, Criticism and Faith, The Early Church and the Coming Great Church, The Integrity of Preaching, Death of Christ, Jesus Lord and Christ, Christ and the Hope of Glory, The Ethic of Jesus in the Teaching of the Church, Life in Christ Jesus, and The Church and the Reality of Christ. He also has contributed to The Interpreter's Bible, The Interpreter's Dictionary of the Bible, and the Oxford Annotated Bible.[59] Although committed to the best literary and critical approach to the New Testament, his theology was definitely Christo-centric. He was one of the most highly appreciated members of the Faculty; and students were drawn to him, not only for his scholarship but also for his concern for their interests. He was an important instrument for the development of the collection in the field of New Testament. He, with other colleagues, insured that the best materials in this field were added to the Library.

One of these persons who abetted him in the task was Frederick Grant, whose education was received at Lawrence College, Nashotah House, General Theological Seminary, and Western Theological Seminary. He was President of Seabury-Western Theological Seminary from 1927-38 and was called from this post to New York. He was a member of the General Convention of the Protestant Episcopal Church, a member of the Committee on Marriage and Divorce, a member of the Committee on the Constitution and Canons of the Protestant Episcopal Church, Chairman of the Committee on Christian Education of

the Diocese of Chicago, Vice-President of the American Association of Theological Schools, a member of the Committee on the
revision of the American Standard Revised Version of the Bible,
a member of the Versions Committee of the American Bible So-
ciety, and one of three observers of the Anglican Communion
at the Vatican Council. His books include An Introduction to
New Testament Thought, Hellenistic Religions, How to Read the
Bible, Ancient Roman Religion, The Gospels, Their Origin and
Growth, Ancient Judaism and the New Testament, Basic Christian
Beliefs, Translating the Bible, Roman Hellenism and the New
Testament, and Dictionary of the Bible. He was Editor-in-
Chief of the Anglican Theological Review for thirty years.[60]

Grant was an extremely tolerant and friendly professor.
His lectures always reflected depth in scholarship and kind-
ness toward those who differed with him. He literally loved
to study and assumed that students shared this affection. He
was in his retirement a frequent visitor to the Library,
which he helped to build through his numerous recommendations
for materials in the field of New Testament.

An appointee to the Old Testament department was
Samuel Lucien Terrien, who had studied at the Sorbonne, Ecole
du Louvre, Ecole Francaise de Jerusalem, and Union. He came
to New York from the College of Wooster, where he had been an
instructor. His books include The Psalms and Their Meaning
for Today, Introduction and Exegesis of Job, Job: Poet
of Existence, Lands of the Bible, and LeLivre de Job.
He also contributed to the Interpreter's Bible and the

Interpreter's Dictionary of the Bible.[61] One of the leading
interpreters of the Book of Job, he was engaged in a literary
dialogue which attracted national attention in religious
circles at the time that Archibald McLeish's J. B. was
appearing on Broadway. As a prominent Old Testament scholar,
he made numerous recommendations for contemporary materials
in his field.

Developments of the Late Thirties

The outstanding cash gift to the Library during the
era was a legacy of the late David Hunter McAlpin, the son of
the man for whom the Collection was named, in the amount of
$5,000 additional for the McAlpin Foundation.[62] The son had
graduated from Princeton and Bellevue Medical College, prac-
ticing medicine in New York until 1901, when his father died.
He abandoned a promising medical career at this time and with
his brothers managed his father's estate.[63]

The gift meant about $175 more income for the school,
making the total yield of the McAlpin monies $3,675. The funds
were to be used for additions to the McAlpin Collection and
also binding and repair of books in other sections of the
Library. Gillett continued to select the books for the Collection,[64] which was not used as much as before, because of the
Depression. Scholars had ordinarily come to New York to use
the McAlpin materials, and the times made such visits impossible
for many.[65]

Other gifts during 1934-35 included hundreds of manuscript sermons of the Reverend Jonas Coe, who died in 1822

while serving as Pastor of the First Presbyterian Church in Troy, New York. These were contributed by Professor William Adams Brown. The remnant of the library of Francis Brown was also given by his widow.[66]

An acquisition problem at the time was associated with the high price of the franc and the mark. German continuations were becoming unusually expensive, with the price of the mark going from twenty-four cents to over forty cents in a brief period. More theological books were written in German than in any other language besides English, and the reduction of these subscriptions was serious in a theological collection which attempted to be global in scope.[67]

Lucy W. Markley, classifier of books on religion at the University of Chicago, came to the staff during this era as Assistant Librarian. It was planned that she would relieve Rockwell of detailed administration in order that he could devote more time to disposing of duplicates which had been accumulating for thirty years.[68] She had Bachelor of Divinity and Doctor of Philosophy degrees from Chicago.[69]

The Contribution of Julia Pettee

Lucy Markley was also appointed to replace Julia Pettee, who planned to retire on June 30, 1939. Miss Pettee supervised the reclassification of approximately 165,000 books during her thirty years at the school. The Library, with the exception of "books printed before 1701 in the McAlpin Collection, the periodicals, many pamphlets, and some remnants" were rearranged by the new classification schedules during her tenure. The remnants included "about half of the section of Christian literature, a group of sermons and a large section of practical piety, hortatory and devotional literature, and some Americana."[70]

When she came to Union, the Library was arranged by the fixed location system, with a catalog consisting of many different alphabetical files, "except for the author list, useless for any purpose but check lists for the Librarian." Gillett had prepared, in addition, a classed catalog for the collection; and this became one basis for the Union Classification Scheme developed by Miss Pettee.[71]

Her main task was to provide a classification scheme and to classify the books in the Library by this system. She, therefore, had resisted pressure to suspend this work of reclassifying in order to catalog gifts. When she retired, many of the pamphlets from the McAlpin Collection, the Frederick Ferris Thompson Collection, and many other gifts remained to be cataloged. She, however, had finished the scheme and established the lines upon which the dictionary catalog was to be continued. She retired with the satisfaction of seeing the Library in a classified order and the dictionary catalog nearly completed. About Rockwell, who called her to Union, she wrote:

> He found me at Rochester and has always held before me a fine vision of the potential greatness of the Seminary library and high professional ideals of its administration.[72]

Her contribution was expanded through the published classification scheme, which has helped the system to become

one of the most widely used in seminary libraries. A preliminary classification scheme had been published in mimeographed form in 1924, but the work was greatly enlarged and
revised in 1939. She was assisted in this latter venture,
not only by her subordinates but also by Professors Bewer,
Hume, and Frame,[73] as well as Professor Alexander Marx of the
Jewish Theological Seminary and Joshua Block of the New York
Public Library.[74]

The new edition of the scheme was immediately reviewed
by several library journals. Colman J. Farrell of St. Benedict's
College, writing in Catholic Library World, lauded it for its
liberal annotations of schedules for individual authors of
early Christian literature. He also thought her schedules for
Reformation and post-Reformation non-Catholic authors were
superior to those of the Library of Congress schedules. He
said that "The treatment of the Catholic Church is generous,
fair, and understanding."[75]

Maurice Tauber, in writing for The Library Quarterly,
predicted that the scheme would have some effect upon the
"procedures of classifiers and catalogers in all libraries
having theological collections." This was true in part because
Pettee's scheme had some lists, such as the "Post-apostolic
Greek and Latin fathers" and the tables for "Hymnology," not
available elsewhere. Tauber criticized the work for "minor
errors, such as misspelled words, unsatisfactory translitera-
tions, and inconsistencies in typographical steup," yet recognized that the scheme was a well-done and useful piece of work.[76]

The published system has numerous definitions, scope notes, and "see" references. It, like many other such schemes, has a general class group at the beginning, form divisions, and supplementary tables. The latter includes those for countries, states, denominations, societies, institutions, and individual authors. The brief notation is mixed, with the figures being read decimally. The work is concluded with a relative index.

Miss Pettee retired at this time; and after a brief interlude as a consultant and classifier of religion at Yale, she moved to Mayflower Farm, Salisbury, Connecticut. Her early published works include an essay, "A Problem in Social Economy" in the Vassar _Miscellany_. The _Library Journal_ has published such articles as "Dissertations and Program Literature," "Book Marking with Tools," "Graded Catalogs," "A Projected Information Bureau of Cromwell's Time," "Wanted—Catalogers," "Factors in Determining Subject Headings," "Code Revision—What Do Catalogers Want?," and "The Development of Authorship Rules as Found in the Anglo-American Code." She is best known, however, for her books on Union's classification scheme and subject headings.

The scheme was published in the fall of 1939; and, at the same time, a partnership was worked out between Union and Auburn Theological Seminary. The latter school had been begun in Auburn, New York eighteen years before the New-York Theological Seminary had been started. Auburn's enrollment was low and its financial resources were limited. When the retirement of several professors at Auburn was announced, representatives of the school came to New York to seek association with Union. The plan which was developed attempted to protect the continuance of both Boards. The only two professors left at Auburn, Robert Hastings Nichols and Walter S. Davison, were appointed to posts in New York.[77]

One of Nichols' students wrote of him:

He was respected as a fine scholar and a splendid teacher. His course in American Church History was well received and he was recognized as one of the great authorities in that field of study. He taught a seminar on the Creeds of Christendom, and students agreed that it was the most helpful course taught on the meaning of the Protestant faith. He was a tireless champion of the liberal tradition. . . .[78]

Another student wrote of Davison:

He not only knew his students while they were at Union, but ten years later could call them by name. His personal interest has helped many a student in the interpretation of Scripture, in prayer and in the devotional life. He has been beloved a teacher, counsellor and friend.[79]

Nichols' recommendations for materials in the field of Church History reflected his interest in liberal Protestantism. Contemporary books on the history of that branch of Christendom were, therefore, in abundance at Union during this era. Davison's nominations for Library materials were more irenic and were related to his interest in the parish ministry.

Approximately 14,000 books were brought from Auburn to Union, where they were absorbed into the Library. Auburn was given the responsibility for the Lending Library for Alumni, which had been established earlier at Union.[80]

Although Rockwell was technically the Librarian, Lucy
Markley increasingly assumed the responsibility of the office
during these years. One of the things this first woman director accomplished was to solve a problem which had plagued the
male librarians for decades. This was brought about through
a vote of the Directors to appropriate one-third of the income
from certain special funds to provide cataloging expenses.
Thus, for the first time, a reasonable amount of unrestricted
book money was available. As usual, about half of the acquisitions were in the form of gifts, with the largest donations
in 1939-40 coming from faculty members, Columbia University,
the R. R. Bowker Company, and the New York Times, the latter
two contributing review copies of new books.[81]

The End of an Era

Rockwell announced at this time that he would retire
from the Faculty, of which he had been a member for thirty-
four years.[82] He was replaced by Lucy Markley, who was, in
turn, replaced as head of the catalog department by Ruth C.
Eisenhart. The new cataloger had been on the staff of Yale
University Library from 1932 to 1940 and had been at Union
for two years before her appointment as head of the department.[83]

Downs, in his book, Resources of New York City
Libraries, wrote that the collection contained at this time
such rarities as an early Bamberg edition of the Babylonian
Talmud published in Venice in 1520-29 and the first edition
of the Jerusalem Talmud. He went on to note that Union had
"all the great polyglots." Other unusual Bibles included

fifty-five Hebrew Bibles printed before 1801, 115 Latin Bibles printed from the fifteenth to the eighteenth centuries, the "Great Bible" of 1641, and the first printing of the first edition of the King James version.[84]

Outstanding patristics included many Benedictine editions of the Fathers, Migne's Patrologiae, the Berlin Corpus and the Vienna Corpus; and the Texte und Untersuchungen zur Geschichte der Altchristlichen Literatur was present, as were special collections on the Gospel of Peter and works by and about John Chryostom, Tertullian, Augustine of Hippo, and Jerome. Another area of unusual strength was said to be the works written for sixteenth and seventeenth century French Huguenots. Another unusual collection was that of church law, including, for example, Catholic periodicals, works by Italian canonists of the fifteenth and sixteenth centuries, textbooks on canon law, church council collections, papal documents, and Protestant legal materials.[85]

A work purchased during the year was a manuscript of the Gospels in Greek, which was bought from Vassilios Iatropoulous of New York, who had purchased it in Moscow. This was the description of the work:

> Pap., 259 ff., 24 x 18 cm. Written in Italy, mid 14th c.,; on Italian paper, with watermarks indicating a date in the 1340's. 4 headpieces, 1 tailpiece, initials; 1 drawing of an initial on facing page. Bound in 17th [?]& c. calf, tooled and gilt, with panel stamp on back cover.[86]

President Coffin wrote of Rockwell, who retired at this time:

269

He startled and amused the Board of Directors by
telling them that the growth of the Library neces-
sitated much more room for the stacks, and suggested
that the entire dormitory (Hastings Hall) be emptied
of students and turned into shelves for books. He
added many valuable volumes to our collection by his
constant watch over sales abroad and by frequent
trips to see for himself what was being offered for
sale. The wars and the consequent poverty brought
important collections on the market, and he had his
eye out for purchases which we needed to complete
our possessions in various subjects. His colleagues
kept pressing him for current publications; but his
major interest was in books already standard.[87]

Although he was no longer Librarian, his interest in

the collection continued during his residence in New York.

He was of assistance in many ways to two succeeding Librarians

until his death in 1958.[88]

FOOTNOTES

[1]Minutes of the Board of Directors of Union Theological Seminary in the City of New York, April 20, 1926.

[2]Reinhold Niebuhr, This Ministry: The Contribution of Henry Sloane Coffin (New York: Charles Scribner's Sons, 1954), p. 103.

[3]Morgan Phelps Noyes, "The Contribution of Henry Sloane Coffin," in Henry Sloane Coffin, A Half Century of Union Theological Seminary, 1896-1945, An Informal History (New York: Charles Scribner's Sons, 1954), pp. 114-30.

[4]Ibid., pp. 114-15.

[5]Ibid., pp. 158-61.

[6]Ibid., pp. 161-62.

[7]Who's Who in America, 1964-65, XXXIII (Chicago: Marquis-Who's Who, 1964), pp. 2055-56.

[8]Ibid., p. 1484.

[9]Ibid., p. 153.

[10]Ibid., p. 904.

[11]Union Theological Seminary. Library, Report in Alumni Bulletin of the Union Theological Seminary, I (June-July, 1926), p. 154.

[12]Leaders in Education, 3d ed. (Lancaster, Pennsylvania: The Sciences Press, 1948), p. 486.

[13]Seymour De Ricci and W. J. Wilson, Census of Medieval and Renaissance Manuscripts in the United States and Canada, II (New York: Kraus Reprint Corporation, 1961), pp. 1648-49.

[14]Union Theological Seminary. Library, Report in Alumni Bulletin, II (October-November, 1927), p. 184.

[15]Ibid.

[16]Ibid., p. 186.

[17]Ibid.

271

[18] Union Theological Seminary. Library, _Catalogue of the McAlpin Collection of British History and Theology_, I, compiled and edited by Charles Ripley Gillett (New York: Union Theological Seminary, 1927), p. vi.

[19] _Ibid._, p. vii.

[20] _Ibid._, pp. viii-ix.

[21] _Ibid._, p. xi.

[22] Union Theological Seminary. Library, Report in _Alumni Bulletin_, II (June-July, 1928), p. 167.

[23] _Ibid._, p. 168.

[24] _Ibid._, p. 169.

[25] "Ballard, Edward Lathrop," _Who Was Who in America_, I (Chicago: The A. N. Marquis Company, 1942), p. 52.

[26] Union Theological Seminary. Library, Report in _Alumni Bulletin_, II (June-July, 1928), p. 169.

[27] _Ibid._

[28] Union Theological Seminary, Catalogue, 1929-30 (New York: Union Theological Seminary, 1929), p. 22.

[29] Directors, _op. cit._, March 12, 1929.

[30] Frank W. Price, "Specialized Research Libraries in Missions," _Library Trends_, IX (October, 1960), pp. 176-77.

[31] Missionary Research Library, _Occasional Bulletin_, VI (December 6, 1955), p. 9.

[32] Coming: A Missionary Library," _Alumni Bulletin of the Union Theological Seminary_, IV (February-March, 1929), p. 73.

[33] Union Theological Seminary, _Catalogue_, 1929-30, pp. 23-24.

[34] Directors, _op. cit._, January 8, 1929.

[35] Union Theological Seminary. Library, Report, 1963, p. 10.

[36] Directors, _op. cit._, March 12, 1929.

[37] Union Theological Seminary. Library, Report in _Alumni Bulletin_, IV (June-July, 1929), p. 177.

[38]Ibid., p. 178.

[39]Ibid., p. 179.

[40]William Stetson Merrill, Code for Classifiers (Chicago: American Library Association, 1928), pp. vii-viii.

[41]Ibid., pp. 181-82.

[42]Ibid., p. 182.

[43]"Sloane, William," Who Was Who in America, I (Chicago: The A. N. Marquis Company, 1942), p. 1134.

[44]Directors, op. cit., May 13, 1932.

[45]Directors, op. cit., March 8, 1932.

[46]Ibid., November 15, 1932.

[47]Union Theological Seminary. Library, Report, May 17, 1932, pp. 1-2.

[48]Ibid., pp. 4-5.

[49]Ibid., p. 5.

[50]Ibid.

[51]Union Theological Seminary. Library, Report, May 23, 1933, p. 6.

[52]Ibid.

[53]Ibid., pp. 6-7.

[54]Ibid., p. 9.

[55]Ibid., p. 8.

[56]Coffin, op. cit., pp. 135-37.

[57]Who's Who in America, 1964-65, p. 2012.

[58]Ibid., p. 1675.

[59]Ibid., p. 1119.

[60]Ibid., p. 777.

[61]Ibid., p. 1992.

[62]Union Theological Seminary. Library, Report, May 22, 1935, p. 2.

273

[63]"McAlpin, David Hunter," The National Cyclopaedia of American Biography, XXXIII (New York: James T. White & Company, 1947), p. 305.

[64]Union Theological Seminary, Library, Report, May 22, 1935, p. 2.

[65]Ibid., May 23, 1933, p. 12.

[66]Ibid., May 22, 1935, p. 2.

[67]Ibid., p. 3.

[68]Ibid., 1939.

[69]C. C. Williamson and Alice L. Jewett, eds., Who's Who in Library Service (New York: The H. W. Wilson Company, 1933), p. 290.

[70]Union Theological Seminary. Library, Report, 1939, p. 1.

[71]Ibid., pp. 3-4.

[72]Ibid., pp. 5-6.

[73]Ibid., pp. 1-2.

[74]Union Theological Seminary. Library, Classification of the Library of Union Theological Seminary in the City of New York (New York: Union Theological Seminary, 1939), p. v.

[75]Colman J. Farrell, "Classification of the Library of the Union Theological Seminary in the City of New York," Catholic Library World, XI (February, 1940), p. 155.

[76]Maurice F. Tauber, "Classification of the Library of UTS in the City of New York," The Library Quarterly, X (July, 1940), pp. 428-29.

[77]Coffin, op. cit., pp. 166-68.

[78]Ibid., p. 168.

[79]Ibid., p. 169.

[80]Ibid., p. 168.

[81]Union Theological Seminary. Library, Report, April 30, 1940, pp. 1-2.

[82]New York Times, March 7, 1942. 14:3.

274

[83]Union Theological Seminary. Library, Report, June 30, 1942, pp. 7-8.

[84]Robert Bingham Downs, Resources of New York City Libraries (Chicago: American Library Association, 1942), pp. 224-29.

[85]Ibid., pp. 229-32.

[86]Seymour de Dicci, Supplement to the Census of Medieval and Renaissance Manuscripts in the U. S. and Canada, originated by C. U. Faye, continued and edited by W. H. Bond (New York: The Bibliographical Society of America, 1962), p. 386.

[87]Coffin, op. cit., pp. 52-53.

[88]Union Theological Seminary. Library, Report, 1958, p. 13.

Chapter IX

THE LIBRARIANSHIP OF LUCY
WHITNEY MARKLEY, 1942-51

World War II Years

The administration of Lucy Whitney Markley, who
succeeded William Walker Rockwell as Librarian in 1942, began
with the nation engaged in a global war. One of the first
projects of her librarianship was that of packing early manuscripts and printed books, including the McAlpin Collection,
in cartons for storage. This hindered the research use of
the materials but was deemed to be a necessity because of the
War.[1]

The most important gift of her first year was an
ornamented Indic manuscript given by Robert E. Hume, on his
retirement. The work was written in Lao with characters on
palm leaves. Purchases during the year included Hume's library,
nearly 700 numbers of Methodist conference minutes bought from
the Methodist Historical Society, and many publications of the
Oriental Institute at the University of Chicago. A new insurance program was adopted at the close of her first year, and
at this time the cash valuations of various parts of the collection were said to be:

Manuscripts kept in the vault		¢ 2,500
Incunabula		10,000
16th century imprints, not a part of any special collection		15,000
17th century imprints, not a part of any special collection		12,000
Thompson Collection		10,000
Americana		3,000
McAlpin Collection		60,000
Special Sets:		
Mansi, Sacrorum Conciliorum	$ 1,000	
Migne, Patrologiae, Series Graeca, and Series Latina	2,000	
Acta Sanctorum	1,000	
Ugolino, Thesaurus Antiquitatum	500	
Monumenta Germaniae Historica	2,500	
British Museum, Catalogue of Printed Books (2 editions)	2,500	
Bibliothèque Nationale, Catalogue Général	1,000	
		10,500
Remainder of the collection (approximately 250,000 items)		300,000 [2]

A significant gift of this era was 3,500 books from
the office of William Adams Brown, which were to form an open
shelf collection in the doctrinal and philosophical field and
in ecumenics. The theological and philosophical books were
said to represent his interest during most of his life and
those on ecumenics the new interest of his later years.[3] It
was planned to expand this William Adams Brown Ecumenical
Library, and the responsibility for the development of this
collection was given to the Curator and the Librarian of the
Missionary Research Library.[4]

Another gift came from the Yale University Press,
which, upon the retirement of President Coffin, gave many books
with Yale imprints. Union faculty members selected 124 volumes
from this source; the gifts included Babylonian studies, history, literature, and linguistic studies.[5]

The end of World War II at this time made it possible to make available the rare books which had been stored, and those who used them began to resume their studies. The Columbia Libraries borrowed, for example, 300 items from the McAlpin Collection for an exhibit in recognition of the ter-centenary of the publication of Milton's Areopagitica. The Cologne Missal of 1520 was also borrowed by the Cloisters for their Easter exhibition. The total use of the principal special collections for the year was:

Collection	Items Used
McAlpin	793
America	14
Early Continental Imprints	105
Frederick Ferris Thompson	8 [6]

A new appointee to the Faculty at this time was John T. McNeill, who came from a post as Professor of European Christianity at Chicago. He had studied at McGill University, Westminster Hall in Vancouver, and Chicago, the latter of which had awarded to him the Ph.D. degree. His published books at the time of his appointment included Unitive Prot-estantism, Makers of Christianity, Christian Hope for World Society, and Medieval Handbooks of Penance.[7] His coming to the Faculty was fortunate for the Library because of his many recommendations for materials in the field of church history. One of America's foremost church historians, he was responsible for the addition of many retrospective items to the collection as well as the acquisition of the better materials which were being produced during his period of service to Union.

Soon after, Paul Scherer came to the Faculty from the pastorate of the Holy Trinity Lutheran Church in New York. He had been educated at the College of Charleston and Lutheran Theological Seminary in Mt. Airy, Philadelphia. The first part of his career had been spent as an Instructor in the latter seminary. He was appointed at Union as Brown Professor of Homiletics and helped to improve the preaching ability of many young theological students during his fourteen years of service. He served for part of that time as an associate editor of The Interpreter's Bible; and his books include When God Hides, Facts That Undergird Life, The Place Where Thou Standest, For We Have This Treasure, Event in Eternity, and Love Is a Spendthrift.[8] Scherer was one of America's greatest preachers and yet was extremely patient in teaching neophytes the principles of homiletics. Always a highly literate man, he insisted that his students read current novels and drama in addition to sermons as they attempted to communicate the Christian message. He was, therefore, partially responsible for the acquisition of large quantities of secular material in the Library as well as the most current literature in the field of homiletics.

Another new man was James Muilenberg, who had degrees from Hope College, Nebraska, and Yale. He had previously been an Instructor in English at Nebraska and Yale, an Associate Professor of Biblical Literature at Mt. Holyoke, the Dean of the College of Arts and Science at the University of Maine, and a Professor of Old Testament Literature and Semitic

Languages at Pacific School of Religion. He held memberships
in the American Schools of Oriental Research, the Society of
Biblical Literature and Exegesis, the American Oriental
Society, the National Association of Biblical Instructors,
the National Council of Religion in Higher Education, and Phi
Beta Kappa. He was the author of <u>The Literary Relations of
the Teaching of the Twelve Apostles and the Epistle of
Barnabas</u>, <u>History of Religion of Israel</u>, and a monograph
dealing with the beginning of the Revolution of 1688. He
also contributed to <u>Excavations of Tell-en-Nasbeh</u> and the
<u>Interpreter's Bible</u>.[9]

He was an exciting lecturer who was responsible for
sending generations of students flocking to the Library for
materials for term papers and theses. He became so engrossed
in his subject that his lectures, which represented the
finest in Biblical scholarship, became almost dramatic
productions. A thorough student himself, he, with Terrien,
insisted that the Library keep its materials current in this
important area of theological education.

Post-War Developments

The end of the War brought a boon to the Library.
This came about through the efforts of the Library of Congress,
in cooperation with the Department of State and the Armed
Forces, in acquiring and bringing to the United States copies
of every war-time publication of any value, which they had
been able to get without theft, from western European countries.
Many university and large college libraries, as well as the
principal public and special libraries, indicated their areas

of interest and agreed to buy the materials which would be
sent to them in these fields, paying the fee of $1.00 per
item.[10]

The Union Library was the only seminary library to
take part in this program, obtaining first priority thereby
in materials on Protestant and Orthodox Christianity and non-
Christian religions. The Catholic University of America had
first priority on Catholic materials, but Union had second
choice on these materials. The program provided that the
Library of Congress should take the materials which were wanted
for its own collection before any other priorities were established. The sum of $2,160 was deposited by Union with the
Library of Congress, and books began to arrive immediately.
The funds were taken from reserve accounts which had been
planned for post-war buying of European materials.[11]

The Library was also strengthened at this time through
substantial acquisitions from the libraries of James Moffatt,
Harry Emerson Fosdick, and Charles Jefferson, one of New York's
leading pastors. Approximately 2,600 volumes, for example,
were selected from the latter's library.[12]

An interesting purchase during this post-war era was
a manuscript, which was acquired from Dawsons of London in
1947. It was described thus:

Nicolaus de Lyra: Postilla in Danielem (ff. 1-38)
--Johannes Gallensis: Postilla in Apocalypsim
(ff. 39-107).
   Vel., 107 ff., 25 x 19 cm. Written in France
(Paris?), after 1328. 6 grotesque drawings in
margins. Bound in heavy boards, repaired.[13]

A second edition of a <u>List of Theological Subject</u>
<u>Headings and Corporate Church Names Based upon the Headings</u>
<u>in the Catalogue of the Library of Union Theological Seminary</u>
was published at this time. A tentative list had been published
in mimeographed form by the Seminary. The preliminary list
had been revised as reclassification had progressed at Union,
where a card file of subject headings was kept. The new edition incorporated the Library of Congress subject headings in
theology in order to make it more useful to large libraries.[14]

The variations were brought about through such means
as adaptations for use in a special theological collection,
those which were adventitious, and those created before the
Library of Congress subheadings had become widely adopted.
The Appendix, with its list of official names for denominational
bodies with brief descriptive notes, has proven useful to catalogers, for whom the work was designed.[15]

Union decided a year later to withdraw from the Library
of Congress Cooperative Acquisitions Project, through which
it had been buying war-time publications from Europe. Although
the program had resulted in the school's acquiring some interesting materials, they were not deemed to be important enough
to justify their purchase price plus the processing costs.
The Project was succeeded by the Farmington Plan; and Union
was in this program from the beginning, taking all Protestant
works. Catholic University agreed to buy the Catholic works,
and the University of Chicago became responsible for non-
Christian religious material.[16]

The most important purchase in the field of sacred
music for the year was the photolithographic reissue of the
works of Bach in forty-six folio volumes. Half of the funds
for this came from an appeal to friends of the School of Sacred
Music, and half came from regular book funds. It was the most
important purchase in the field in many years.[17]

The last of the war reserve money was used at this
time to buy the library of the late Pastor Weiss of the Protestant Church in Paris. The collection was especially strong
on French Calvinism and the Protestant churches of France.
Only about one out of four items purchased proved to be duplicates; the Library added, therefore, nearly 900 volumes from
this source.[18]

The school budgeted $1,000 for purchases in the first
full year of cooperation with the Farmington Plan at this time,
but only $448.86 were spent. Current publications were re-
ceived from Sweden, Switzerland and France during this year,
but the procedures for securing the books were found to be
slow. Six more countries were added in 1949; yet the receipts
were far below early expectations, for the school only acquired
240 items in this way during the year.[19]

The development of the Library was, as always, depend-
ent upon the interests of the Faculty; and some of the more
influential members of that body had become by this period
interested in the ecumenical theology springing from Europe
as a result of the Barthian revolt. Bennett and Van Dusen
bought heavily, for example, from the writings of Aulen, Barth,

Brunner, and Visser 't Hooft. Niebuhr's recommendations were
for scholarly works on social, economic and political lines,
with little emphasis on "light and readable" works. Bennett's
recommendations were strongly oriented toward political matters
and Continental theology.[20]

Lucy Markley left Union during this era and joined
the staff of Garrett Biblical Institute at Evanston, Illinois.
The appointment of Robert Fullerton Beach of Garrett as her
replacement was announced in the New York Times on April 12,
1951.[21]

FOOTNOTES

[1]R. H. Nichols, "The Library," <u>Alumni Bulletin</u>, XVIII (April, 1943), p. 6.

[2]Union Theological Seminary. Library, Report, 1943, pp. 2-4.

[3]<u>Ibid</u>., 1944, p. 9.

[4]Union Theological Seminary, <u>Catalogue, 1945-46</u> (New York: Union Theological Seminary, 1945), pp. 31-32.

[5]Union Theological Seminary. Library, Report, 1945, p. 9.

[6]<u>Ibid</u>.

[7]J. W. Schwarz, ed., <u>Religious Leaders of America</u>, II, 1941-42 (New York: 277 Broadway, 1942), p. 774.

[8]<u>Who's Who in America</u>, 1964-65, XXXIII (Chicago: Marquis-Who's Who, 1964), p. 1768.

[9]<u>Ibid</u>., p. 1445.

[10]Union Theological Seminary. Library, Report, 1946, p. 5.

[11]<u>Ibid</u>.

[12]<u>Ibid</u>., p. 6.

[13]Seymour de Ricci, <u>Supplement to the Census of Medieval and Renaissance Manuscripts in the U. S. and Canada</u>, originated by C. U. Faye, continued and edited by W. H. Bond (New York: The Bibliographical Society of America, 1962), p. 386.

[14]Julia Pettee, <u>List of Theological Subject Headings and Corporate Church Names Based upon the Headings in the Catalogue of the Library of Union Theological Seminary, New York City</u>, 2d ed. (Chicago: American Library Association, 1947).

[15]<u>Ibid</u>.

[16] Union Theological Seminary. Library, Report, 1948, p. 3.

[17] Ibid., p. 5.

[18] Ibid., 1949, p. 3.

[19] Ibid.

[20] Ibid.

[21] New York Times, April 12, 1951, 35:7.

Chapter X

THE LIBRARIANSHIP OF ROBERT
FULLERTON BEACH, 1951-74

The Pre-Union Background of Beach

Robert Fullerton Beach was born in Brooklyn on July 14, 1911. He was educated at Wesleyan University and the School of Library Service of Columbia. He was awarded the Bachelor of Library Science and the Master of Library Science degrees from the latter school. He was a reference and circulation assistant at the Yale University Library from 1933 to 1936 and was on the staff of Berea College Library from 1936 to 1943. He was the Librarian of Garrett Biblical Institute from 1946 to 1951.[1]

Beach was a tall, affable man who combined scholarship with a personal interest in the patrons of the Library. He endeared himself to students through his concern for meeting their bibliographical needs as well as through his continuing interest in their careers beyond their Seminary years. He was a highly respected member of the Faculty, where he held the rank of associate professor.

Developments of the 1950's

Two major building projects were underway at the time Beach was appointed. The first was an audio-visual center

with equipment and facilities which were unsurpassed in any
theological seminary. This addition was opened on October 22,
1951 and was part of a five-story structure in the quadrangle
known as Auburn Hall. Facilities in this building included
lecture rooms, studios, preaching rooms, and a radio control
room.[2]

Another project begun at this time was an expansion of
the School of Sacred Music through a grant of $200,000 from
the James Foundation, established in 1941 through the will of
Authur Curtiss James. The plans included the remodeling and
finishing of James Memorial Chapel Tower, organ and piano
practice rooms, a studio, and library space.[3]

Gifts to the Library during this early portion of
Beach's administration included an unusual missal published
in Cologne in 1644, given by a priest at the neighboring Corpus
Christi Catholic Church. Another gift was a Nekcsei-Lipcz
Bible from the Library of Congress. This was a copy of a
fourteenth century manuscript from Hungary which had hand
illuminations in bright colors.[4]

Another contribution received at the school was a be-
quest of $250,000 from Mrs. Thomas W. Lamont.[5] This was in
addition to another gift of $50,000 which had been made a few
years earlier at the time of the death of Mr. Lamont, Chairman
of the Board of J. P. Morgan & Company. He had left $9,535,000
for charitable and educational purposes, including $5,000,000
to Harvard College.[6]

An important purchase during the period was a seven-volume reference work by Ernst Bücken entitled <u>Handbuch der Musikwissenschaft</u>.[7] This was an important addition for the use of the School of Sacred Music. The Library of this School by this time included about 1,800 books and pamphlets belonging to the Hymn Society; and, in addition, approximately 4,000 volumes in the main collection had to do with music. The School also had a collection of approximately 800 anthems and large choral works. The classes of 1951 and 1952 contributed records for the beginning of a recorded sacred music collection for use in the new audio-visual center.[8]

The new facilities for the School in James Memorial Chapel Tower were finished at this time. Part of the space provided was designated for a library room for housing the Alumni repertory collection and reference materials.[9]

The Library received at this time a large number of books from the estate of Professor David E. Roberts,[10] who had died at the age of forty-four. Educated at Occidental College and Union, he had been the Traveling Fellow of the class of 1934 and had in this capacity spent a year in Europe. He had returned to Union as a teacher of philosophy of religion and systematic theology and had become, in 1940, the Dean of Students, in which office he remained until 1946, when he began to teach on a full-time basis again. He was a member of the American Philosophical Association and the American Theological Society, Chairman of the Board of Protestant Student Work from 1936 to 1940, a member of the Board of Managers of

the Intercollegiate Branch of the Young Men's Christian
Association from 1944 to 1950, the Chairman of the Westminster
Foundation at Columbia from 1946 to 1950, and a member of the
Commission of Religion and Health of the National Council of
Churches from 1947 until his death.[11]

He was one of the most personable members of the Union
Faculty. A scholar who recommended many contemporary titles
in his fields for purchase in the Library, he was also extremely
cordial in his relationships with students, many of whom were
entertained in his apartment. He also took a keen interest
in the field of psychiatry and religion. A David E. Roberts
Memorial Book Fund was established upon his death, therefore,
to buy books in this area in honor of this man who had spoken
meaningfully to many readers through his book, Psychotherapy
and the Christian View of Man.

The Seminary had developed excellent financial resources
by this time; and many developments were made possible because
of this improved condition. The endowment stood, for example,
at $9,000,000, which was more than twice the amount available
for any other seminary in the nation. The budget for 1953-54
was $1,039,222.[12] Additional income was provided through a
gift of $525,000 from the Rockefeller Foundation to educate
young religious leaders from various parts of the world,
twenty-seven of whom were to be invited each year to study at
Union. Adherents of every religion were to be eligible for
the grants made possible through this fund.[13]

Another Rockefeller grant in the amount of $10,375,000 was given to six interdenominational seminaries and the American Association of Theological Schools. Union's share was an outright gift of $1,000,000 for endowment plus $500,000 payable on the basis of each dollar for every dollar raised for capital needs, which were estimated to be $6,125,000.[14]

The improved financial structure made possible the bringing of some of the leading scholars from various parts of the world to the Faculty during the late 1940's and the 1950's. Many young professors were added as well as seasoned teachers whose publications were widely accepted as authoritative.

Among the latter was Lewis Joseph Sherrill, a graduate of Austin College, Presbyterian Theological Seminary in Louisville, and Yale, from which he received the doctorate. He was a member of the southern branch of the Presbyterian Church. His books include The Rise of Christian Education, Guilt and Redemption, The Struggle of the Soul, and The Gift of Power. During an era when religious education had accepted almost in entirety the philosophical presuppositions of John Dewey, Sherrill was one of the pioneers in restoring a theological basis for the field. His recommendations for the Library, therefore, included not only books on methodology but also doctrinal literature which he felt was pertinent to the subject.

A returnee to the Faculty was Mary Ely Lyman, who had degrees from Mount Holyoke, Union, and Chicago. She was the

widow of Professor Eugene W. Lyman of the Union Faculty. She
had, before her return to Union, been a teacher in the Rockville,
Connecticut High School, the Y. W. C. A. General Secretary
at Mount Holyoke College, the Frederick Weyerhaueser Professor
of Religion at Vassar, a Lecturer in English Bible at Union,
an Associate in Religion at Barnard College and Columbia, the
Dean and Professor of Religion at Sweet Briar, and a Visiting
Lecturer at the American School of Oriental Research in
Jerusalem. She was a member of the National Association of
Biblical Instructors, serving as President in 1945; the Society
of Biblical Literature and Exegesis; and the American Theological Society. She was the author of Knowledge of God in
Johannine Thought, Paul the Conqueror, The Fourth Gospel and
the Life of Today, The Christian Epic, Jesus, In Him Was Life,
and A Study-Guide to the Gospel of John.[15]

She was the epitome of New England graciousness. In
addition to being a fine teacher, she, during her years at
Union, was a hostess who entertained many of the students in
her apartment. During these occasions, the conversation was
comparable to the exquisite cuisine. An unreformed liberal,
her recommendations for purchases on the English Bible reflected
her theological stance, although she was, of course, happy to
have neo-orthodox Biblical studies added to the collection.
Union and its Library has a little more distinction because
of the nearly thirty-year connection of this lady with the
school.

Another Faculty member added at this time was Robert
Edwin Seaver, who has subsequently become Professor of Speech

and Director of the Program in Religious Drama. His formal education was received at Northwestern and Columbia. He holds membership in the Speech Association of America, the American Educational Theatre Association, the General Committee of the Division of Christian Life and Work, and the Commission on Drama of the Department of Worship and Arts of the National Council of Churches, and Trinity Parish of the Episcopalian Church. He is a former professional actor who has appeared with Maurice Evans, Basil Rathbone, and Frank Sinatra.[16]

The Program in Religious Drama has required the addition of thousands of books of currently-produced plays for the Library, and Seaver has been instrumental in the acquisition of many of these. Union's holdings in this area are, to say the least, unusual for a theological seminary.

A new appointee in the church history department was Robert Handy, a graduate of Brown, Colgate Rochester Divinity School, and Chicago. He had been Pastor of the Baptist Church in Mt. Prospect, Illinois from 1943 to 1945, Instructor in the Baptist Missionary Training School in Chicago from 1948 to 1949, and Instructor in Humanities at Shimer College in Mt. Caroll, Illinois from 1949 to 1950. He holds membership in the American Historical Association, the American Studies Association, and the American Society of Church History. He is the author of We Witness Together and Members One of Another and has shared in writing American Christianity.[17] A cordial, interesting teacher, he has made numerous recommendations for the improvement of the Library's holdings of contemporary and retrospective materials on the history of American Christianity.

Miner Searle Bates, who had taught for many years at the University of Nanking, was appointed Professor of Missions at this time. His published works include Religious Liberty: An Inquiry and The Prospects of Christianity throughout the World, the latter of which was edited with Wilhelm Pauck. In his post at the Seminary, Bates helped to prepare hundreds of missionaries for the major denominations of Protestantism. He, in the process, made many recommendations for contemporary materials for the Missionary Research Library, as well as for missions material for the general collection. He and his wife were also genial hosts to generations of students and visiting missionaries at Union.

Another appointee was Daniel Day Williams, who was elected to a Professorship of Systematic Theology. His education was received at Denver, Chicago Theological Seminary, and Columbia. Before coming to Union, he was Pastor of the First Congregational Church in Colorado Springs, Dean of the Shove Memorial Chapel and Instructor in Religion at Colorado College, Professor of Christian Theology at Chicago Theological Seminary and the Federated Faculty of the University of Chicago, and Associate Director of the Theological Education Survey. He is the author of The Andover Liberals, God's Grace and Man's Hope, What Present-Day Theologians Are Thinking, and The Minister and the Care of Souls. He was the co-author of The Advancement of Theological Education and contributed to The Theology of

Reinhold Niebuhr; A Companion to the Study of St. Augustine, The Shaping of American Religion, The Empirical Theology of H. N. Wieman, and Alfred North Whitehead.[18] He was a representative of the process school of theology, which harks back to the naturalism of the earlier part of this century. He helped to restore the respectability of liberalism in the curriculum; and this development shaped, to a degree, the direction in which the collection has grown. Two of the works which he wrote or helped to produce, What Present-Day Theologians Are Thinking and The Advancement of Theological Education, were heavily used in Protestant seminaries.

Wilhelm Pauck also came to Union from Chicago Theological Seminary and the University of Chicago Federated Faculty. His education was received at the Real Gymnasium of Berlin-Steglitz and the University of Berlin. He was a Fellow of the American Academy of Arts and Sciences and served as President of both the American Theological Society and the American Society of Church History. He was the author of Das Reich Gottes auf Erden, Karl Barth--Prophet of a New Christianity?, The Heritage of the Reformation, and Luther's Lectures on Romans. He was the co-author of The Church against the World, Religion and Politics, and The Ministry in Historical Perspectives. He contributed to Environmental Factors in Christian History and Religion and the Present Crisis.[19] His recommendations for Library acquisitions reflected his interest in retrospective and contemporary materials in the field of church history.

The first incumbent of the Henry Sloan Coffin Professorship of Practical Theology was Paul Waitman Hoon. His education was received at the University of Cincinnati, Yale, Union, Marburg, Cambridge, and Edinburgh. He was Assistant Minister of the Chester Hill Methodist Church in Mt. Vernon, New York; and a Minister in New Milford, Connecticut; Bridgeport, Connecticut; New Rochelle, New York; and Germantown, Pennsylvania. He was the author of the Exposition of the Epistles of St. John in the Interpreter's Bible.[20]   A Methodist who was highly appreciative of the Anglo-Catholic tradition, he stressed the liturgical renewal in his classes and his nominations for current materials in the Library. A slight man with white hair, he is remembered by his former students for his courtesy, cordiality, and practicality.

Ralph D. Hyslop came in 1955 from a post as Professor of Historical Theology and History of Christianity at the Pacific School of Religion to become Professor of Ecumenical Studies and Associate Director of the Program of Advance Religious Studies. He was a Congregationalist and had degrees from the University of Wisconsin, Chicago Theological Seminary, and Edinburgh. Immediately before joining the Union Faculty, he spent a year in Geneva with the World Council.[21] He recommended many contemporary books for the Library on the ecumenical movement.

James D. Smart became, the following year, the Jesup Professor of Biblical Interpretation. He was educated at the University of Toronto, Marburg, and Berlin. He was a Pastor

in Ailsa Craig, Galt, and Peterboro in Ontario, as well as in
Toronto. He also served as Editor-in Chief of Curriculum
Publications for the Presbyterian Church in the U. S. A. from
1944 to 1950. His books include What a Man Can Believe, God
Has Spoken, A Promise to Keep, The Recovery of Humanity, The
Teaching Ministry of the Church, The Rebirth of Ministry,
Servants of the Lord, The Interpretation of Scripture, and
The Creed in Christian Teaching.[22] His recommendations for
Library purchases reflected his interest in current Biblical
studies and Christian education. He was influential in re-
storing a theological orientation to the educational program
of liberal Protestantism.

Roger L. Shinn became the William E. Dodge, Jr. Professor
of Applied Christianity in 1960. He was educated at Heidel-
berg (Ohio) College, Union, and Columbia. He served as
Chairman of the Department of Philosophy at Heidelberg,
Professor of Theology at Vanderbilt, and Professor of
Christian Ethics at the latter institution. His religious
activities included the presidency of the Board of Homeland
Ministries of the United Church, membership on the Executive
Committee of the International Congregationalist Council,
membership on the General Committee of the Department of
Church and Economic Life and the General Committee of the
Department of Racial and Cultural Relations of the National
Council of Churches, and a position on the Religious Advisory
Council of the President's Commission on Government
Contracts. He also held membership in Americans for Demo-
cratic Action, American Veterans Committee, American

Theological Society, American Society of Christian Social
Ethics, and the Religious Research Association. He was the
author of Beyond This Darkness, Christianity on the Mount,
Life, Death and Destiny, The Existentialist Posture, and The
Educational Mission of Our Church.[23] His recommendations for
Library materials were based on his scholarly interest in
contemporary materials in the fields of theology and social
ethics.

During the same year that Shinn came to Union, William
David Davies was named Edward Robinson Professor of Biblical
Theology. Born in England, his education was received at
Cambridge and the University of Wales. He served as Pastor
of a parish in Cambridgeshire, England; Assistant Tutor in
Chestnut College of Cambridge; Professor of New Testament
Studies at Yorkshire United College; and Professor of
Biblical Theology at Duke. He held membership in the Society
for Biblical Literature and Exegesis, Studiorum Novi
Testamenti Societas, American Schools of Oriental Research,
and the Society of Old Testament Studies of England. He was
the author of Paul and Rabbinic Judaism, Torah in the
Messianic Age and/or The Age to Come, Christian Origins and
Judaism, and The Setting of the Sermon on the Mount. He was
also the co-editor of The Background of the New Testament and
Its Eschatology, which was a festschrift in honor of Charles
H. Dodd.[24] Said to be a diligent task-master in leading his
students to use the Library, his nominations for acquisitions reveal not only his British background but also his

interest in the best retrospective and contemporary materials in the field of New Testament studies.

Carl Ellis Nelson was named Professor of Religious Education and Psychology at this time. His education was received at Lamar Junior College in Beaumont, Texas; A. and M. College at College Station, Texas; Austin College; Austin Presbyterian Theological Seminary; the University of Texas; and Columbia. The latter school awarded him the doctorate in 1955. Before his appointment at Union he had held positions as Associate Minister and Director of Student Work at University Presbyterian Church in Austin; Chaplain of the State School for the Blind in the same city; Professor in Religious Education at the Austin Presbyterian Theological Seminary; Instructor in Bible at the University of Texas; Director of Youth Work for the Board of Christian Education of the Presbyterian Church, U. S.; and Director of Research, the Texas Legislative Council's study of Higher Education in the State of Texas. He was transferred to the Skinner and McAlpin Professor of Practical Theology in 1960, and he published a volume entitled Love and the Law with John Knox Press in 1963.[25] He made important recommendations for the development of the collection, especially in the field of religious education.

Another appointee was Robert Wood Lynn, who subsequently became Auburn Professor of Religious Education. He was educated at Princeton and Yale before coming to Union for doctoral study. He was active in the American Society of Church History and the Committee on the Nature of the

Minister of the General Assembly of the United Presbyterian Church in the U. S. A. He also served on the Editorial Board of Christianity and Crisis. He also published a book on Protestant Strategies in Education.[26] He was said to be one of the stimulating younger members of the Faculty and recommended many titles in the field of Christian education for addition to the Library.

Beach ranked well with these members of the Faculty; and his professional organization, the American Theological Library Association, expressed its appreciation of his abilities by electing him President for 1954-56. As the Inter-Church Center was being constructed, he was contacted about the bibliographical needs of people who would work in that building. Libraries were planned within the Center, but the wish of the leaders of the National Council of Churches was that a minimal amount of duplication of materials and services should take place.[27]

The Library received two archival additions of importance at this time. Ralph Hyslop gave some papers on the World Council of Churches' second assembly held at Evanston, Illinois. These had to do with the "Main Theme" discussions and included minutes of the "Main Theme" Coordinating Group and reports of the secretaries of fifteen "Main Theme" groups on discussion. The latter collection was the only one in existence. Frederick Grant, at the same time, gave a series of papers on the discussions between the Protestant Episcopal and the Methodist Churches conversations on unity. These included materials on the ministry, polity, and Holy Communion.[28]

Three other interesting gifts were received during this era. The first came from Columbia and included a selection of German theological works from the Deutsches Haus on the campus of that school. The second and third were Mary Baker Eddy material. One was a positive microfilm copy of correspondence between Mrs. Eddy and Mrs. Augusta Stetson. The other was an album of general correspondence to and from Mrs. Eddy.[29]

Beach received an Assistant Librarian at this time with the appointment of William M. Robarts to the staff. A former pre-ministerial student, he had worked in the libraries at the University of Tennessee and Columbia. Barbara Griffis was appointed at the same time as the Ecumenical Librarian.[30] Ruth Eisenhart was involved, in the meantime, editing the Cumulated Supplement to the Union Classification scheme published in 1939. She was also in charge of issuing the current lists of changes and additions which come out semi-annually. The Librarian was also serving on the American Theological Library Association's Board, which directed the publication of the new Index to Religious Periodical Literature, whose general editor was Lucy Markley. Other services provided at this time included the provision of assistance to Professor Conald Wolfe of Brooklyn College in connection with the preparation of a definitive edition of Milton's prose works to be published by Yale University Press. Wolfe was serving as the editor of the materials and made extensive use of McAlpin items in working on the project.[31]

Gifts to the Library during the era included approximately 300 books from Mary Ely Lyman and substantial contributions from the collections of Professors Frame and Sherrill. Annual purchases included approximately one hundred dollars' worth of materials on religious drama to reinforce the new program in that field. These were paid for by the Rockefeller Foundation. The Old Dominion Foundation, supported by Paul Mellon, was also giving about $1,000 a year for materials on psychiatry and religion.[32]

A long-range development program was announced at this time by President Van Dusen. The total of $16,000,000 for projects in this plan were broken down as follows:

New residence offices, lecture and seminary rooms	$3,100,000
Faculty salaries	3,500,000
Modernization of present plant and equipment	3,800,000
Advanced religious studies	2,500,000
Pastoral counseling, psychiatric studies, internships	1,250,000
Scholarships	700,000
Enlarged extension services	475,000
Religious drama	400,000
School of Sacred Music	250,000 [33]

Within eighteen months, $4,225,000 had been raised toward this program.[34]

Developments of the 1960's

John L. Young was appointed to the Library staff at this time. He came to Union with a Bachelor of Divinity degree from the University of Chicago and a Master of Arts degree from the Columbia School of Library Service. He subsequently performed in an excellent manner as the Reference Librarian.[35] Soon after, Joseph Tucker, a graduate of Union in the class of 1953, came to the staff, where he continued as Periodicals Librarian. George C. Cook, Jr. came from Harvard and the Columbia School of Library Service at the same time as Assistant in the Catalog Department.[36] Richard H. Pachella, who subsequently received graduate degrees from Harvard and the School of Library Service of Columbia and been appointed Rare Book Librarian, came to the staff in September, 1960.[37]

The opening of the Interchurch Center near the Seminary brought about a modest increase in the use of the Library. Inter-library loans were made to the three major libraries there and also direct lending privileges were extended to staff members of the Center.[38]

Two large orders for microfilm copies of McAlpin items were received at this time. The first was part of a national project of University Microfilms, and the second was from Osaka City University in Japan. The Collection stood at the time at approximately 18,000 items, but new titles were being added each year. Another large order for materials for microfilming came from the Foundation for Reformation Research in St. Louis. The Ecumenical Institute at Evanston, Illinois, also requested a complete copy of the shelf list of the Ecumenical Library. Approximately 3,000 cards were copied for this project. A copy of each card added to the shelf list was subsequently provided for the shelf list at Evanston.[39]

Two significant manuscripts came as gifts at this
time. The first was a six-volume bound set of sermons of
Stephen Grosvenor Hopkins, an Auburn alumnus and son of Samuel
Miles Hopkins, Professor of Church History at Auburn from
1847 to 1893. These were given by Julia Hopkins, a daughter.
The other gift was a group of papers from the estate of Henry
Preserved Smith turned over to the Library by Professor
Muilenburg.[40]

Gifts of approximately $500 each were common during
this era from Time, Inc. These were contributed in acknowledgement of service rendered by the Library to the publication of
Time.[41] Henry Luce's presence on the Directorate of the Seminary was probably responsible, in part, for this gift.

The Missionary Research Library was mentioned at this
time in an issue of Library Trends, in which its Librarian
wrote that the collection was supervised by a joint committee
of twelve, representing the Division of Foreign Missions of
the National Council of the Churches of Christ in the United
States of America and the Seminary. Funds were secured from
approximately 100 missionary agencies and a number of individuals. The move of the Interchurch Center into the neighborhood
had brought, he wrote, historical records and present activities
of many missionary boards into nearer purview. At the same
time, interest in the Missionary Research Library was expanded
because of the new Center.[42] This Library was chartered by
the University of the State of New York and incorporated as
a non-profit institution under the Education Law of the State
of New York in 1961.[43]

Herbert C. Jackson was appointed Director of this
Library in 1961. He studied at the University of Nebraska,
William Jewell College, Southern Baptist Theological Seminary,
and Yale, the latter of which awarded him the Ph.D. degree.
He had taught missions at three Baptist seminaries before his
appointment at Union.[44] One of his first decisions was to
transfer materials on Alaska and Hawaii, in view of their
statehood, from his collection to the general Library or from
"foreign missions" to "home missions."[45]

Early the next year it was announced that the John
Foster Dulles Collection on the Church and International Order
had been created in the Library. Materials for this Collection
were bought in part through royalties from <u>The Spiritual
Legacy of John Foster Dulles: Selections from His Articles
and Addresses</u>. The work was edited by President Van Dusen
and published on the first anniversary of the death of the
Secretary of State.[46]

Other gifts during 1961 included a large collection
on Congregational Christian-Evangelical and Reformed union
negotiations which had belonged to William Walker Rockwell.
These were contributed by his wife. A second gift was a
"unique collection of letters and other papers" for the years
1946 to 1959 from the Conference on Church Union commonly
called the Greenwich Plan. Another contribution was a microfilm from the Library of Harvard Divinity School containing
some unpublished writings of Dietrich Bonhoeffer, who had
studied at Union.[47]

An important service provided during this year was
the offering of a course in "Theological Literature and
Librarianship" taught by Beach in the summer session of the
School of Library Service of Columbia. Another was brought
about through cooperation with G. K. Hall & Company in the
publication of the <u>Shelf List</u> of the Library. The first run
included 100 sets, which included 210,000 entries.[48]

Services performed during the next academic year,
1961-62, included a visit by Beach to Chicago Theological
Seminary to analyze the program there and to recommend steps
for its library development. Ruth Eisenhart, in the meantime,
served on the American Library Association's Committee on Catalog Code Revision as a member of the Sub-Committee on Religious
Headings and as a consultant representing the American Theological Library Association. She also prepared a paper on "Cataloging Liturgical and Other Religious Texts" for the International Conference on Cataloguing Principles held in Paris
in October, 1961, and attended the Conference as a member of
the American delegation.[49]

The inauguration of the Auburn Resident Pastors Program,
enabling ministers to come to Union for extended periods of
time for study, also provided opportunities for service to
these men. The expressions of appreciation for the program
included statements such as this:

> In looking back over the last two weeks spent at
> Union . . . it would seem to me that the high point
> was the free use of the Library which was made
> available to us.[50]

Several important gifts were made at this time, the
first of which was two complete sets of the mimeographed
papers of the Third Assembly of the World Council of Churches
held in New Delhi in 1961. These were contributed by Blanche
Britton, long-time Registrar of the Seminary. President
Van Dusen gave the second contribution, a "unique collection
of letters and papers dealing with his many activities in the
World Council of Churches."[51]

The most important gift, however, was the beginning
of the matching funds made available through the American
Theological Library Association Library Development Program.
Shared in by nearly every seminary accredited by the American
Association of Theological Schools, the program was financed
by Rockefeller money. While weaker schools used this for
current materials, Union spent a good deal of its funds made
available in this way for the replacement of retrospective
sets by modern reprints and positive copies.[52]

Additions to and services of the ecumenical aspects
of the Library were abetted during this period through Catholic-
Protestant conversations, the Second Vatican Council, and the
Montreal Faith and Order Conference. The collection was increasingly used by Catholic scholars, some of whom called it
the finest source of materials on their faith to be found in
the United States. Priests of this body admitted to the
graduate program of the Seminary found a plethora of materials
on Catholicism.

Despite its ecumenicity, the Library was, however, basically Protestant. One bit of evidence for this was that fact that when Lawrence S. Thompson, Director of the University of Kentucky Libraries, planned a project entitled "The History of Ideas in Europe," designed to make scholarly materials more generally available to libraries, he turned to Union for data on this branch of Christendom. He supervised the microcard reproduction of approximately 60,000 pages of the Library's holdings on "The Reformers, Their Precursors and Opponents in the Age of Luther" as part of the program.[53]

The 1960's, in addition to these developments, were noteworthy for appointments to the Faculty. Almost every one of these persons, from John C. Bennett, who was inaugurated as President on April 10, 1964, to the lowliest instructor, probably made some contribution to the growth of the collection.

One of the professors, James Alfred Martin, Jr., was named to the Danforth chair of Religion in Higher Education. His formal education was received at Wake Forest, Duke, Union, and Columbia. He served as Assistant Pastor of the Roxboro, North Carolina Baptist Church, Instructor of Philosophy and Psychology at Wake Forest, and Crosby Professor of Religion at Amherst College. He held membership in the Society for Religion in Higher Education, the American Theological Society, and the Society of Theological Discussion. He was the author of Empirical Philsophies of Religion and Fact, Fiction, and Faith. He also, with J. A.

Hutchinson, wrote <u>Ways of Faith</u>.[54] Although the literature
in the area of religion and higher education is scanty in
comparison with the traditional divisions of theological
study, Martin insured that most of the materials produced
found their way to Union's stacks.

Another new professor was Edmund Augustus Steimle, who
was named to the Brown Chair of Homiletics. A graduate of
Princeton and the Lutheran Theological Seminary in
Philadelphia, he served as a teaching fellow in the latter
institution before becoming Pastor of the Lutheran Church of
Our Savior in Jersey City, New Jersey. He later became Pastor
of the University Lutheran Church in Cambridge, Massachusetts, from where he was called to the Lutheran Theological
Seminary again as Hagan Professor of Practical Theology. He
came to Union from this post.[55] As Scherer's successor, he
carried on the tradition of recommending contemporary
materials in the field of preaching for the Library.

Next came Robert S. Baker in 1961 as Director of the
School of Sacred Music. He received the degree of Doctor of
Sacred Music from the Seminary in 1944. He was, at the time
of his appointment as Director, Organist-Choir Director at
the Fifth Avenue Presbyterian Church and Organist at Temple
Emmanuel-El. He served as Chairman of the National
Convention of the American Guild of Organists. He composed
several published works and recorded for RCA Victor.[56] He,
of course, took an active interest in the growth of the
Library of Sacred Music.

Another appointee at this time was Paul Louis Lehmann. He attended Ohio State University and Union. As the ranking student of the class of 1930, he was awarded the Seminary Travelling Fellowship and spent the year 1932-33 at Zurich and Bonn. He taught at Elmhurst College, Eden Theological Seminary, Wellesley College, Princeton Theological Seminary, and Harvard Divinity School. His books include <u>Forgiveness: Decisive Issue in Protestant Thought</u>, <u>Re-educating Germany</u>, and <u>Your Freedom Is in Trouble</u>. He had a prominent role in the World Conference on Faith and Order in 1952.[52] As one of the nation's leading theological scholars, he made many significant recommendations for the improvement of the Library's holdings in systematic theology.

Also new in the decade was James Mase Ault in the field of Practical Theology. He came from the pastorate of the First Methodist Church of Pittsfield, Massachusetts. He also held similar positions in Leonia and in East Rutherford, New Jersey. An alumnus of 1949, he was a member of the National Council's Department of Church and Economic Life.[58] His nominations for Library materials reflected his interest in the practical concerns of the parish minister.

Another new professor was John Macquarrie. He received M.A., B.D. and Ph.D. degrees from Glasgow. He served during World War II in the Royal Army Chaplains Department and was for a period in charge of German Prisoner of War chaplains in the Middle East. After the War he was minister of St. Ninian's Church, Bechin, Scotland, until he became a member of the Faculty of the University of Glasgow.

He served as a member of the Church and Nation Committee of the Church of Scotland and as a Chaplain in the Territorial Army for thirteen years. He and Professor E. S. Robinson of the University of Kansas translated Martin Heidegger's _Being and Time_.[59] His books include _An Existentialist Theology_, _The Scope of Demythologizing_, _Twentieth-Century Religious Thought_, and _Studies in Christian Existentialism_.[60] His recommendations for Library acquisitions were consistent with his interest in existentialism and demythologization of the New Testament.

Another new professor was James Alvin Sanders, whose education was received at Vanderbilt, Ecole des Hautes Etudes at the University of Paris, and Hebrew Union. He came to New York from Colgate Rochester Divinity School, where he was Joseph B. Hoyt Professor of Old Testament Interpretation. He was a member of the American Schools of Oriental Research, the Society of Biblical Literature and Exegesis, the National Association of Biblical Instructors, and the National Association of Professors of Hebrew. He wrote _Suffering as Divine Disciple in the Old Testament and Post-Biblical Judaism_ and _The Old Testament in the Cross_.[61] In his experience at Union, he made a contribution to the growth of the Old Testament collection by recommending retrospective and contemporary titles for purchase.

New in the fall of 1965 was Johannes Christiaan Hoekendijk, who was named Professor of Missions. His education had been received at the Missionary Training

Institute at Oegstgeest, the University of Leiden, and the
University of Utrecht. During the War he served as Pastor
for refugees and prisoners of war in Geneva and as an army
chaplain in the Pacific area. Since the war he had been
Missions Consul to Indonesia, General Secretary of the
Netherlands Missionary Council in Amsterdam, Secretary for
Evangelism of the World Council of Churches, Professor of
Pastoral Theology and Missions and Professor of Church
History of the Twentieth Century at Utrecht. He held
memberships in the Academic Council of the Netherlands,
Deutsche Gesellschaft für Missionswissenschaft, and the
Utrecht Society of Arts and Sciences. His Publications
include World Missions during World War II, Church and Nation
in German Missiology, Evangelism in France, The Church Inside
Out, and The Future of the Church, the Church of the Future
as well as 100 articles on missionary and ecumenical
subjects.[62] He helped the collection to be developed in an
even greater ecumenical and international direction.

Also new in the fall of 1965 was Richard Frederic
French, who came from the Presidency of New York Pro Musica
to become Professor of Sacred Music. He was educated at
Phillips Exeter Academy and Harvard. Before World War II he
served as Assistant Dean of Harvard College; and, following
the War, he returned to Cambridge as Assistant Professor of
Music and Director of Graduate Studies in the Music
Department. He became in 1952 the Vice-President of
Associated Music Publishers, from where he moved to New York Pro
Musica. He had recently translated into English the only

Russian book on the music of Stravinsky.[63] In his new post
he helped to strengthen the holdings of the Library of Sacred
Music.

The Library staff included at this time, in addition
to those already mentioned, Mary Ann Freudenthal, Head of the
Circulation Department; Barbara Marjorie Griffis, Kenneth W.
Ludwig, Mrs. Julius McDonald, and Mrs. William C. Smith,
Assistants in the Cataloging Department; Jack W. S. Wallens,
Religious Education and Sacred Music Librarian; and Robert E.
Schroeder, Acquisitions Librarian.[64]

Principal borrowers at this time, outside the Union
constituency, included American Heritage, Time, Drake University, Drew University, Duke University, Methodist Board of
Missions, the National Council of Churches, and the United
Presbyterian Missions Library. The latter, located at the
Interchurch Center, was the heaviest borrower; and through it
loans extended by Union were sent to Presbyterian ministers
in various parts of the nation.[65]

The Ecumenical Library received at this time a group
of pamphlets and papers belonging to Peter Ainslie, an early
leader in the ecumenical movement, contributed by his son,
who graduated from the Seminary in 1955. This collection was
especially rich in materials about the Stockholm Conference
of 1925 and early Faith and Order documents. The World Council
of Churches also sent a group of duplicates during the year.[66]

Loans at the time included an early manuscript of
Thomas Aquinas to the Stadtbibliothek at Mönchengladbach,

Germany; a first edition of Milton's <u>Areopagitica</u> to the University of Notre Dame for an International Galileo Conference; and a copy of the Koberger Bible, the first illustrated printed German Bible dating from 1483, to the Vatican Pavillion of the World's Fair.[67]

Beach closed his annual report for this year with this paragraph:

> It cannot be urged too strongly that no immediate solution to the Library's space problem is in sight. <u>Total future expansion space for stack collection is estimated at not more than five years.</u> Within this grace period major space must be developed, if possible adjacent to the present Library plant. The best wisdom of those responsible, here at the Seminary, will have to be explored to assure the continuing growth and development of Union's library program.[68]

During the next year, 1965, the Library received the papers of Abbe Livingstone Warnshuis, a missionary in China, who lived between 1877 and 1958, from his wife. These documents included correspondence, diaries, sermons, lecture notes, minutes, and other papers related to his work with the Federal Council of Churches, the International Missionary Council, the National Council of Churches of China, and the World Council of Churches.[69] In the following year, the Library received the papers of Hunter Corbett, a Presbyterian missionary, who lived between 1835 and 1920, and his son-in-law, Harold F. Smith, a missionary and university teacher in China. The documents included diaries, scrapbooks, notes, letters, and articles on Chinese missions and schools.[70]

On July 1 of the next year, 1967, the Missionary Research Library became a part of the Union Seminary Library

administratively and operationally. While the National
Council of Churches continued partial financial support of
the Missionary Research Library, the major portion of the
operating budget was assumed by Union; Beach became Director
of the Missionary Research Library while continuing to serve
as Librarian of the Seminary.[71] The integration of the
Missionary Research Library, the largest library in the world
devoted to missions, made available to users of Union's
Library material on missions, social conditions and cultures
in Asia, Africa, the Middle East, Latin America and the
Pacific.[72]

To the integrated collection, at this time, came the
papers of Matilda Calder Thurston, a missionary in China, who
founded and served as the first president of Ginling, the
first Christian women's college in that country. During the
early seventies, the wife of Emory Ross, a missionary in
Zaire, gave his papers to the Union Library.[73]

These papers were received at about the same time as
the papers of Harry Frederick Ward, the former professor at
Union, were given to the Library. The papers of Lorenzo
Warriner Pease, a pioneer missionary in Cyprus, were also
added to the archival collections. In 1971, the papers of
Harry Emerson Fosdick were given by his family and
transferred to Union from Riverside Church.[74]

In the following year, the gifts included Proces-
sionale Leodiense, a vellum manuscript completed in 1575 and
dedicated to Gerardus cardinal van Grosbeeck; this gift was
contributed by Mrs. William Walker Rockwell in memory of her

husband, the former librarian at Union. Some gifts given anonymously included Grotius' In consultationem G. Cassandri annotata published by Elsevir in Leyden in 1642 and Albertus Pighius' Controversariu praecipurarum in comitiis Ratisponensibus tractatarum...explicatio published in Cologne by Melchior in 1542 and Robert Pinkerton's Russia: or, Miscellaneous Oberservations, which included seven translated sermons by Archbishop Ambrose of Kazan and Metropolitan Michael of St. Petersburg.[75]

Additional gifts of note were contributed in 1973 when the Library received more than fifty titles from the Friends Monthly Meeting in Scarsdale, New York. One of these works was the 1698 edition of Charles Leslie's anti-Quaker tract, The Snake in the Grass: or Satan Transform'd into an Angel of Light. William Cave's Apostolici published in 1687 was received at this time from Hildegard Dietz, while Francis T. P. Plimpton contributed manuscript sermons of Jedediah Morse and James Pike.[76]

Robert Beach, following twenty-three years of service to the Seminary, announced that he would retire on June 30, 1974. In addition to his contributions to the Library, he was active in the American Theological Library Association and on the summer session faculty of the Columbia University School of Library Service from 1960 until 1970, during which time he taught in six alternate sessions a course on "Theological Libraries and Librarianship".[77]

FOOTNOTES

[1] *Who's Who in America, 1964-65*, XXXIII (Chicago: Marquis-Who's Who, 1964), p. 131.

[2] *New York Times*, October 23, 1951, 32:8.

[3] *Ibid.*, November 21, 1951, 27:4.

[4] Union Theological Seminary. Library, Report, 1952, p. 6.

[5] *New York Times*, January 3, 1953, 1:3.

[6] *Ibid.*, February 11, 1948, p. 1:4.

[7] Union Theological Seminary. Library, Report, 1953, p. 6.

[8] Ellouise W. Skinner, *Sacred Music at Union Theological Seminary, 1836-1953; An Informal History* (New York: Union Theological Seminary, 1953), p. 46.

[9] *Ibid.*

[10] Union Theological Seminary. Library, Report, 1955, p. 7.

[11] *New York Times*, January 5, 1955, 23:5.

[12] Henry Sloane Coffin, *A Half Century of Union Theological Seminary, 1896-1945, An Informal History* (New York: Charles Scribner's Sons, 1954), pp. 246-47.

[13] *New York Times*, April 23, 1954, 24:3.

[14] *Ibid.*, December 19, 1955, 29:8.

[15] *Who's Who in America, op. cit.*, p. 1246.

[16] Union Theological Seminary, Biographical Information Sheet (Mimeographed).

[17] *Who's Who in the East* (Chicago: Marquis-Who's Who, 1963, p. 392.

[18] *Who's Who in America, 1964-65, op. cit.*, p. 2169.

[19] Ibid., p. 1556.

[20] Ibid., p. 950.

[21] Union Theological Seminary, Union Theological Seminary Alumni Bulletin, II (May, 1955), 3.

[22] Who's Who in America, 1964-65, op. cit., p. 1858.

[23] Ibid., p. 1829.

[24] Ibid., p. 481.

[25] Union Theological Seminary, Biographical Information Sheet (Mimeographed).

[26] Ibid.

[27] Union Theological Seminary. Library, Report, June 30, 1956, p. 2.

[28] Ibid., p. 7.

[29] Ibid.

[30] Ibid., 1957, p. 10.

[31] Ibid., 1958, pp. 3, 9.

[32] Ibid., p. 8.

[33] New York Times, May 12, 1958, 27:5.

[34] Ibid., October 28, 1959, 24:6.

[35] Union Theological Seminary. Library, Report, 1959, p. 10.

[36] Ibid., 1960, p. 10.

[37] Ibid., 1961, p. 9.

[38] Ibid., 1960, p. 2.

[39] Ibid.

[40] Ibid., p. 8.

[41] Ibid., p. 7.

[42] Frank W. Price, "Specialized Research Libraries in Missions," Library Trends, IX (October, 1960), pp. 175-85.

[43]Union Theological Seminary, Catalogue, 1962-63 (New York: Union Theological Seminary, 1962), p. 31.

[44]The Union Seminary Tower, VIII (May, 1961), p. 2.

[45]Union Theological Seminary. Library, Report, 1961, p. 4.

[46]New York Times, January 14, 1961, 13:8.

[47]Union Theological Seminary. Library, Report, 1961, pp. 4-5.

[48]Ibid., pp. 9, 11.

[49]Ibid., 1962, p. 9.

[50]Ibid., p. 11.

[51]Ibid., pp. 3-4.

[52]Ibid., 1964, p. 13.

[53]Ibid., 1963, p. 4.

[54]Who's Who in America, 1964-65, op. cit., p. 1292.

[55]The Union Seminary Tower, VII (February, 1961), 2.

[56]Ibid., VIII (May, 1961), 1.

[57]Ibid., IX (May, 1962), 4.

[58]Ibid., VIII (May, 1961), 1.

[59]Ibid., IX (May, 1962), 1.

[60]Letter from John Macquarrie, July 10, 1965.

[61]Who's Who in America, op. cit., p. 1751.

[62]Union Theological Seminary, Biographical Information Sheet (Mimeographed).

[63]Ibid.

[64]Union Theological Seminary. Library, Report, 1964, p. 13.

[65]Ibid., pp. 3-4.

[66]Ibid., pp. 4, 6.

[67] Ibid., p. 15.

[68] Ibid., p. 16.

[69] Union Theological Seminary. The Burke Library, Some Special Collections, March 20, 1985, p. 15.

[70] Ibid., p. 14

[71] "Missionary Research Library to Merge with Union Theological Seminary Library, ATLA Newsletter, XIV (May 13, 1967), p. 57.

[72] Fay M. Blake, "Union Theological Seminary Library," The Bookmark, XXIX (November, 1969), p. 57.

[73] Union Theological Seminary. The Burke Library, op. cit., pp. 5, 6, 12.

[74] Union Theological Seminary. The Burke Library, op. cit., pp. 5,6, 12.

[75] Union Theological Seminary. Library, Report, 1972, p. 10.

[76] Ibid., 1973, p. 14.

[77] ATLA Newsletter, XXI (May 18, 1974), p. 103.

Chapter XI

RECENT DEVELOPMENTS, 1975–85

The Librarianship of Robert Maloy, 1975–79

In 1975, Robert Maloy came from the post as Librarian
of the Claremont Graduate School of Theology to Union
Theological Seminary in the City of New York as the Director
of the Library. One of the first major actions of his
administration was the abandonment of the Petee scheme of
classification for the Library and the adoption of the
Library of Congress Classification system.

In May of 1976 an agreement was reached between the
Union Library and the International Bonhoeffer Society for
Archive and Research by which the latter group agreed to
furnish the Library with copies of unpublished Bonhoeffer
manuscripts as they became available. The Bonhoeffer
collection at Union was also to include a comprehensive
collection of sources with special attention for English-
language materials.[1]

Other important collections acquired at this time
included sermons, letters, and a diary from the papers of
Paul Ehrman Scherer, a long-time member of the Union faculty,
and the papers of Henry Pitney Van Dusen, former President of

321

Union, who was active in the World Council of Churches, the
Presbyterian Board of foreign Missions, and the American
Association of Theological Schools.[2] In January of 1977,
Paul A. Byrnes began to devote half of his time to organizing
the archival collections containing such papers.[3]

In 1979, Robert Maloy left Union Seminary to become
the Director of Libraries at the Smithsonian Institution in
Washington, D. C.; Richard Spoor was named as his successor
as Director of the Library.

The Librarianship of Richard Spoor, 1979-

Richard Spoor had been a member of the Union Library
staff in a variety of posts in which he had served, for
example, as the head of the reference department and as head
of bibliographic control and collection development. He also
had been involved with planning better physical facilities
for the Library, the process for which arose from the Library
Committee of the Board of Directors.

In the first year of his role as Director of the
Library, he issued the second edition of a document titled
The Shape of Things to Come, which was used by the architects
in designing improved facilities. On March 13, 1979, the
Executive Committee of the Board of Directors commissioned
the firm of Mitchell/Giurgola Architects to renovate the
Library's physical facilities,[4] and construction began in mid-
summer of 1980.[5]

At this time, Union received a challenge grant from
the Kresge Foundation in the amount of $250,000, building on

a similar gift of $600,000 awarded to Union by the National
Endowment for the Humanities received two years earlier. The
Andrew W. Mellon also contributed $500,000 at this time to
maintain the quality of the Library, with priority being
given to preservation activities.[6]

Other major gifts for the renovation came from the
Austin Memorial Foundation, the Bodman Foundation, Mr. and
Mrs. Walter Burke, the Clark Foundation, the Arthur Vining
Davis Foundations, the Caleb C. Julia W. Dula Educational
and Charitable Foundation, the Sherman Fairchild Foundation,
Mr. and Mrs. Harry W. Havemeyer, Mrs. Horace Havemeyer, Sr.,
Mr. and Mrs. John N. Irwin II, Mr. and Mrs. Timothy Light,
Mr. and Mrs. David H. McAlpin, Sr., Mr. and Mrs. Eugene M.
Moore, Dr. and Mrs. Steven C. Rockefeller, and Mr. and Mrs.
Stephen A. Wise, in addition to numerous other donors.[7]

On April 25-26, 1983, the Library, on which $3,200,000
had been spent to enlarge, renovate, and reorganize, was
rededicated. President Donald Shriver announced at this time
that the Board of Directors had renamed the Burke Library of
Union Theological Seminary in the City of New York to honor
the long-time member and immediate past chair of the
Seminary's Board of Directors.[8]

The Burke Library, which includes approximately
600,000 items, participates in several cooperative programs.
It is affiliated, for instance, with more than 150 libraries
through its membership in the New York Metropolitan Reference
and Reserarch Library Agency. It also has cooperative

programs with other similar institutions through its membership in the New York Area Theological Library Association.
The Library staff also contribute to the production of a
microfiche union catalog of the post-1975 holdings of the
Burke Library and the libraries of Harvard Divinity School.[9]

Through the State University of New York network, the
Burke Library is a member of Online Computer Library Center,
a national automated system of library copperation. Through
its affiliation with Columbia University, the Library also
participates in the programs of the Research Libraries Group,
a consortium of major research libraries, the major purpose
of which is to enhance capabilities for research by
improving the availablity and management of information.[10]

FOOTNOTES

[1]Union Theological Seminary. Library. "Agreement between the International Bonhoeffer Society for Archive and Research, English Language Section, and Union Theological Seminary Library on the Bonhoeffer Regional Archive and Research Collection," May, 1976, p. 1.

[2]Union Theological Seminary. The Burke Library, "Some Special Collections," March 20, 1985, pp. 4, 6.

[3]Robert Maloy, "The Library: A Report, 1966/67-1974/77 and Beyond", July 1977, p. 135.

[4]"UTS Library Planning Newsletter," August 1979, p. 1.

[5]"UTS Library Planning Newsletter," September. 1980, p.1.

[6]Union Seminary Library Receives Two Grants," ATLA Newsletter, XXIX (November 14, 1981), p. 22.

[7]"A Celebration of Word, Symbol, and Space Marking the Reopening and Rededication of the Library, Union Theological Seminary in the City of New York," April 25-26, 1983, p. 12.

[8]"Union Theological Seminary Library in New York Rededicated and Renamed," ATLA Newsletter, XXXI (August 13, 1983), p. 13.

[9]Union Theological Seminary, Catalog, 1984-1985 (New York: Union Theological Seminary, 1984), p. 22.

Summary and Conclusions

Summary

The Founding of the Seminary and Its Library

Union Theological Seminary in the City of New York
has been a center of theological controversy since its establishment in 1836. The school was founded in an era of serious
division in American Presbyterianism. Its earliest Directors
and Faculty members, with one exception, were affiliated with
the liberal branch of that schism. The institution has, therefore, from its inception been identified with liberal Calvinism.

The fact that the school has been a theological storm
center may account in part for the fact that its Library is
one of the finest theological collections in the western hemisphere. The school has not been satisfied, for example, to
have only one side of a theological argument represented in
its collection; but for nearly 130 years the institution has
attempted to have available materials on various facets of
the central theological issues dividing American Christianity.

The fact, too, that the school has from its beginning
been in the left-wing of the reformed tradition of Protestantism
may account in part for the development of its Library. One
evidence of this emphasis is found in the founders' refusal
to be allied with the ecclesiastical organizations of the
Presbyterian Church because of their fear of the orthodox

group which had control of the General Assembly during that period. A stress on freedom with a de-emphasis on the doctrine of total depravity have been characteristic of the school's various theological positions, despite the fact that it was probably the first American seminary to give serious consideration to Karl Barth's neo-orthodoxy. In contrast, then, to schools which consider that a theological library should reflect a given set of orthodox tenets, the collection at Union for many years has included works from a variety of approaches. In institutions with the freedom of inquiry which is an important part of the school's tradition, intellectual incisiveness is most naturally cultivated and scholarship is most mature.

Another important characteristic of Union, which has been true from its beginning, has been its ecumenicity. While the school was established by Presbyterians, the founders were the most ecumenical in the denomination. They were opposed to the establishment or strengthening of denominational organizations to perform functions which, in their opinion, were being satisfactorily executed by non-denominational groups. This desire for inclusiveness, which was reflected in the name of the institution, has been influential in the development of the collection. While Presbyterianism is well represented there, for example, so are the other major branches of Protestantism, Orthodoxy, and Catholicism, as well as non-Christian religions and secular causes. This development is the culmination of one of the purposes of the founders.

Another characteristic of the Seminary from its origin has been the influence of laypeople in its development. The first meeting of those interested in founding the school was attended by four clergymen and five laypeople; and one-half of the first Directorate was composed of laypeople. The business people who have guided the school's progress through the intervening years have made several vital contributions to the growth of the Library. First, they have provided most of the funds for the purchase of materials. Second, they have supervised the expenditure of these monies in a generous but efficient manner. Third, by their contracts with secular society, they have prevented the school from becoming theologically introverted. The Library, for example, has never been only a collection of theological literature; it has, from its beginning, included secular materials which would seem out of place in an institution which was dominated by the clergy.

Fourth, these laypeople, from the era of the founders, have worked to develop the type of institution which would produce excellence in the ministry. The preamble to the 1836 Constitution, which is still used, in stating the objectives of the institution, indicated that one of the principal purposes of the school was to be the enlistment of "genius, talent, enlightened piety, and missionary zeal" for the ministry.[1] While other qualities of the effective minister are mentioned, enlightenment is stressed throughout the preamble.

The Directors have been insatiable in their demand for this excellence. Their pride was reflected in their claims,

at the time the school was established, that all other theological institutions were inadequate. The founders made it
clear that they would be satisfied in their proposed institution with nothing but the best. This desire for excellence
has been important insofar as it has influenced the institution
to strive for high standards; yet the haughtiness of some of
these people, who have included some of New York's wealthiest,
is strangely inconsistent with the ideals of the Nazarene,
the propagation of whose teachings the Seminary was purportedly
designed to advance.

Great libraries, however, are not often built by poor
and humble donors; and despite the criticisms which may be
levied against Union's founders, they were interested in the
development of the collection. Their earliest plans included
provisions for this purpose. Their attempt to secure the
finest scholars available for the Faculty was also important
for the history of the Library, for they must have realized
that in this field good scholars cannot be secured and kept
without good bibliographical tools.

In the first academic year, then, a Library Committee
was appointed. Professor Henry White was placed in charge
of the collection, and $1,000 were allocated for books. The
materials purchased were supplemented by gifts from the collections of religious people in New York and environs. This meager
start was, however, quickly supplemented by the purchase of
one of the most important European libraries imported into the
United States during the nineteenth century.

Although it was the most significant purchase in the
history of the Library in terms of the value of its contents,
the acquisition of the Van Ess collection did not substantially
enhance the development of the collection in the fulfillment
of the principal objectives of the institution. It was useful
for scholars interested in church history and Biblical studies,
but its value to the student body was negligible. The balance
of the Library with approximately 14,000 volumes in non-English
languages and only about 1,000 volumes in English was inadequate
for a student body of 100, few of whom were able to read any
non-English languages except Greek and Hebrew. The purchase
of the Library was, however, fortuitous in the long-range development of Union's collection; and the $5,000 spent for it,
during a period when the annual budget of the school amounted
to approximately $10,000, have been repaid in terms of use by
scholars and by the fame brought to the institution through
its acquisition. The addition of the Van Ess Library was, in
fact, the most important development in the early history of
the Library. By acquiring one of the most scholarly theological
libraries in the United States through this purchase, a tradition of library awareness was begun at the Seminary.

The Librarianship of Edward Robinson

Although Henry White, R. B. Patton and others served
for brief periods as Librarian during this period, the first
person to serve in this capacity for any substantial period
was Edward Robinson, who began his service to the school in
1840. Because of the feeble financial circumstances of the

institution during the eleven years in which he was Librarian, little progress was made in the development of the collection. His most important role in connection with the Library was the one he played in securing the Van Ess collection before he became Librarian.

Although his librarianship was marked by an absence of budgeted funds for the purchase of books, a small number of materials was added through gifts of books and money by friends of the Library, as well as through the sale of duplicates. Yet, these gifts in eleven years resulted in the addition of only 2,000 books, for an annual average of 188 volumes.

Robinson worked diligently during the decade as a member of a Faculty with two full-time professors, who were responsible for offering courses in all departments of theological education for a student body of 100. He continued, in addition, to publish many Biblical studies. The time that he was expected to devote to the Library was reflected in a financial statement in which he was reported to have been paid $2,000 for his professorship and $100 for his role as Librarian.[2]

The state of the Library at the close of his administration justified Henry B. Smith, his successor as Librarian, in asserting that

The literary character of the Seminary is slight, its zeal in theological science is little, the need of a comprehensive range of theological studies and books has got to be created.[3]

The Librarianship of Henry Boynton Smith

Smith could not be accused of failing to attempt to remedy the situation. One of the first things he did, on assuming the role of part-time Librarian, was to get a budget approved for the Library for the first time in the institution's history. Although this budget for materials averaged only approximately $750 per year during his administration, it was a start in the right direction and was better than the haphazard financing for the Library which had been characteristic of the first fifteen years of the school's existence.

The limited financial resources available for the development of the Library during this period were strengthened through the results of a series of endowment campaigns designed to underwrite the current program of the school as well as a projected expansion in facilities. This, in fact, was probably the most important development in the school's program during Smith's administration as Librarian. During this period the institution began to accumulate permanent funds which were to enable it to strengthen its entire program, including the development of its Library.

Among the significant acquisitions for the collection, in addition to regular purchases amounting to an average of approximately $750 per year during Smith's administration were substantial gifts from the libraries of Edward Robinson and David Dudley Field, as well as the Sprague Collection of 2,000 pamphlets.

These were eclipsed, however, by a long series of gifts selected by Ezra Hall Gillett and paid for by David H. McAlpin. These materials included nearly all of those available on the Deistic movement in England, as well as a large number of Dissenting, Unitarian, and Universalist works. Gillett's entire library, which was especially strong on American theology and history, was given to Union upon his death.

The Librarianship of Charles Augustus Briggs

Charles Augustus Briggs, whose name is associated with one of the most famous heresy trials in American history, was appointed Librarian upon the death of Smith. He introduced more innovations in the Library than any of his successors; and his freedom to do this may have been related to the fact that his father, a wealthy New York business man, was Chairman of the Directors' Finance Committee during many years of his appointment.

He, like his predecessors, was a part-time Librarian, who devoted most of his time to teaching. Yet, he had a more critical approach to his task than had they. One of his first actions as Librarian was to prepare a report for the Directors on the needs of the Library. In his investigation of the Library preparatory to making this report, he felt that its contents were in a chaotic condition. He was also critical of the weaknesses of the collection in fulfilling the educational objectives of the institution. He thought, in this connection, that most of the materials were too scholarly for the patrons who most frequently used the collection. He criticized also the meagerness of the financial support of the collection as being too meager, the book catalog as being worn, and the physical facilities as being too small. His principal recommendations were for an endowment of $50,000 and for a full-time Librarian,[4] both of which goals were accomplished during his administration.

He began efforts immediately to improve conditions. He supervised, for example, the reclassification and recataloging of the collection according to the scheme used by the Astor Library[5] as adapted by himself.[6] The collection was also strengthened through the development of a "model theological library" in the Reference Room as a memorial to Henry B. Smith[7] as well as through the purchase of Smith's library.[8]

The first of Briggs's two major recommendations was achieved through a gift from Governor E. D. Morgan in the amount of $400,000 for the construction of a new Library building on Park Avenue and the endowment of the collection.[9] The budget for the Library was immediately raised to $3,500,[10] which represented a substantial increase over the budget of $750, which had been typical of Smith's administration.

McAlpin continued his strong financial support of the Library throughout Briggs's administration, and most of the resources provided by this benefactor were used for purchasing materials for the famous Collection of British History and Theology named for him. While, prior to Briggs's administration, the McAlpin Library monies had been spent principally for materials on the Deistic controversies of the late seventeenth and early eighteenth centuries, Briggs used the funds during his librarianship for the purchase of literature by the Westminster and Puritan Divines and for books and pamphlets written during England's Civil War and the era of the Commonwealth.[11] This collection was increased to approximately

12,000 titles by Briggs and is one of the largest collections in existence of materials from this era.[12]

The Library grew from 30,000 to 50,000 volumes during the seven years of Briggs's administration. He achieved, during his incumbency, most of the goals he had set for the Library at the beginning. The last to be achieved was his second major recommendation; the appointment of a full-time Librarian was realized in 1883, when Charles Ripley Gillett assumed that office.

Briggs, one of the most controversial scholars in the field of religion during the latter part of the nineteenth century and the early part of the twentieth, was never satisfied for Union to become a school for ministers but insisted that it be a center of theological education to which scholars from every nation and denomination would come for study. He knew that if this objective were realized that its Library would have to be strengthened, and he was unrelenting in his demands that it be the finest collection of theological literature in the western hemisphere.

The Librarianship of Charles Ripley Gillett

Gillett's administration was less brilliant than was that of Briggs, but Gillett's term extended over a much longer period and probably included more growth than any of the nineteenth-century librarians. His first year in his new office included the announcement of David McAlpin's largest gift to the Library in the amount of $10,500,[13] the receipt of nearly 7,000 volumes and 5,381 pamphlets from the library of Edwin

Hatfield, which Gillett characterized as the "richest gift ever made to the seminary library,"[14] and expanded plans for new buildings on Park Avenue. Soon after, Gillett was given the task of supervising the move of 60,000 volumes three miles to the new buildings.[15]

One of his innovations was the introduction of a subject index which was related to the fixed location scheme used by the Library.[16] A large amount of the backlog, which had been accumulating for years, was also cataloged during his incumbency.[17]

The strength of the Library during this period lay in its special collections, such as the Van Ess Library, the Bird Collection of works on hymnology, the McAlpin Collection, the Gillett Collection, and the Isaac Hall New Testaments in Greek, the Samuel McAuley Jackson books on Zwingli, and the Henry Boynton Smith Library of Philosophy. This specialization was the Library's misery as well as its grandeur, for the book budget was secured from permanent funds assigned to some of these collections, leaving inadequate amounts for the purchase of current books required for a well-rounded collection. Despite various attempts, Gillett was never able to solve this problem. He, in fact, made recommendations for the expansion of this system of designated funds for certain areas of the collection, which, had they been adopted, would have made the administration of the monies even more inflexible.

The introduction of more seminars with opportunities for independent research, electives into the curriculum, representatives from various denominations for lectures, an honors

course, and the graduate program all had influence on the
expansion of the collection during this era. During Gillett's
administration, the Library grew from 50,000[18] to 94,000[19]
and thus became the largest theological collection in the
United States.

The Acting Librarianship of
William Walker Rockwell

When Gillett became Registrar, William Walker Rockwell
was appointed Librarian; and the first years of his administration saw the construction of the new buildings on Morningside
Heights. Other important events of the early years of his
incumbency included the beginning of the Library of Religious
and Moral Education. Julia Pettee, the new Cataloger, began
classifying the collection according to the Union Classification scheme, which she developed at this time.

Rockwell's acting librarianship was short-lived, en-
during for only five years. He was replaced as the administrator of the collection by Henry Preserved Smith.

The Librarianship of Henry Preserved Smith

Smith's administration began with the establishment
of the James Library Endowment Fund in the amount of $250,000
from the sale of the former location of the Seminary. The
influence of World War I made it difficult for the Librarian
to acquire European materials, which were more important in
theology than in some other fields.

Some rare materials were acquired at this time from
the widow of Frederick Ferris Thompson, a New York business

man. The Hymn Society of America deposited its collection at Union at this time, strengthening the holdings in religious music.

Smith was an outstanding scholar; but, like many of his predecessors as Librarian, his time was divided between teaching and administration of the collection. Experience had demonstrated that supervising the activities of the Library was a full-time responsibility; and William Rockwell was appointed to that duty in 1925, upon Smith's retirement.

The Librarianship of William Walker Rockwell

Rockwell had a proclivity to establish special collections, the administration of which has sometimes been burdensome to his successors. His administration began with the acceptance of the Missionary Research Library, which has made an excellent addition to Union's holdings in the field. Other collections begun by him included the Lending Library for Alumni and the Sacred Music Library. Fortunately, the Library of Auburn Seminary, which joined Union during his administration, was assimilated into the general collection.

The five-volume Catalogue of the McAlpin Collection was published at this time and has become a standard bibliographical source in theological collections and large secular libraries. The latter part of his administration saw the appointment of Lucy Markley as his Assistant and the retirement of Julia Pettee, who had, by this time, reclassified most of Union's holdings and thus developed the Union classification scheme. The new Assistant became the Librarian upon Rockwell's retirement in 1942.

The Librarianship of Lucy Whitney Markley

The William Adams Brown Ecumenical Library was established during her administration and was formed largely from the library of the professor whose name it bore. She also encouraged the school, the only seminary to do so, to participate in the Library of Congress Cooperative Acquisitions Project. Although this program was short-lived, Union agreed to buy Protestant works in its successor, the Farmington Plan.

Her administration was brief, and in 1951 she left to join the staff of Garrett Biblical Institute and was replaced by Robert Fullerton Beach of that institution.

The Librarianship of Robert Fullerton Beach

The quickened interest in ecumenicity during the 1950's and 1960's had a strong influence on the development of the Library, with Beach acquiring many of the major papers of various ecumenical conferences. The Rockefeller Foundation also made it possible to develop the collection in the area of religious drama, and the Old Dominion Foundation paid for many purchases in the field of psychiatry and religion. Another special collection developed was the one named for John Foster Dulles; these holdings were strong on materials on the church and international order.

The Librarianship of Robert Maloy

One of the major actions of Beach's successor, Robert Maloy, was the abandonment at Union of the Petee scheme of classification and the adoption of the Library of Congress Classification. Maloy also oversaw the establishment of the Bonhoeffer Collection at Union and the organization of the archival collections.

The Librarianship of Richard Spoor

The years during which Richard Spoor has been the director of the Library have been noteworthy for the enlargement, renovation, and reorganization of the Library. He also has increased the cooperation of the Library with many other networks and resource sharing organizations in making the splendid resources at Union available to scholars throughout the world.

Conclusions

This study of the history of a seminary library "unsurpassed among the theological collections of this country"[20] has implications for administrators, faculty members, benefactors, and librarians of other seminaries as they attempt to improve their libraries. The growth of this Library has relevance for the development of objectives, administration, personnel, finances, and curricula of other similar institutions as well as for the expansion of their collections and services.

In formulating long-range purposes, a seminary does well, for example, to be as ecumenical as possible. Opening its doors to faculty members, students, and patrons from as wide a constituency as possible will result in a collection which represents many points of view. Accompanying this will be the objective of building a climate in which free inquiry may take place in the field of religion. The school should also see itself as more than a center for the education of ministers and should seek to be a "theological university" to which people from many nations may come for study in various fields of endeavor. The library, at least, should understand its role as being wider than serving only its student body and faculty.

Union's experience also has demonstrated the value of appointing seminary administrators who are appreciative of scholarship and yet who are able to raise money. Theological education depends almost entirely upon gifts for its support; and Union's success, at least, has been related to the securing of wealthy laypeople to share in its program planning and to support it financially. Some means of securing Library support from these persons have been to share the bibliographical needs and achievements with them and to be generous in naming collections for them. Union's experience has also demonstrated the wisdom of locating a theological school in a large city, which is more apt to have wealth, students, books, and capable people, from which good theological libraries are made.

The latter is the most important quality of these four ingredients of an excellent theological collection. If a school wants a superior collection, it must have an excellent faculty to assist in the selection of its materials. The librarian should be a scholar also; but even superior people, such as Briggs, Rockwell, and Beach, have depended heavily on subject specialists for the development of the collection.

Endowment seems to be the most satisfactory answer to the problems of financing this development. Because the library will benefit in nearly every conceivable way from steady financial support, every effort should be expended to build up a school's permanent funds.

Those responsible for the library will be wise, also, to keep the curriculum of the school as current and as excellent as possible. While stressing scholarship, emphasis should also be placed on current trends in society which demand the attention of the Church. The theological library which contains only religious materials is irrelevant. It must, like the curriculum, reflect the Church's interest in such problems as international order, racial injustice, and emotional illness.

Granted adequate financing, the greatest need of theological education, the collection should be built according to a long-range plan. Yet, the program must be flexible enough to allow for the purchase of a bargain, such as the Van Ess Library, even though it may not meet the immediate needs of the school. Other areas of heavy buying should include periodicals, because much of current discussion in the field of religion is available only in this form. Items which add to the uniqueness of the collection, such as manuscripts, unusual collections acquired by individuals, and materials for existing fields of specialization, should be bought as freely as possible. Trips to Europe, searching of sales catalogs, and attendance at book sales are necessary to acquire the retrospective materials essential to the improvement of inadequate collections.

Because of the strong emphasis on older materials, however, the Seminary may well accept gifts in the form of books and periodicals as well as in money. Publications of religious societies, conference reports, and manuscript materials have also been among the many rich gifts accepted by Union. If gifts are welcome, this fact should be advertised through the public relations media of the school. Union has had unusually good fortune in accepting large collections as loans, such as the Missinary Research Library and the Library

of the Hymn Society of America. These have usually become
permanently located at the Seminary.

The collection of a seminary should also be related
to other libraries in its vicinity. Union's experience has
shown the wisdom of locating first near the Lenox and the Astor
Libraries and later near that of Columbia. The goal of becoming
the theological section of a cooperative metropolitan library
system is an excellent ambition for any theological institution.
A parallel role may be played in the nation through regular
reporting to the National Union Catalog.

The collection should be shared, too, with as wide a
constituency as possible. Union has, for example, from its
origin loaned to others than its Faculty and student body.
The mailing services for ministers is also a policy worthy of
wider repetition. A seminary which builds an excellent

collection has a responsibility, like Union, to publish its
catalog, to make its materials more available to scholars.

Aside from adequate financing, perhaps the most important quality for building a theological collection, however,
is a dissatisfaction with the status quo. Those responsible
for a large or a small theological library do well to have
the attitude expressed by Henry Boynton Smith in a letter
written in 1850:

> The literary character of the Seminary is slight,
> its zeal in theological science is little, the need
> of a comprehensive range of theological studies and
> books has got to be created.[21]

344

A solution to this problem was given fifty years later
by Charles Ripley Gillett:

> . . . The development of a library takes time and
> money, and a complete library cannot be ordered over
> night. It requires study, consultation, selection,
> caution, and a wide range of knowledge. It must be
> built upon plans which embrace the future as well as
> the present, and regard must also be made to the
> shortcomings of the past.[22]

This applies to Union as well as to the other "theological
collections of this country"[23] which it presently surpasses.

FOOTNOTES

[1]Minutes of the Board of Directors of Union Theological Seminary in the City of New York, January 11, 1836.

[2]Charles Ripley Gillett, "Detailed History of the Union Theological Seminary in the City of New York" [New York, 1937] (Typewritten), pp. 231-32.

[3]George Lewis Prentiss, The Union Theological Seminary in the City of New York: Historical and Biographical Sketches of Its First Fifty Years (New York: Anson D. F. Randolph and Co., 1889), pp. 65-66.

[4]"Report by Dr. Briggs, May 7, 1877," "Extracts from Source Materials Used in Preparing a History of Union Theological Seminary," ed. by Charles Ripley Gillett [New York, 1937] (Typewritten), p. 64-A.

[5]Charles Ripley Gillett, "The Library of the Union Theological Seminary, Its Proper Position, Its Present Condition, Its Pressing Needs, April 1899" (Typewritten), p. 421.

[6]Prentiss, op. cit., p. 356.

[7]Union Theological Seminary, Catalogue of the Officers and Students of the Union Theological Seminary in the City of New York, 1877-78 (New York: Wm. C. Martin, 1877), p. 15.

[8]Directors, op. cit., March 12, 1878.

[9]Ibid., April 5, 1880 and April 11, 1881.

[10]Minutes of the Finance Committee of Union Theological Seminary in the City of New York, May 3, 1880.

[11]Union Theological Seminary. Library, Catalogue of the McAlpin Collection of British History and Theology, comp. and ed. by Charles Ripley Gillett (New York: Union Theological Seminary, 1927), I, v.

[12]Prentiss, op. cit., pp. 354-55.

[13]Directors, op. cit., January 8, 1884.

[14]Charles Ripley Gillett, "The Library, General Catalogue, and the Alumni," in George Lewis Prentiss, The Union

Theological Seminary in the City of New York: Its Design
and Another Decade of Its History, with a Sketch of the Life
and Public Service of Charles Butler, LL.D. (Asbury Park,
New Jersey: M., W., & C. Pennypacker, 1899), p. 357.

[15]Charles Ripley Gillett, "Report of the Librarian of
Union Theological Seminary to the Directors of the Seminary
for the Year, May 1, 1884 to May 1, 1885."

[16]Ibid., May 1, 1885 to May 1, 1886, p. 1.

[17]Ibid., May 10th, 1887, p. 1.

[18]Ibid., May 1, 1884 to May 1, 1885, p. 2.

[19]Ibid., May 12, 1908.

[20]Union Theological Seminary, Catalogue, 1964-65,
p. 29.

[21]Prentiss, The Union Theological Seminary in the
City of New York: Historical and Biographical Sketches of
Its First Fifty Years, op. cit., pp. 65-66.

[22]Gillett, "The Library of the Union Theological Seminary, Its Proper Position, Its Present Condition, Its Pressing
Needs," op. cit., Sections 13-14.

[23]Union Theological Seminary, Catalogue, 1964-65,
op. cit., p. 29.

Bibliography

A. BOOKS

Coffin, Henry Sloane. A Half Century of Union Theological Seminary, 1896-1945, An Informal History. New York: Charles Scribner's Sons, 1954.

Downs, Robert Bingham. Resources of New York City Libraries, A Survey of Facilities for Advanced Study and Research. Chicago: American Library Association, 1942.

Hatfield, Edwin F. The Early Annals of Union Theological Seminary in the City of New York. New York: No. 30 Clinton Place, 1876.

Lane, William Coolidge and Charles Knowles Bolton. Notes on Special Collections in American Libraries. ("Library of Harvard University, Bibliographical Contributions," edited by Justin Winsor, No. 45) Cambridge, Mass.: Issued by the Library of Harvard University, 1892.

Latourette, Kenneth Scott. The Nineteenth Century Outside Europe ("Christianity in a Revolutionary Age," Vol. III) New York: Harper & Brothers, Publishers, 1961.

Morison, Samuel Eliot and Henry Steele Commager. The Growth of the American Republic, Vol. I. New York: Oxford University Press, 1956.

Niebuhr, Reinhold. This Ministry: The Contribution of Henry Sloane Coffin. New York: Charles Scribner's Sons, 1954.

Pettee, Julia. List of Theological Subject Headings and Corporate Church Names Based upon the Headings in the Catalogue of the Library of Union Theological Seminary, New York City. 2d ed. Chicago: American Library Association, 1947.

Prentiss, George Lewis. The Union Theological Seminary in the City of New York: Historical and Biographical Sketches of Its First Fifty Years. New York: Anson D. F. Randolph and Co., 1889.

_____. The Union Theological Seminary in the City of New York: Its Design and Another Decade of Its History, with a Sketch of the Life and Public Services of Charles Butler, LL.D. Asbury Park, N. J.: M., & C. Pennypacker, 1899.

Ricci, Seymour De and W. J. Wilson. Census of Medieval and Renaissance Manuscripts in the United States and Canada, Vol. II. New York: Kraus Reprint Corporation, 1961.

_____. Supplement to the Census of Medieval and Renaissance Manuscripts in the United States and Canada, originated by C. U. Faye, continued and edited by W. H. Bond. New York: The Bibliographical Society of America, 1962.

Skinner, Ellouise W. Sacred Music at Union Theological Seminary, 1836-1953; An Informal History. New York: Private Printing, 1953.

[Smith, Elizabeth L.]. Henry Boynton Smith, His Life and Work. New York: A. C. Armstrong & Son, 714 Broadway, 1881.

Tauber, Maurice F. et al. Technical Services in Libraries. New York: Columbia University Press, 1953.

Thompson, Robert Ellis. A History of the Presbyterian Churches in the United States ("The American Church History Series," edited by Philip Schaff et al., Vol. VI) New York: The Christian Literature Co., 1894.

Winsor, Justin. "Address," Public Exercises on the Completion of the Library Building of the University of Michigan, December 12, 1883. Ann Arbor: University of Michigan, 1884.

B. PUBLICATIONS OF THE GOVERNMENT, UNIVERSITIES, AND LEARNED SOCIETIES

American Theological Library Association Library Development Program. Bulletin No. 2: A.T.L.A. Library Development Program, October 1, 1961. New Haven, Conn.: A.T.L.A. Library Development Program, October 1, 1961.

Johnston, W. Dawson and Isadore G. Mudge. Special Collections in Libraries in the United States. U. S. Bureau of Education Bulletin, 1912, No. 23. Washington: U. S. Government Printing Office, 1912.

Michigan. University. Board of Regents. Proceedings, 1891-96, 1906-10, 1914-17. [Ann Arbor: University of Michigan, 1891-96, 1906-10, 1914-17].

New York (State) Laws, Statutes, etc. Laws of the State of
        New-York Passed at the Sixty-Second Session of the
        Legislature Begun and Held in the City of Albany, the
        First Day of January, 1839. Albany: Printed for
        W. & A. Gould & Co., [etc.], 1839.

                C. PUBLICATIONS OF UNION THEOLOGICAL SEMINARY
                        IN THE CITY OF NEW YORK

Gillett, Charles R. "The McAlpin Collection of British
        History and Theology," Union Theological Seminary
        Bulletin, Vii (January, 1924), pp. 1-29.

McAuley, Thomas. Extracts from a Speech Delivered by Dr.
        McAuley at the Dedication of the Edifice Belonging
        to the New-York Theological Seminary, 12th Dec. 1838
        [New York, 1839?].

New-York Theological Seminary. Catalogue of the Officers and
        Students of the New-York Theological Seminary, 1839-
        40. New York: Printed by William Osborn, 1839, 1840.

_____. Constitution and By-Laws of the New-York Theolog-
        ical Seminary, Founded on the 18th of January, A. D.
        1836. New York: Printed by William Osborn, 88
        William-street, 1839.

Nichols, R. H. "The Library," Alumni Bulletin, XVIII (April,
        1943), 6.

Rockwell, William Walker. "Henry Preserved Smith," Alumni
        Bulletin, II (April-May, 1927), 138.

The Union Seminary Tower, VI-XII (1959-65).

Union Theological Seminary. Alumni Bulletin, III (1927),
        unpaged.

_____. Appeal in Behalf of the Union Theological Seminary
        in the City of New York. New York: Union Theological
        Seminary, 1864.

_____. Biographical Information Sheets (Mimeographed).

_____. Catalogue. 1841, 1843-44, 1848-87, 1889-1964.
        New York: Union Theological Seminary, 1841, 1843-44,
        1848-87, 1889-1964, 1984-85.

_____. "Coming: A Missionary Library" Alumni Bulletin of
        the Union Theological Seminary, IV (February-March,
        1929), 73.

350

_____. Constitution and Laws of the Union Theological Seminary in the City of New York, Founded on the 18th of January, A. D. 1836. New York: Union Theological Seminary, 1847, 1853, 1858, 1867, 1876, 1885, 1886, 1893, 1896.

_____. The Dedication of the New Buildings of the Union Theological Seminary in the City of New York, November 27, 28 and 29, 1910. New York: Union Theological Seminary, 1910.

_____. Endowments of the Union Theological Seminary in the City of New York. New York: Union Theological Seminary, 1890.

_____. General Catalogue of Union Theological Seminary in the City of New-York. New York: Union Theological Seminary, 1876, 1898, 1908.

_____. The Laying of the Corner-Stone of the New Buildings of the Union Theological Seminary and the Inauguration of the Reverend Professor Francis Brown as President of the Faculty. New York: Union Theological Seminary, 1908.

_____. "The Missionary Library," Alumni Bulletin of the Union Theological Seminary, IV (February-March, 1929), 83.

_____. One Hundredth Anniversary, 1836-1936. New York: Union Theological Seminary, 1936.

_____. Services in Adams Chapel at the Dedication of the New Buildings of the Union Theological Seminary, 1200 Park Avenue, New York City, December 9, 1884. New York: Printing House of William C. Martin, 1885.

_____. Statement of the Most Important Facts and Dates Connected with the History of the Union Theological Seminary from the Election of President Charles Cuthbert Hall, D.D., LL.D. to the Laying of the Corner Stone of the New Buildings on Morningside Heights, Prepared by William Adams Brown, Ph.D., D.D., for the Board of Directors. New York: Irving Press, 1909.

_____. Union Theological Seminary Alumni Bulletin, I-V (1954-63).

Union Theological Seminary. Library. Catalogue of the McAlpin Collection of British History and Theology, V Vols., comp. and ed. by Charles Ripley Gillett. New York: Union Theological Seminary, 1927-30.

_____. Classification of the Library of Union Theological
Seminary in the City of New York. Rev. and enl. ed.
New York: Union Theological Seminary, 1939.

_____. Reports, 1918, 1920-31 in Union Theological Seminary
Bulletins, I-VIII (May, 1918-July, 1925) and Alumni
Bulletin of the Union Theological Seminary, I-VII
(June-July, 1926-November, 1931).

D. ARTICLES IN MULTI-VOLUME SETS

Allison, W. H. "Theological Libraries," in The New Schaff-
Herzog Encyclopedia of Religious Knowledge, XI:336-41,
ed. Samuel Macauley Jackson et.al. New York: Funk
and Wagnalls Company, 1911.

"Ballard, Edward Lathrop," Who Was Who in America. Chicago:
The A. N. Marquis Company, 1942, p. 52.

Brown, William Adams. "Theological Seminaries," The New
Schaff-Herzog Encyclopedia of Religious Knowledge,
XI, 376-79, ed. Samuel Macauley Jackson et al. New
York: Funk and Wagnalls Company, 1911.

Christie, Francis A. "Jackson, Samuel Macauley," Dictionary
of American Biography, ed. Allen Johnson and Dumas
Malone, IX, 553-55. New York: Charles Scribner's
Sons, 1937.

"Dodge, Cleveland H.," The National Cyclopaedia of American
Biography, XXVI, 407. New York: James T. White, 1937.

Frame, James Everett, "Vincent, Marvin Richardson," Dictionary
of American Biography, ed. Dumas Malone, XIX, 279-80.
New York: Charles Scribner's Sons, 1937.

"Harkness, Edward Stephen," Who Was Who in America. Chicago:
The A. N. Marquis Company, 1942, p. 521.

"Hastings, Thomas Samuel," The National Cyclopaedia of American
Biography, VII, 317-18. New York: James T. White
Company, 1897.

"Law, Walter William," The National Cyclopaedia of American
Biography, XXXI, 73, New York: James T. White Company,
1944.

Leaders in Education. 3d ed. Lancaster, Pennsylvania:
The Sciences Press, 1948.

"McAlpin, David Hunter," The National Cyclopaedia of American
Biography, XXXIII, 304-05. New York: James T. White
Company, 1947.

Muzzy, David Seville, "Butler, Charles," Dictionary of
American Biography, ed. Allen Johnson and Dumas Malone,
III, 359-60. New York: Charles Scribner's Sons, 1937.

Rockwell, William Walker. "Prentiss, George Lewis," Dictionary
of American Biography, ed. Allen Johnson and Dumas
Malone, XV, 189-90. New York: Charles Scribner's
Sons, 1937.

Schwarz, J. C. Religious Leaders of America. 2 vols. New
York: 277 Broadway, 1941-42.

Shaw, William Bristol. "Dodge, William Early," Dictionary of
American Biography, ed. Allen Johnson and Dumas Malone,
V, 152-53. New York: Charles Scribner's Sons, 1937.

_____. "Fayerweather, Daniel Burton," Dictionary of
American Biography, ed. Allen Johnson and Dumas Malone,
VI, 306. New York: Charles Scribner's Sons, 1937.

_____. "James, Daniel Willis," Dictionary of American
Biography, ed. Allen Johnson and Dumas Malone, IX,
573-74. New York: Charles Scribner's Sons, 1937.

"Sloane, William," Who Was Who in America. Chicago: The
A. N. Marquis Company, 1942, p. 1134.

"Thompson, Frederick F.," The National Cyclopaedia of American
Biography, VI, 140-41. New York: James T. White
Company, 1929.

Who's Who in America, 1964-65, XXXIII. Chicago: Marquis-
Who's Who, 1964.

Who's Who in Music. New York: Hafner Pub. Co., 1962.

Who's Who in New York. New York: Lewis Historical Publishing
Company, Inc., 1947.

Who's Who in the East. Chicago: Marquis-Who's Who, 1963.

Who's Who in the Protestant Clergy. Encino, California:
Nygaard Associates, 1957.

Williamson, C. C. and Alice Jewett, eds. Who's Who in Library
Service. New York: The H. W. Wilson Company, 1933.

E.   UNPUBLISHED MATERIALS

Farris, Donn Michael. "A Survey of the Library of the Union
Theological Seminary in New York City." Unpublished
Master's project, School of Library Service, Columbia
University, 1950.

Gillett, Charles Ripley. "Detailed History of the Union Theological Seminary in the City of New York." [New York, 1937.] (Typewritten.)

_____. Extracts from Source Materials Used in Preparing a History of Union Theological Seminary." [New York, 1937.] (Typewritten.)

_____. Letters to Miss Edith Humphrey, 325 Hancock St., Brooklyn, N. Y., June 25, 1901; G. P. Putnam's Sons, 27 W. 23d, New York, N. Y., September 9, 1901; and G. E. Stechert, 9 E. 16th St., New York, N. Y., September 9, 1901.

_____. "The Library of the Union Theological Seminary, Its Proper Position, Its Present Condition, Its Pressing Needs, April 1899." (Typewritten.)

_____. Report of the Librarian, Union Theological Seminary, 1884-88, 1889-90, 1891-92, 1893-95, 1896-1901, 1903-06, 1907-08.

Macquarrie, John. Letter, July 10, 1965.

Maloy, Robert. "The Library: A Report, 1966/67-1974/77 and Beyond," July 1977.

Minutes of the Alumni Association of Union Theological Seminary in the City of New York, 1842-.

Minutes of the Board of Directors of Union Theological Seminary in the City of New York, 1835-.

Minutes of the Building Committee of Union Theological Seminary in the City of New York, 1881-1884.

Minutes of the Committee on Site and Buildings of Union Theological Seminary in the City of New York, 1905-11.

Minutes of the Executive Committee of Union Theological Seminary in the City of New York, 1846-.

Minutes of the Faculty of Union Theological Seminary in the City of New York, 1837-.

Minutes of the Finance Committee of Union Theological Seminary in the City of New York, 1840-.

Parker, John W. "Report of a Study Made of the Library of Union Theological Seminary in the City of New York." Unpublished Master's project, School of Library Service, Columbia University, 1951.

Rockwell, William W. Librarian's Report to the Board of Directors of Union Theological Seminary, 1909-10.

_____. Union Theological Seminary. "A Celebration of Word, Symbol, and Space Marking the Reopening and Rededication of the Library, Union Theological Seminary in the City of New York," April 25-26, 1983.

_____. "In Memoriam William Adams, D.D., LL.D., Union Theological Seminary, 1873-1880-." (Typewritten.)

_____. "Union Theological Seminary, 1874-1899, Address Presented by the Faculty to the Reverend Charles Augustus Briggs, D.D. . . . to Commemorate the Twenty-Fifth Anniversary of His Connection with the Institution January 19th, 1899." [Handwritten.]

_____. Union Theological Seminary. Library. "Agreement between the International Bonhoeffer Society for Archive and Research, English Language Section, and Union Theological Seminary Library on the Bonhoeffer Regional Archive and Research Collection," May, 1976.

_____. Catalogue of the Van Ess Collection [n.p., 18--?].

_____. Growth of Library: The Total Number of Additions to the Library from May 1, 1940 to April 30, 1941. (Typewritten.)

_____. Union Theological Seminary. Library. Planning Newsletter, August, 1979; September, 1980.

_____. Report, 1917, 1932-35, 1939, 1940-64, 1972-73.

_____. Review of the Library, 1951-1961. And a Look Ahead. (Typewritten.)

_____. Statement of the Work of the Catalogue Department, May 1st, 1930 to May 1st, 1931.

_____. Union Theological Seminary. The Burke Library. Some Special Collections. New York: Union Theological Seminary, March 20, 1985.

Union Theological Seminary. Registrar. "Registrar's Archives," 1836-1899.

F. NEWSPAPERS AND PERIODICALS

ATLA Newsletter, XIV, May 13, 1967; XXI (May 18, 1974) XXIX (Nov. 14, 1981); XXXI (Aug. 13, 1983).

Blake, Fay M. "Union Theological Seminary Library," The Bookmark, XXIX (November, 1969), 57.

Eisenhart, Ruth C. "The Classification of Theological Books," Library Trends, IX (October, 1960), 257-69.

The Evening Post: New York, May 8, 1888, p. 4

Farrell, Colman J. "Classification of the Library of the UTS
    in the City of New York," Catholic Library World, XI
    (February, 1940), 155.

Harper's Weekly, February 9, 1884, p. 95.

Missionary Research Library Occasional Bulletin, VI (December 6,
    1955), 9.

New York Evangelist, April 16, 1836; October 14, 1837;
    February 13, 1841; July 6, 1843.

New York Observer, December 10, 1836; May 6, 1837; July 16,
    1842.

New York Times, September 12, 193, 10:8; May 21, 1924, 1:4;
    November 27. 1924. 18:8; December 25, 1924, 18:8;
    January 4, 1925, II, 1:7; January 30, 1940, 1:2, 5:5,
    6; May 20, 1925, 1:4; May 31, 1925, 18:1; February 11,
    1948, 1:4; November 12, 1948, 25:3; April 12, 1951,
    35:7; October 23, 1951, 32:8; November 12, 1951, 27:4;
    January 3, 1953, 1:3; April 23, 1954, 24:3; January 5,
    1955, 23:5; December 19, 1955, 28:8; May 12, 1958, 27:5.

Pettee, Julia, "A Classification for a Theological Library,"
    Library Journal (December, 1911), pp. 611-24.

Price, Frank W. "Specialized Research Libraries in Missions,"
    Library Trends, XI (October, 1960), 175-85.

Raeppel, Joseph E. "Julia Pettee," ALA Bulletin, XLVII
    (October, 1953), 417-19.

Rockwell, William Walker. "The Library of Union Theological
    Seminary," The Columbia University Quarterly, XIII
    (March, 1911), 211-13.

Tauber, Maurice F. "Classification of the Library of UTS
    in the City of New York," The Library Quarterly, X
    (July, 1940), 428-30.

Time, August 14, 1964, p. 36.

Church, State and Society in the 19th Century

Anglo-German comparison.

Ed. by Adolf M. Birke, Kurt Kluxen
1984. 164 p. (Prince Albert Studies 2) bd. DM 58,—
(3-598-21402-2)

A universal, comprehensive interpretation of religion and church in the age of modernization can only be established through an international comparative study. The Prince Albert Society took the lead at its conferencen in Coburg in September 1983 and made use of the English and German developments to begin a comparative study.

The English contributions deal with the transformation of the state control over the church, with the internal structural crises of the Anglican Church in the 19th century, and with an episode of Prussian-British cooperation, the creation of an Anglo-Prussian bishop's seat in Jerusalem. The German contributions take up the basic questions from the era of Prussian-Protestant church development and deal with the spectrum of political catholicism as well.

Further contributions point to the fruitful intellectual exchange between the two nations before the time of German-British antagonism and world wars.

K·G·Saur München·New York·London·Paris

K·G·Saur Verlag KG · Postfach 71 10 09 · 8000 München 71 · Tel. (089) 79 89 01
K·G·Saur Inc. · 175 Fifth Avenue · New York, N.Y.10010 · Tel. (212) 982-1302

International Bibliography of Jewish History and Thought

Ed. by Jonathan Kaplan
1984. XVIII, 483 p. bd. DM 128,— (3-598-07503-0)

This solidly researched bibliography of Jewish history and
thought from ancient to modern times provides a listing of over
2,000 works of major importance in Hebrew, English, German,
Spanish, Portuguese and French. The entries are organized in
the first section by historical period and then by shorter time
periods or topics of significant interest. The second section
provides a listing of works on the history of Jewish com-
munities, arranged geographically. Works are listed
alphabetically by author, but Hebrew works are grouped
together in each section and subdivision as are all other European language works. Cross references connect the two lists.
Each entry is annotated in the language of publication Two
author/editor/translator indexes — in Hebrew and European
languages — provide further access to the entries for the
educator, student and librarian.

K·G·Saur München·New York·London·Paris

K·G·Saur Verlag KG · Postfach 71 10 09 · 8000 München 71 · Tel. (0 89) 79 89 01
K·G·Saur Inc. · 175 Fifth Avenue · New York, N.Y.10010 · Tel. (212) 982-1302

Bibliotheca Trinitariorum

International Bibliography of Trinitarian Literature

Ed. by Erwin Schadel

Vol. I: Author Index
1984, CXII, 624 p. Bd. DM 120,— (3-598-10572-x)

Vol. II: Index Volume
1985. ca. 300 p. Bd. ca. DM 58,— (3-598-10573-8)

This bibliography, which presents and sights a voluminous amount of historical material, was undertaken and worked out with a systematic purpose. Its intent is, in the present post-nihilistic search for identity, to encourage the unfolding of the meaning in the space of trinitaria metaphysics. It intends to be a wider-reaching completion of its counterpart, the **Bibliotheca anti-trinitariorum** which was published 300 years ago.

Vol. 1 is an alphabetical author-title listing which arranges individual modern authors chronologically, so that if applicable, the development of a particular method of approach is made clear. The "opera omnia" of patristic and medieval writers were examined, insofar as available. The editions of important single works of these authors (including translations) have been noted.

The 2nd volume will index the listed titles according to form, subject, and history, so that detailed scientific studies are possible.

K·G·Saur München·New York·London·Paris

K·G·Saur Verlag KG · Postfach 71 10 09 · 8000 München 71 · Tel. (0 89) 79 89 01
K·G·Saur Inc. · 175 Fifth Avenue · New York, N.Y.10010 · Tel. (212) 982-1302